天津市2010年度哲学社会科学规划基金项目 TJYW10-2-595

文 体 翻 译

A Guide to Translation of Stylistic Varieties

主　编　刘著妍
副主编　付晓燕　王　莘

图书在版编目(CIP)数据

文体翻译/刘著妍主编. —天津:天津大学出版社,2013. 1
ISBN 978-7-5618-4609-4

Ⅰ. ①文… Ⅱ. ①刘… Ⅲ. ①文体 - 翻译 Ⅳ. ①H052

中国版本图书馆 CIP 数据核字(2013)第 027465 号

出版发行 天津大学出版社
出 版 人 杨欢
地 址 天津市卫津路 92 号天津大学内(邮编:300072)
电 话 发行部:022-27403647
网 址 publish. tju. edu. cn
印 刷 天津泰宇印务有限公司
经 销 全国各地新华书店
开 本 169mm×239mm
印 张 14
字 数 334千
版 次 2013 年 3 月第 1 版
印 次 2013 年 3 月第 1 次
定 价 39. 00 元

前　　言

传统的文体学主要分析文学家的文学风格和作家作品的语言特点。20 世纪 80 年代，人们从语言功能的角度把各种传递信息的语篇划为实用文体。文体通常分为文学文体和非文学文体，非文学文体也称为实用文体或应用文体。非文学文体通常分为新闻报刊、广告、科技、法律、政论、经贸、旅游等，文学文体通常分为诗歌、散文、小说、戏曲等。翻译学是一门综合性很强的学科，是一个复杂的系统，涉及翻译中的每一个要素——原本、译本、译者、受众、经验、方法、技巧、原则、目的、条件、审美等。综上所述，一种文体的翻译可以同时借鉴不同的理论与翻译策略，文体翻译理论体系的不断创立与发展见证着其他学科及领域的科研的同步发展与创新，同时不同的翻译理论与翻译策略对一种文体功能的体现也不尽相同，其应用价值更不可小觑。要想成为一个优秀的译者，不仅要准确传递原文的基本信息，还要传达其文体风格和语言特色。译者在翻译时首先必须熟悉原文的文体特征，才能为忠实再现原文奠定基础。不同文体的语言表达方式十分不同。例如，应用文强调实用性，而文学作品的语言则偏重于创造性、形象性和象征性。即便在应用文类中，在翻译这些不同体裁的文字时必须牢牢把握其各自不同的特点，才能使译文在内容与形式两个方面尽可能充分地达到与原文等值。

本书涵盖了跨文化交际中经常碰到的常用文体类型，着重探讨了这类文体的突出特点以及英语与汉语在表达上的差异及互译方法。帮助学习者了解翻译所涉及的语言文体差异和翻译风格，增强文体意识，从而能够在翻译实践中根据翻译的既定目的与功能确定总体翻译策略，并运用恰当的翻译技巧，提高各种不同情况下进行翻译实践的能力。

为了改进翻译教学的现状，使教学与研究和翻译实践紧密结合起来，做到有的放矢，本书将重点转移到篇章的分析与研究上，并突出其“实用”性，精讲有关理论，精选素材并适量设置练习。在介绍各种文体类型时，努力探讨各种文体的突出特点，对比和介绍英、汉两种语言在文体类型上的具体差异和互译对策。本书在编写思路与方法上都进行了新的尝试：第一，观念新，更贴近于翻译教学的实用性与实践性；第二，角度新，从篇章的角度入手，将词句的翻译融入其中；第三，内容新，涉及翻译实践中可能遇到的各类文字的翻译；第四，方法新，强调精讲多练，讲练结合，以练为主，理论联系实际。

全书共分为九章，第一章为文体翻译总论，简要地阐述了翻译的基本理论、文体分类与特征、常用的翻译方法和技巧，使学习者对文体翻译这一学科有一个较系统、全面的认识；第二章至第六章分别介绍了科技、广告、新闻、商务、旅游文体的翻译，论述了各类文体的语言、篇章特点和翻译方法；第七至第九章为散文翻译、小说翻译与诗歌翻译。本书的各章又分成若干小节，分别论述各类文体的各种不同类别。在每一类别总的论述后，都附有一些翻译练习，并深入分析与评论，以帮助学习者通过翻译实例巩固所学内容。有些章节带有附录部分，此部分旨在帮助学习者对翻译中常出现的内容进行梳理。练习的答案按章节顺序集中附于书后。

由于翻译是一种再创作，同样的原文，不同的译者可能有不同的译法。其中确有对错之分，但在更多的情况下只具好差之别。练习答案所提供的译文绝非唯一或标准的版本，仅供参考。文学作品的译文若引自著名译者的译本，均注上了名字。其余大多为本书作者所译。

本书可作为高等院校文体翻译教材，也可供自学或翻译爱好者参考使用。由于内容涉及面较广，在使用本书时不必拘泥于章节的顺序，可根据学生的需要与教学的要求突出某些章节或略过某些内容，或浅尝即止。练习亦不一定全做，可根据学生实际需要适当选择。此书将在使用中不断完善，由于作者水平有限，加之时间紧迫，错误、遗漏和不妥之处在所难免，恳请各位专家、学者提出宝贵意见，以便再版时更正。此书的出版得到了刘常华老师的大力支持，在此表示衷心感谢。在此书的编写过程中，孙晓园、刘蒙蒙、石磊等在材料的整理方面做了很多工作，在此表示感谢！

编者

2012 年 10 月

目　录

Chapter One
Theoretical Preliminary
总论

Three Principles of Tytler(泰特勒三原则)

Alexander Fraser Tytler is a famous Scottish translation theorist. His work *Essay on the Principles of Translation* is the first one among western translation theories. In this book, he put forward the three principles of translation.

(1) A translation should give a complete transcript of the ideas of the original works.

(2) The style and manner of writing should be of the same character as that of the original.

(3) A translation should have all the ease of the original composition.

It is from these three aspects that Tytler elaborates on "loyalty" to the source text. The advent of three principles of translation is a milestone. Before, dichotomy is dominant, which includes content equivalence and formal equivalence. Recently, the three principles of translation are often compared to Yan Fu's translation criteria: faithfulness, expressiveness and elegance. Between the two sets of translation criteria, there are both similarities and differences.

关键词:三原则;忠实;译文应该完全传达原文的意思;译文的风格和笔调应与原文一致;译文应与原文一样流畅;严复:信、达、雅

1. Definition of Translation

Down through the ages, people's definitions of translation are diversified. It differs from person to person. It evolves with time. Changes of the world also help to shape the connotation of translation. From the following definitions, you may have a glimpse of what translation is.

(1) Translating is both a craft and an art, that is to say, it involves an accurate and controlled manipulation of language, tempered by a degree of freedom, imagination and creativeness.

(2) Transferring the meaning of a stretch or unit of language, the whole part of a stretch or unit of language, the whole part of a text, from one language to another.

(3) Translation is like busy matchmakers: they sing the praises of some half-veiled beauty and extol her charms, and arouse an irresistible longing for the original. (Goethe)

(4) The replacement of textual material in one language (source text, ST) by equivalent textual material in another (target language, TL). (Catford)

(5) Translating consists in reproducing in the receptor language the closest natural equivalent of the source language message, first in terms of meaning and second in terms of style. (Nida & Taber)

Exercise: Translate the following sentences.

1) A man may usually be known by the books he reads as well as by the company he keeps; for there is a companionship of books as well as of men; and one should always live in the best company, whether it be of books or of men.

2) A good book is often the best urn of a life enshrining the best that life could think out; for the world of a man's life is, for the most part, the world of his thoughts. Thus the best books are treasures of good words, the golden thoughts, which, remembered and cherished, become our constant companions and comforters. "They are never alone," said Sir Philip Sidney, "they are accompanied by noble thoughts."

3) Youth is not a time of life; it is a state of mind; it is not a matter of rosy cheeks, red lips and supple knees; it is a matter of the will, a quality of the imagination, a vigor of the emotions; it is the freshness of the deep spring of life.

4) It was the best of times, it was the worst of times; it was the age of wisdom, it was the age of foolishness; it was the epoch of belief, it was the epoch of incredulity; it was the season of Light, it was the season of Darkness; it was the spring of Hope, it was the winter of Despair; we had everything before us, we had nothing before us; we were all going direct to Heaven, we were all going direct the other way.

5) 翻译是指把--种语言文字的意义转换成另一种语言文字。简言之,翻译是一种用不同的语言文字将原文作者的意思准确地再现出来的艺术。从以上翻译的定义可以知道,原文的思想必须尽可能得到保持,不可有所增删。译者的任务只是转换文字而不是改变其意思。因此,翻译有两个要素:准确性与表达性。准确性是翻译的首要条件。译者必须谨慎地遵循原文作者的意思,所选用的字词和句式结构必须如实地传达原文的思想。表达性是让译文易于理解。换言之,译者必须用自己的手段尽可能地将原文的思想清楚而有力地表达出来。准确性使译出的思想明确无误,而表达性则使译文生动,具有魅力。

2. Principles and Criteria of Translation

The so-called principles and criteria of translation are actually the two aspects of the same thing. The former lays emphasis on the translator, who should follow these principles whereas translating; while the latter on the reader or critic, who may use the criteria to evaluate translation. Whenever principles or criteria of translation are under discussion in China, Yan Fu's "three-character guide", which was first proposed in 1898, would be mentioned, namely the principle of "faithfulness, expressiveness and elegance" (信、达、雅).

In the past decades, Mr. Yan's principle of translation has been generally regarded as a plumb-line to measure the professional level of translation and a goal for translators to strive after. However, in the application of this principle, people have come to find some limitations to the three characters and put forward a variety of new standards instead.

Three kinds of opinions are expressed on the principle of faithfulness, expressiveness and elegance. The first group maintains the original three characters, and in the meantime, adds some new concepts to the character "雅". According to them, "雅" means far more than the English word "elegance". Apart from the traditional interpretation, it also means classicism, and the adherence to the original style and flavor. The second group, however, argues that the word "雅" is out of place in tradition. While adopting the first two characters of Yan Fu's principle, they discard the character "雅" and try to find some other new criteria instead. Noticeably, there are revisions such as "faithfulness, expressiveness and closeness" (信、达、切), "faithfulness, expressiveness and fitness" (信、达、贴), and so on. The third group of people, by casting away the three-character guide, proposes some new principles or criteria of translation of their own. Of the various popular theories, two of them are the most influential: spiritual conformity (神似) and sublimed adaptation (化境). The former, proposed by Fu Lei, emphasizes the reproduction of the spirit or the flavor of the original, while the latter, advocated by Qian Zhongshu, focuses on the translator's smooth and idiomatic Chinese version for the sake of the Chinese readers.

Despite the variety of opinions, two criteria are almost unanimously accepted, namely the faithfulness and accuracy (忠实、准确), and smoothness (流畅). We may also take these two criteria as the principles of translation in general. By faithfulness and accuracy, we mean being faithful not only to the original contents, to the original meaning and views, but also to the original form and style. By smoothness, we mean not only easy and readable rendering, but also idiomatic expressions in the target language, free from stiff formula and mechanically copying from dictionaries.

Exercise: Check the following Chinese versions with the criteria of faithfulness and smoothness.

1) All your moods are created by your thoughts or "cognitions". "You feel the way you do right now because of the thoughts you have at this moment."

所有的情绪都是由思维产生的,或者说来源于"认识"。"你之所以感到这么做是对的,那是因为你的大脑就是这么想的。"

2) If a designer were to design a bracket to support 100 lb. when it should have been figured for 1,000 lb., failure would be forthcoming.

如果设计者所设计的托架能支撑100磅,当它被设计为1 000磅时,事故一定会出现。

3) Afterwards he found a sunspot which lived long enough to disappear from view on the western limb of the sun, to reappear on its eastern limb, and finally to regain its old position.

后来,他发现有一个停留在太阳西部的边缘上的黑子过了很长一段时间才消失在太阳的东部边缘上,最后再次回到了原位。

4) Great was his joyous pride when he proved to his own satisfaction, by patient experiments of his own, the explanations given in the lectures.

当他由于自己勤奋的试验和讲课中所得到的解释显得满意时,他是兴高采烈的。

5) In 1872, he published the results in a paper titled The *Galvanic Chain, Mathematically Treated.*

在1872年,他以《电流的链,数学化处理》为标题在报纸上出版了这个结果。

6) During one four-year period about 600 years ago the Black Death killed at least 25 million people in Europe.

在一个四年期间的约600年前,黑死病至少使2 500万欧洲人死亡。

7) Scientific discoveries and inventions do not always influence the language in proportion to their importance.

科学的发现与发明,就其重要性的比例而言,并不一定对语言有什么影响。

8) The importance of superconductor in the uses of electricity cannot be overestimated.

超导体在电器应用上的重要性不能被估计过高。

9) The pilot lamp stopped to represent the termination of the operation.

指示灯停止显示操作终止。

10) How wild his white hair looked—as if it had been electrified.

他满头白发,十分凌乱——简直像刚电烫过一般。

3. Text Typology and Functional Classification

文体通常分为文学文体和非文学文体,非文学文体也称为应用文体或实用文体。文学文体通常分为诗歌和散文,或诗歌、散文、小说、戏剧。非文学文体通常分为新闻报刊、广告、科技、法律、政论、经贸、旅游等。

Translating is essentially a text-processing action; different types of texts require different translation strategies. Basing on previous classification of language functions, Newmark builds his own text typology, which divides the source text of translation functions into three main types: expressive, informative and vocative, with each type processing distinctive features in the aspects of author's status, text emphasis, language manner and so on. The text typology by Newmark is quite brief, defined, and easily utilized, which is a guide to translation. He also claims that, in translation practice, few texts are purely expressive, informative or vocative; most include all three functions, with an emphasis on one of the three.

英国当代翻译理论家纽马克运用了功能语言理论,即语言的三大功能,提出了三种文本功能:表达功能(expressive function);信息功能(informative function);呼唤功能(vocative function)。并根据不同的功能提出了相应的翻译策略:语义翻译(semantic translation);交际翻译(communicative translation)。

Reiss is a representative of functionalists. In her view, text typology can serve as a guideline for translation criticism and she hoped the translator could specify the appropriate hierarchy of equivalent levels needed for a particular translation. She classified the text in accordance with the dominant communicative function of a text.

In her translation-oriented text typology, the three main text types she proposed are informative, expressive and operative; each text type is identified by its semantic, lexical, grammatical and stylistic features.

赖斯将语言义本分为:表达功能文本(expressive),强调文本的创造性构建和语言的美学层面,突出文本作者及文本本身;信息功能文本(informative),凡是旨在传递信息、知识、意见等事实的文本,皆属于信息功能文本,文本的重心在于其内容和主题;感召功能文本(operative),旨在通过说服文本读者或者接受者采取某种行动,使其从行为上对文本做出反应,其语言特点是对话式的,文本的重点在于感召。

切斯特曼对赖斯文本类型的分类整理

文本类型	表达功能文本	信息功能文本	感召功能文本
语言功能	表达感情(表达文本作者的态度)	提供信息(陈述事实或事物)	感召读者(使文本接受者产生行动)
语言特点	美学	逻辑	对话
文本重心	文本形式	传递文本内容	对话
译本功能	传达美学形式	传递文本内容	产生预期的效果
翻译方法	再现原文内容与风格	文字通顺易懂,力求清晰明白	可做调整,达到等效

3.1 Expressive Text

Expressive text includes literature, essay, novel, poem, drama, and autography. Translation of these texts is expected to convey both meaning and form, the artistic effect, the unique flavor, such as diction, sentence pattern, rhetoric, as well as other non-conventional use of language. Translators should be keen enough to identify these stylistic elements and try to represent them in their translation.

3.2 Informative Text

This type of text mainly informs the reader about objects and phenomena of this real world. In translation, the translator should concentrate on establishing semantic equivalence between source and target texts; the format of informative text is often standard: a textbook, a technical report, an article in a newspaper or a periodical scientifc paper, a thesis, minutes or agenda of a meeting. By the way, in the translation of Chinese political and economic documents, we ought to keep the tone in the original text and avoid misunderstanding.

3.3 Vocative / Appellative / Operative Text

The term "vocative" in the sense of "calling upon" helps the readership to act, think or feel, actually to "react" in the way intended by the text. Some typical examples of vocative text are notices, advertisements, political and religious speeches, debating speeches, instructions, persuasive writings (requests, cases, theses) and possibly popular fictions and so on.

风格与文本类型

翻译的层次:直译与意译		常见的文本
严格的直译 Literalness	要求比较严格的直译	条约、法典、规章、政府公文; 政治论文及文献
直译要求随文体之样式改变 ↓	基本直译	一般学术理论、科技情报与著作
	一般要求直译,但必须考虑可读性	新闻报道和分析; 报刊特写
	直译与意译兼顾;充分考虑可读性	传记、游记、札记等; 文艺小说
	基本意译,力求获得最佳可读性	舞台或电视剧本; 抒情散文
译文的可读性 Readability	必须完全意译方能达意,力求获得最佳可读性与艺术性	诗歌; 歌词

4. Style and Stylistics

The word "style", itself, has several connotations that make it difficult for the term to be defined accurately. However, in *Linguistic Criticism*, Roger Fowler makes the point that, in non-theoretical usage, the word "stylistics" makes sense and is useful referring to an enormous range of literary contexts, such as John Milton's "grand style", the "prose style" of Henry James, the "epic" and "ballad style" of classical Greek literature, etc. In addition, stylistics is a distinctive term that may be used to determine the connections between the form and effect within a particular variety of language.

4.1 The Concept of Style

The word "style" derives from the Greek or Latin word "stile" or "stilus", which firstly means pointed instrument, used for writing and later indicates a way of writing. It is widely used in music, painting and architecture as well as other social activities. In language use, style has been an object of interest since earliest Greek, concentrating on the study of grammar and rhetoric. It is said that there are more than thirty definitions for style, so it is important to understand its connotations because it can provide us with a basis for analyzing the style of texts. Here are some of the connotations of style.

(1) A person's distinctive language habits, or the set of individual characteristics of language use, or we can put it into: "style is the man itself" or modern terms, and "style" is called "the expression of your personality" without any relationship with the literary significance.

e. g.

Hemingway's style

Henry James' style

Mark Twain's style

(2) Style may refer to a set of collective characteristics of language use, including national style, style of age, etc. The style in this regard includes a range of rules that writers in that particular genre (or age) follow or are expected to follow. The analysis and assessment of style involve examination of a writer's choice of words, his figures of speech, the devices (rhetorical and otherwise), the shape of his sentences (whether they are loose or periodic), the shape of paragraphs — indeed, of every conceivable aspect of his language and the way in which he uses it.

e. g.

Elizabethan style

the style of legal document

the style of news reporting

(3) A characteristic of "good" or "beautiful" literary writings.

e. g.

ornate style

terse style

plain style

(4) Style may refer to the effectiveness of a mode of expression, which is implied in the definition of style as "saying the right thing in the most effective way" or "good manners", as a "clear" or "refined" style advocated in most books of composition. Therefore, style is the artistically and thematically motivated choice. In literature, style involves the novelist's choice of words and phrases, and how the novelist arranges these words and phrases in sentences and paragraphs.

"In the broadest sense, style can be applied to both spoken and written, both literary and non-literary varieties of language; but by tradition, it is particularly associated with written literary text." (Leech)

(5) Linguistics-oriented style: manners indicating prominent linguistic features, devices or patterns, most frequently occur in a particular text of a particular variety of language.

Exercise: Answer the following questions.

1) If given two poems, one by Li Bai (李白), the other by Du fu (杜甫), could you differentiate them?

2) What is the author's habitual use of the language? Similarly, if you were offered

two poems, one by Li Qingzhao (李清照), the other by Xin Qiji(辛弃疾), could you differentiate them?

4.2 Translatability and Untranslatability of Style

Quite a few people regard style untranslatable in that it is impossible to render the characteristics of one language into another and produce the style of the ST for both the objective and subjective reasons.

The noted scholar Alexander Fraser Tytler expresses the idea that style is translatable in his famous *Essay on the Principles of Translation*, in which he puts forward his "three laws of translation".

E. A. Nida and C. R. Taber hold a similar point of view. "Translating consists in reproducing in the receptor language the closest natural equivalent of the source language message, first in terms of meaning and second in terms of style".

From the above quotations, we may draw a conclusion that style can be translated.

4.3 Concepts of Stylistics

Stylistics is a branch of linguistics which studies style in a scientific and systematic way concerning the manners/linguistic features of different varieties of language at different levels. In fact, stylistics suggests a scientific and systematic, rational, objective rather than an impressionistic, fragmentary and intuitive, subjective investigation of style.

"Stylistics", as defined by *Longman English Dictionary*, is the study of style. Leech defines: "Stylistics is the study of the use of language in literature."

The goal of stylistics is not simply to describe the formal features of texts for their own sake, but in order to show their functional significance for their interpretation of the text.

Stylistics is a discipline that studies the ways in which language is used; it is a discipline that studies the styles of language in use.

Stylistics is a branch of linguistics which applies the theory and methodology of modern linguistics to the study of style.

Stylistics is a linguistic approach to literature, explaining the relation between language and artistic function, with motivating questions such as "why" and "how" more than "what". (Leech)

Stylistics is a branch of linguistics which studies the characteristics of situational distinctive uses of language, with particular reference to literary language, and tries to establish principles capable of accounting for the particular choices made by individuals and social groups in their use of language.

4.4 Stylistic Feature

As a branch of applied linguistics, then, stylistics drew upon developments in descriptive linguistics (especially in its earlier stages), and particularly so in relation to grammar, through which it developed many of its models and "tools" for analysis. As is interpreted in this book, stylistic analysis centers upon the formal and linguistic properties of a text and the stylistic features of different varieties are mainly studied on the following items: phonology, lexis, syntax/grammar, and semantics.

4.4.1 The Phonological Category

Phonology is used here to refer to the system of speech sounds in a language, which includes the following aspects:

elision;
sound symbolism;
sound patterning;
rhythm;
rhyme;
pause;
stress;
tempo;
intonation patterns;
alliteration;
assonance;
consonance;
onomatopoeia;
pitch.

4.4.2 The Graphological Category

Graphology is used here to refer to the writing forms, and the signs used in a text, which includes the following aspects:

punctuation;
capitalization;
paragraphing;
italics;
format of printing;
graphic signs;
spelling.

4.4.3 The Lexical Category

Lexis is used here to refer to the choice of words, which includes the following aspects:

general or specific (super ordinate or subordinate);
Anglo-Saxon or Latinate;
conceptual or associative (denotative or connotative);
monosyllabic or polysyllabic (simple or hard);
descriptive or evaluative;
formal or informal (clippings, blends, abbreviations);
standard or nonstandard (slang, jargon);
dynamic or static (verbs);
vulgar or euphemistic;
favorable or unfavorable;
archaic or neologism (old fashioned or new words);
common or rare;
abstract or concrete (nouns).

4.4.4 The Syntactic/Grammatical Category

sentence types;
sentence complexity;
sentence length;
clause types;
phrase types;
grammatical constructions;
word order;
tenses;
voices;
grammaticality.

4.4.5 The Semantic Category

figures of comparison (simile, metaphor, analogy, personification);
figures of replacement (metonymy, allusion, hyperbole, euphemism);
figures of repetition (alliteration, assonance, rhyme);
figures of double meaning (pun, irony, satire);
figures of contrast/juxtaposition (antithesis, oxymoron);
figures of reverse meanings;
figures of resemblance.

Apart from the items mentioned above, the stylistic features may also include such aspects as how the overall discourse patterning and planning, the subject matter, the text layout, and the introduction of materials of different kinds contribute to the conveying of meaning of the whole text. And the students can work on their stylistic analysis under the following guidelines.

(1) Work systematically through the text and note down points we feel of some stylistic significance.

(2) Quantify the frequency of a linguistic feature.

(3) Assess the importance of stylistic features.

(4) Make statements about the overall linguistic picture of the text in question.

5. Stylistics-oriented Translation

A lively debate has continued for many years between those translators who maintain that technical translation does not need to concern itself with matters of style and those who assert that all writings, whether they are technical, journalistic, literary, etc., should be designed to conform to the stylistic conventions that reflect the specific expectations of the target audience. In this regard, style refers to a wide scale of considerations, ranging from the overall structure form of the entire text to lexical choice at sentence fragment level.

Stylistics studies the effect of languages. Different stylistics may demonstrate different language features, which can be shown by lexis and grammar. To differentiate the different stylistics, registers of system-functional linguistics can serve as a channel. Register is comprised of three parts: field of discourse, tenor of discourse and mode of discourse; field of discourse mainly gives a description of what is going on and the language environment; tenor of discourse answers the questions including who has participated, and what is the relationship between addresser and addressee (formal or informal); mode of discourse deals with the medium that has been selected for relaying the message, which is known as speaking (conversation, monologue, etc.) and writing (speech, news, etc.). From the analysis of the register of different stylistics, it can be found that different stylistics should adopt different translation strategies correspondingly.

Lexis is the most basic unit of a text. The overall style of a text is reflected by the choice of each word. In political essays, serious and general words are preferred; while in children literature, simple and "small" words are more likely to appear. Exact and formal words are indispensable to law of English while EST (English for Science and Technology) is characterized by terminologies. Essays and poems are supposed to choose words whose meanings are vague; while ads prefer newly-coined words or figures of speech like pun.

6. Comparative Studies of English and Chinese Language

According to some linguists, noticeably Lian Shuneng, in his *Contrastive Studies on English and Chinese*, ten contrasts indicate the disparity between English and Chinese.

6.1 Synthetic vs. Analytic

English is a synthetic language marked with inflections, while Chinese is an analytic language without any inflection, which is usually implied in the context or explicitly shown in such words as "着、了、过", etc. A synthetic language is characterized by frequent and systematic use of inflected forms to express grammatical relationships. An analytic language is marked by a relatively frequent use of function words, auxiliary verbs, and changes in word order to express syntactic relations, rather than of inflected forms. Look at the following example.

He moved astonishingly fast.
He moved with astonishing rapidity.
His movements were astonishingly rapid.
His rapid movements astonished us.
His movements astonished us by their rapidity.
The rapidity of his movements was astonishing.
The rapidity with which he moved astonished us.
He astonished us by moving rapidly.
He astonished us by his rapid movements.
He astonished us by the rapidity of his movements.

He—His
move—moved—movements
rapid—rapidly—rapidity
astonish—astonished—astonishing

他的行动快得惊人。
他行动的速度快得惊人。
他行动速度之快,令人惊讶。
他的快速行动使我们感到惊讶。
我们对他的快速行动感到惊讶。

6.2 Compact vs. Diffusive

English sentences are compact, tightly combined with connectives or prepositions, while Chinese is diffused and loose in structure.

e. g.

Now the integrated circuit has reduced by many times the size of the computer of which it forms a part, thus creating a new generation of portable minicomputer.

【译文】现在集成电路成了计算机的组成部分,使计算机的体积大大缩小,从而产生了新一代的便携式微型计算机。

A notion has taken hold in the US to the effect that only the people who should be encouraged to bring children into the world are those who can afford them.

【译文】在美国有一个根深蒂固的观点,认为只有对那些抚养得起子女的人,才应鼓励其生育。

6.3 Hypotactic vs. Paratactic

In English, clauses or phrases are coordinated with or subordinated to one another syntactically while in Chinese they are placed one after another without coordination connectives. To clarify the relations between words, phrases and clauses, English more often resorts to overt cohesion, frequently by using various cohesive ties such as relatives (relative or conjunctive pronouns and adverbs, e. g. who, whom, whose, that, when, where, why, how), connectives (coordinate or subordinate conjunctions, e. g. and, or but, yet, so, however, as well as, either... or..., neither... nor..., when, while, as, since, until, so... that..., unless, lest), prepositions, and some others. Chinese sentence concentrates on word order or pragmatic meaning, neglecting whether the sentence is complete or not. In addition, unlike English, which uses conjunctions as a way of connection, the Chinese sentence is formed to express meanings.

The structure of English can be compared to a tree. Chinese is paratactic in that it has no inflections and does not need connectives for sentence organization. The meanings of different parts help indicate the relationship within a sentence. The structure of Chinese can be compared to a bamboo.

Chinese: left-extending, heavy-headed like a lion. For example,

一棵树
一棵大树
一棵枝繁叶茂的大树
花园里一棵枝繁叶茂的大树
李家花园里一棵枝繁叶茂的大树
同里镇李家花园里一棵枝繁叶茂的大树
……

English: right-extending, heavy-tailed like a peacock. For example,

This is the cat.
This is the cat that killed the rat.
This is the cat that killed the rat that ate the cake.
This is the cat that killed the rat that ate the cake that lay in the house.
This is the cat that killed the rat that ate the cake that lay in the house that was built by Jack.
…

e. g.

It is rather for us to be here dedicated to the great task remaining before us: that from these honored dead we take increased devotion to that cause for which they gave the last full measure of devotion; that we here highly revolve that these dead shall not have died in vain; that the nation, under God, shall have a new birth of freedom; and that the government of the people, by the people, and for the people, shall not perish from the earth.

【**译文**】我们应该做的是献身于他们留给我们的伟大任务。我们的先烈已将自己的全部精诚奉献给我们的事业,我们应从他们身上汲取更多的精神力量,努力使他们的鲜血不致白流。在上帝的保佑下,自由将得到新生。我们这个民有、民治、民享的政府将永存于世上。

Exercise: Translate the following sentences.

1) Oil used for this purpose must be of the correct thickness; if it is too thin it will not give sufficient lubrication, and if it is too thick it will not reach all parts that must be lubricated.

2) If I had known it would come to this, I would have acted differently.

3) He is always changing his mind the moment he sees something new.

4) He has never been back to his birthplace since he left it ten years ago.

5) When the conversation gets disagreeable, to say one word more is a waste of breath.

6) It is easy to change rivers and mountains but hard to change a person's nature.

7) In a word, while the prospects are bright, the road has twists and turns.

8) 人不犯我,我不犯人。

9) 枯藤,老树,昏鸦。
小桥,流水,人家。
古道,西风,瘦马。
夕阳西下。
断肠人在天涯。

10) 对人太苛求,没有什么道理,自己也容易失望。

6.4 Complex vs. Simplex

English sentences are long and complex, while Chinese sentences are short and simple. Sentences of short rhythm are used in Chinese and sentences of short or medium length hold a major part in Chinese. The frequent use of punctuation in Chinese is also a good way to achieve the simple style. As for English, complex sentences with embedded clauses are commonly seen. Subordination is one of the most important characteristics of contemporary English.

Exercise: Translate the following sentences.

1) Many man-made substances are replacing certain natural materials either because the quality of the natural product can not meet our ever-increasing requirement, or, more often, because the physical properties of the synthetic substance, which is the common name for man-made materials, have been chosen, and even emphasized, so that it would be of the greatest use in the fields in which it is to be applied.

2) There is no more difference, but there is just the same kind of difference, between the mental operations of a man of science and those of an ordinary person as there is between the operations and methods of a baker or of a butcher who weights out his goods in common scales and the operation of a chemist who performs a difficult and complex analysis by means of his balance and finely graduated weights.

3) 有时候,在工作中重要的是能否处理好人际关系(interpersonal skills),而不是有多大的才能(professional skills)。人际关系就是一种善于听取别人意见,体察别人的需要,虚心接受批评的能力。善于处理人际关系的人敢于承认错误,敢于承担自己的责任,这是对待错误的一种成熟和负责任的态度。

4) 中国已经成功地发射了第一颗试验通信卫星。这颗卫星是由三级火箭推动的,一直运转正常。它标志着我国在运载工具和电子技术方面进入了一个新阶段。

6.5 Impersonal vs. Personal

Westerners believe that the universe is divided into two opposites: man and nature, subject and object, mind and matter, the divine and the secular, which is reflected in the language, is expressed as subjects being "impersonal subject". By contrast, Chinese people have very strong consciousness of subjective participation. Personal subject is expressed in Chinese language. There are more impersonal structures used as the subject in English than in Chinese. As a result of the difference, the conversion of English impersonal subject into Chinese personal subject is often employed in translation.

Exercise: Translate the following sentences.

1) An idea suddenly occurred to me.

2) A great elation overcame them.

3) From the moment we stepped into the People's Republic of China, care and kindness surrounded us on every side.

4) The thick carpet killed the sound of my footsteps.

5) 人们已认识到维持生命必需的食物主要有三种。第一种是碳水化合物,这些碳水化合物广泛存在于动植物世界中,包括糖、淀粉及纤维分子,它们为人体提供能量。

6.6 Active vs. Passive

The passive voice is extensively used in English, while Chinese sentences are usually active. For example, it is admitted that, it is asserted that, it is believed that, it is claimed that, it is felt that, it is found out that, it is noticed that, it is pointed out that, it is regarded that, it is stressed that, it is suggested that, it is thought that... (人们承认,人们主张,人们相信,人们宣称,人们发现,人们知道,人们注意到,人们指出,人们注

意,人们强调,人们建议,人们认为,……)

Exercise: Translate the following sentences.

1) 他准备给我一份工作,这使我大吃一惊。

2) 很抱歉,因为雨太大,参观博物馆得推迟到明天了。

3) 请全系师生于星期三下午两点在会议室集合,听报告。

4) 采取"一国两制"适合中国国情, 并非权宜之计。

5) 那个孩子受了重伤,医院立即把他收下了。

6) 凡是做功,都是把能从一种形式转换成另一种形式。

7) 1964 年 10 月,中国成功地爆炸了第一颗原子弹,这把基辛格吓了一跳。

8) 要制造飞机,就必须仔细考虑空气阻力问题。

6.7 Static vs. Dynamic

English is static, with agent nouns being frequently used to replace verbs, while Chinese is dynamic, with more verbs being used in a single sentence. In English, nouns can be characterized as "stative" (English is featured by its predominance of nouns over verbs). English makes more use of nouns, adjectives, and prepositions, and is therefore more static. Conversely, Chinese often employs verbs, adverbs, verbal phrases, repletion and duplication of verbs, and is therefore more dynamic.

Exercise: Translate the following sentences.

1) Thus the best books are treasures of good words, the golden thoughts, which, remembered and cherished, become our constant companions and comforters.

2) He is a good eater and good sleeper.

3) The sight and sound of our jet planes filled me with special longing.

4) Television is the transmission and reception of images of moving objects by radio waves.

5) One after another, speakers called for the downfall of imperialism, abolition of exploitation of man by man, liberation of the oppressed of the world.

6) 住在楼上的人家提着水桶去楼下的水龙头打水。

7) 他上下班一般坐地铁。

8) 采用这种新装置可以大大降低废品量。

9) 林则徐认为,要成功地禁止鸦片买卖,就得首先把鸦片销毁。

10) 中国加入世贸组织,将为中国,乃至亚洲以及世界各国、各地区的经济发展注入新的活力。

6.8 Abstract vs. Concrete

In expressing the same idea, English seems more abstract while Chinese, more concrete. For example,

He is *a valuable acquisition* to the team.

虚译:他是该队一种宝贵的获取。

实译:他是该队不可多得的新队员。

Nowadays a student heading for college may pack *a frying pan* along with his books.

实译:如今上大学的学生除了带他的书上学校以外,还可以带上一个平底煎锅。

虚译:如今大学生在学校里不仅要读书还要做饭吃。

Good secretaries are like *gold dust*.

【译文】好的秘书是不可多得的宝贵人才。

For many families, especially in Tokyo, two *incomes* are a necessity.

【译文】对于许多家庭来说,夫妻俩都去上班赚钱是迫不得已的事,在东京尤其如此。

He contemplates retiring with *a hand on the helm*.

【译文】他打算退位但依然听政。

Exercise: Compare the following translation version.

1) 因此,我们的苦闷基本上比西方人更少、更小;因为苦闷的强弱是随欲望与野心的大小而变化的。

【译文】Therefore, our metal sufferings, as compared with westerners', are fewer and less intense, since whether our sufferings are strong or weak is determined by whether our desires and ambitions are big or small.

改译:Therefore, we generally suffer less depression than westerners, as the degree of the suffering varies directly with that of our desire and ambition.

2) 花园是人间的乐园,有的是吃不了的大米白面,穿不完的绫罗绸缎,花不完的金银财宝。

【译文】The garden was a paradise on earth, with more food and clothes than could be consumed and more money than could be spent.

3) 中华民族自古以来很少把人看成高于一切。

【译文】The Chinese people have seldom considered man above anything else.

改译: The Chinese people have seldom believed in human supremacy.

4) 农业社会的人比工业社会的人享受差得多,因此欲望也小得多。

【译文】People in the agricultural society enjoy themselves less than those in the industrial society, so they have less desire.

改译: People in the agricultural society have less enjoyment than those in the industrial society, hence less desire.

5) 许多人把自己开店当做理想。可是开门七件事:柴、米、油、盐、酱、醋、茶。当然最重要的应该是要有钱,因为只有钱才能解决这一切。

【译文】People hope to start their own business to realize their dreams, but there are a lot of things that have to be considered at first. Of course, money can solve all these.

6.9 Indirect vs. Direct

Some English sentences seem to be indirect in affirmation while Chinese sentences are straightforward.

Exercise: Translate the following sentences.

1) I couldn't feel better.

2) I couldn't agree with you more.

3) He can't see you quickly enough.

4) This book is quite beyond me.

5) Every person has the right to be free from hunger.

6) If you have a car, you are independent of trains and buses.

6.10 Substitutive vs. Repetitive

Generally speaking, there are not so many repetitions used in English as in Chinese.

Exercise: Translate the following sentences.

1) 我们说,长征是历史记录上的第一次,长征是宣言书,长征是宣传队,长征是播种机。

2) 质子带正电荷,电子带负电荷,而中子既不带正电荷,也不带负电荷。

3) He hated failure; he had conquered it all his life, risen above it, and despised it in others.

7. An Overview of English and Chinese Thought Patterns

Language does not exist in a vacuum. It serves and is modeled by other systems in the human mind. Because it is used for conveying ideas, it must be spoken and understood easily and efficiently, and its structure and function are forced to stay within the limits imposed by people's processing capacities. Because it is used for communication within a complex social and cultural system, its structure and function are modeled by these factors as well.

Differences of Thinking Modes

English	Chinese
Analytical Mode of Thinking	Synthetic Mode of Thinking
Thought pattern: objects are studied by analyzing their parts.	Thought pattern: objects are studied from an overall point of view.
Subject-unconsciousness	Subject-consciousness
Aesthetic values: no emphasis is given to antinomy and balance. Clarity and precision are aesthetic principles.	Aesthetic values: emphasis on the beauty of balance. Symmetry and parallel connection are aesthetic principles.
English is functional because of the Indo-European emphasis on reasoning and logic.	Chinese is imaginative because of the Chinese emphasis on intuition and images.

7.1 Linear vs. Circular / Spiral

English people are inclined to linear thinking which focuses on reason and logic. Their discourse organization also turns out to be linear. The gist of the statement is often given at the beginning of the text, and the paragraph is usually made by an integrated unity with its idea expressed directly. However, Chinese people have the tendency to delay the topic and illustrate indirectly with the main point of information shown finally after an elaborate stating of the related situation. So Chinese thought pattern is a cyclical one.

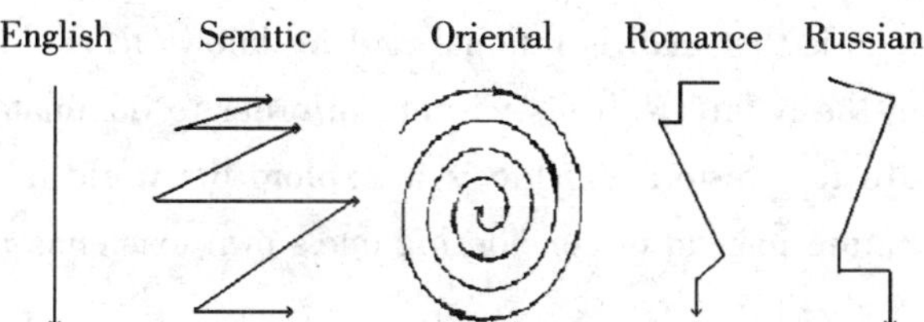

7.2 Ethical Thinking vs. Cognitive Thinking

Due to the limited prospect of geographic environment and the farming economy of China in ancient days, the Confucian thought was formed. From the view of Confucianism, it is the existing rules and ethics that will make man understand and be aware of the world better. As Professor Lian Shuneng states, "The Confucians are concerned about the principles man should obey rather than the principle of the nature and about the meaning of life rather than the essence of the nature."

Lin Yutang, the famous Chinese linguist, also has pointed out that Chinese make use of feelings to conciliate since they know that theories cannot be relied on. Their thoughts take both the theories and feelings into accounts and man's behavior is required to be in accordance with the proper feelings. This is the main character of Chinese thinking principle. On the contrary, the western culture is developed from the maritime climate and special geographic environment. Therefore, the westerners are fond of astronomy and geography because the knowledge of astronomy and geography can make their lives safe and comfortable, and gradually, the cognitive tradition to investigate the nature and to obtain from the nature is built in their culture. According to the different focuses on the philosophy ideas, the Chinese thinking mode is more ethical while the westerners' is more cognitive.

7.3 Figurative Thinking vs. Abstract Thinking

Another chief feature of Chinese thinking mode is to be figurative because Chinese prefer to be aware of the nature and principles of the objects with knowledge and experience they have owned and use them to build up concrete things or objects to explain the principles from the view of their philosophy ideas. In the history of Chinese literature, the image analytic method is widely used and provided. So, the forming of Chinese characters can be resulted from this figurative thinking mode of Chinese. Most of the original Chinese characters were created just as symbols or collections of symbols of the things in the nature. Compared with Chinese figurative thinking, the westerners' thinking mode is comparatively more abstract. This attributes to the rational and logical thinking tradition of the westerners. As to the western philosophy, the sign of distinguishing man and other existing things is that man is rational and he knows to explore the world and to reveal the mysteries of the nature with his wisdom in order to dominate the world with his laws and principles. To the westerners, life is to explore the world in order to understand it and challenge the nature instead of considering one's own existence and moralities, etc.

Chapter Two
Translation of Science and Technology
科技文体翻译

Functional Equivalence(功能对等)

Functional equivalence, or dynamic equivalence, is proposed by American linguist and translator Eugene A. Nida. Throughout his life, Nida has devoted himself to the translation of *Bible*. During this process, he developed his own translation theory, which is considered one of the classics in the field of translation. Functional equivalence means more than the equivalence in terms of word. It refers to the equivalence in terms of the functions. Functional equivalence includes four aspects:

(1) lexical equivalence;

(2) syntactic equivalence;

(3) discourse equivalence;

(4) stylistic equivalence.

Among the four aspects, Nida considers meaning is more important than form.

关键词:功能对等;动态对等;词汇对等;句法对等;篇章对等;文体对等

EST Translation

The English of EST is actually a big variety, including the English of chemistry, the English of physics, the English of mathematics, the English of biology, the English of medicine, etc. Generally speaking, the English of all scientific fields has something in common on which we base our studies. Sci-tech literature has these characteristics: long complex sentences, use of passive voice, noun phrases with crowding pre-attributives and post-attributives. Besides invariable present tense, logic coherence, well-knit structure and precise definitions, clear, fluent, compact, plain, brief, non-emotional language is another feature of EST text. It is impersonal, formal in mode of speech, objective and accurate in statement, standard in language, unadorned in stylistics, strict in logic, concentrated in technical terms.

1. Comparison between EST and Literature English

EST is a communicative style to exchange information—sentences in EST may have more than one modifier, qualifier or additional element, which produces long and complex sentences.

Literature English tends to seek elegant style or carry strong personal emotions or inclinations of the authors.

2. Five Categories of EST

(1) Works, papers and reports on science and technology, lab reports and programs.

(2) A variety of sci-tech information and written materials.

(3) Structure descriptions and operating procedures in operative manuals (of apparatus, instruments, machines, tools, etc.).

(4) Language used in talks, meetings and conversations concerning science and technology.

(5) Commentaries in such audio materials as films, videos, etc.

除此之外,科技英语也可以分为:科技著作、科技论文和报告、实验报告和方案;各类科技情报和文字资料;科技使用手段,包括仪器、仪表、机械、工具等的结构描述和操作说明;有关科技问题的会谈、会议交流用语;有关科技的影片、录像等有声资料的解说词;科技发明、发现的报道;科学幻想小说。

3. Stylistic Feature of EST

3.1 Lexical Feature

EST has a wealth of abbreviations, coinages and borrowed words primarily concerned with the commonly used words. Here, abbreviations consist of four kinds of words: blends, initializes, acronyms, and clipped words.

Lexical feature of EST vocabulary usually consists of common words with specific meaning, highly technical words such as anode(阳极), hydroxide (氢氧化物), isotope (同位素), and enormous number of semi-technical words, noun compounds, nominalization, bloom of new terms, newly coined words and various word-formation ways.

科技文体是一种独立的文体形式,科技词汇的大量涌现形成了其词汇特点,其词汇形态大致可以分为三类:单词式,如行星(planet),摆(pendulum);复合式,如传送系统(carrier system)、短路器(circuit-breaker);短语式,如数据处理装置(data processing installation)、应答系统(enquiry-response system)。构词法的掌握对翻译有很大裨益。另外,科技文章词汇翻译需要注意选取符合技术规范的词语。例如,以下词汇在其不同的使用领域有其自身的翻译规律。

e. g.

beacon 信号灯——警告过程

bank 银行——存储块区

pocket 口袋——存储桶

mask 面罩——屏蔽

3. 1. 1 Borrowing

English in its development has managed to widen its vocabulary by borrowing words from other languages. Greek, Latin, French and Spanish have all played an active role in this process.

翻译此类术语时一般按音译即可,必要时用增词法作解释。

e. g.

Xerox 静电复制(出自商标名)

Kuru 库鲁病(出自新几内亚的地名)

IBM System IBM 系统(出自公司名)

3. 1. 2 Compounding

Compounding is the way to join two separate words to produce a single form.

复合词的意义可以通过各部分意义相加得出总体意义,但也有不少例外。翻译时应格外注意其隐喻色彩与意象的特征,如靶心(bull's eye)、航向与指挥(cat-and-mouse)、高频高压电源屏蔽罩(dog-house)。

e. g.

brain-trust 智囊团

green-house 温室

field-test 现场测试

abdominal-delivery 剖宫产

3. 1. 3 Blending

Two words are blended by joining the initial part of the first word and final part of the second word, or by joining the initial parts of the two words.

此类术语采用"掐头去尾"的方法构成,翻译时应首先弄清其代表的原词含义,再将两者意义相加。

e. g.

taikonaut = taikong + astronaut 航天员

minicomputer = miniature + computer 微型计算机
transistor = transfer + resistor 晶体管
telex = teleprinter + exchange 电传
copytron = copy + electron 电子复写(技术)

3.1.4 Abbreviation / Clipped Words

A clipped word means the word shortened from a longer word by cutting a part off the original so that we use what remains instead (A great number of English words have undergone the process of abbreviation in their etymological history, and it is also called clipping).

e. g.

fridge = refrigerator 冰箱
lab = laboratory 实验室
tech = technology 技术
flu = influenza 流感
telecom = telecommunication 电信

3.1.5 Acronym / Initialism

Both initialism and acronym are the words formed by joining the initial letter of technical terms in EST. Initialism is the words pronounced letter by letter, while acronym is the words from initial letter but pronounced as a normal word. Most words of initialism and acronym are so common that their full names are seldom given in the writing.

e. g.

Acronym:
radar = radio detecting and ranging 雷达
SARS = Severe Acute Respiratory Syndrome 严重急性呼吸综合征,非典型性肺炎
laser = light amplification by stimulated emission of radiation 激光
AIDS = Acquired Immune Deficiency Syndrome 艾滋病
Initialism:
WWWW = World Wide Web Worm 网络蠕虫病毒
UFO = Un-identified Flying Object 不明飞行物,飞碟
SST = supersonic transport 超音速运输机
ADP = Automatic Data Processing 自动数据处理
EDPM = Electronic Data Processing Machine 电子数字处理机
GSV = Guided Space Vehicle 制导宇宙飞船
GPS = Global Positioning System 全球定位系统
LCD = Liquid Crystal Display 液晶显示

RAM = Random Access Memory 随机存取存储器

AS = air scoop 空气收集器

= air seasoned 风干的(木柴)

= air speed 航空站

= American Standard 美国标准

= atmosphere and space 大气层与宇宙空间

= automatic sprinkler 自动洒水车

= automatic synchronizer 自动同步器

3.1.6　Affixation

Affixation is an important means of coining new English words and technical terms, with prefix and suffix as inseparable elements.

英语构词法主要有合成、转化和派生,其中派生就是加前、后缀,其出现频率远远高于其他方法。翻译时对词缀概念的了解很重要。

e. g.

macroclimax 大气候

macrospore 大孢子

bathythermograph 海水测温仪器

deoxyribonucleic 脱氧核糖核的

3.1.7　Proper Nouns

There are many EST terms transformed from proper nouns such as the names of people, place, book and film. There are many physical terms that are named after the name of physicists.

e. g.

Newton 牛顿

Watt 瓦特

Ampere 安培

Pascal 帕斯卡

Volt 伏特

Joule 焦耳

Farad 法拉

3.1.8　Complex and Changeful Word Meaning

A term may have many different meanings, which can be distinguished according to the specialty, collocation, content and so on.

有些词在不同专业中都要使用,但不同专业中却有不同的含义,如"transmission"可以译成:"发射、传播"(无线电工程学);"传动、变速"(机械学);"透射"(物理学)；“遗传”(医学)。又如“base”，可以译成“底座”(机械学)；“碱”(化学)；“基极”(电子学)；“底边”(数学)；“基地垒”(体育学)。

3.1.9 Bloom of New Terms

Along with the development of science and technology, there are many new EST terms coming into being.

e. g.

Google 用搜索引擎搜索信息

email 电子邮件

web page 网页

webzine 网络杂志

3.1.10 Coinages

Coinages refer to the newly invented words or phrases characterized by expressiveness and brevity. Coinages proceed from the whimsical creation of EST writers through compounding or analogy.

e. g.

information superhighway 信息高速路

airbus 空中巴士

3.2 Amplification and Omission in Lexical Translation

3.2.1 Amplification

修辞性增译

Speed and reliability are the chief advantages of the electronic computer.

速度**快**、可靠性**高**是电子计算机的主要优点。

A new kind of computer—small, cheap, fine—is attracting increasing attention.

一种新型计算机越来越引起人们的注意——这种计算机**体积小**、**价格低**、**性能优**。

概括性增译

The advantages of the recently developed composite materials are energy saving, performance efficient, corrosion resistant, long service time, and without environmental pollution.

最新开发的复合材料具有节能、性能好、抗腐蚀、寿命长和无污染**五大**特点。

The vapor pressure changes with the temperature, the pressure, and the kind of liquid.

蒸气压力随温度、压力和液体类型这**三个**因素的变化而变化。

逻辑性增词

I was taught that two sides of a triangle were greater than the third.

我学过,三角形的两边**之和**大于第三边。

This shows that the resistance of an electric conductor is inversely proportional to its cross-section area.

这表明,导体电阻的**大小**与导体横切面的**大小**成反比。

增译复数含义

Note that the words "velocity" and "speed" require explanation.

请注意,"速度"和"速率"这**两个**词需要加以解释。

For reasons the alternating current is more widely used than the direct current.

由于**种种**原因,交流电比直流电用得更为广泛。

3.2.2 Omission

省译冠词

A photon of solar energy excites ***a*** chlorophyll molecule within ***a*** plant cell's chloroplast, causing it to give off ***an*** electron.

太阳能的光子激发植物细胞叶绿素分子,使它释放出电子。

Small dose of toxins can induce ***a*** host to manufacture anti-toxins.

小剂量的毒素能使受体产生抗毒素。

省略代词

If ***you*** reduce the volume which a gas occupies to one-third, the pressure increases three times.

如果把气体所占的体积压缩到1/3,那么压力便会增加3倍。

One material can be distinguished from another by ***their*** physical properties.

根据物理性质,可以把一种材料与另一种材料区分开来。

省略介词

Most of the patients ***with*** neuron circulatory asthenia are unwilling to accept psychotherapy as such.

多数神经循环无力患者不愿意接受这种精神疗法。

Non-linear computer-based video editing is now feasible ***for*** most home computer users.

大多数家用电脑用户均可在非线性基础上进行视频编辑。

Exercise: Translate the following sentences.

1) The letter I stands for the current in Amperes, E the electromotive force in Volts and the R the resistance in Ohms.

2) Commission depends on the quantity of goods ordered.

3) Gas expands with temperature.

4) Water pressure increases with depth.

5) This report summed up the new achievements made in thermoplastic and thermosetting plastic.

3.3 Syntactic Feature

The primary purpose of EST is to supply information and to achieve clarity, conciseness and accuracy. As for the sentence length, there are more long sentences. Sentences of more than 30 words are by no means rare in EST writings, and they often contain several clauses and non-finite verb phrases as pre- and post- modifiers. About one-third of the verbs in EST writings are in passive voice.

3.3.1 Frequent Use of It-introduced Sentences

e. g.

It is possible to make concrete of any required strength within reasonable limits.

3.3.2 Frequent Use of Passive Voice

According to some linguists, the number of passive sentences in scientific and technological articles is ten times that of other articles. In the textbooks for physics and chemistry at least one-third of the verbs are passive voice. In order to explain clearly and draw the readers' attention to the objects, phenomena and processes, there is the need to put it in a clear prominent position. Passive sentences are widely used because of the following factors.

(1) Compared to active voice, passive voice is more objective, which attaches great importance to objectivity.

(2) Passive voice can better highlight the objects.

(3) In many cases, passive voice is briefer than active voice.

(4) Passive voice in English has its marked features like: be + v-ed.

e. g.

As oil *is found* deep in the ground, its presence cannot *be determined* by a study of the surface. Consequently, a geological survey of the underground rock structure must *be carried out*. If it *is thought* that the rocks in a certain area contain oil, a "drilling rig" *is assembled*. The most obvious part of a drilling rig *is called* a "derrick". It *is used* to lift sections of pipe, which *are lowered* into the hole made by the drill. As the hole *is being drilled*, a steel pipe *is pushed* down to prevent the sides from falling in. If oil *is struck*, a cover *is* firmly *fixed* to the top of the pipe and the oil *is allowed* to escape through a series of valves.

【译文】石油埋藏于地层深处。因此,仅仅靠研究地层表面,是无法确定有无石油的,必须对地下的岩石结构进行地质勘测。如果确定了某一区域的岩石蕴藏着石油,就在此安装钻机。钻机最明显的部分是机架,用来提举一节一节的钢管。这些钢管被压入井孔。一边钻井,一边下钢管,以防止周围土层塌陷。一旦出油,就紧固管盖,让油从各个阀门喷出。

Exercise: Translate the following sentences.

1) Contraction during cooling of heated solids is made use of in riveting.

2) If the mixture of the two gases, oxygen and hydrogen, is heated, something will happen that will cause the hydrogen atoms to lose their electrons.

3) New sources of energy must be found, and this will take time.

4) Communication satellites are used for international living transmission throughout the world.

5) Many code vessels are fabricated partly in the shop and partly in the field especially boilers.

6) These voice messages can be accessed later by the person to whom they are addressed.

7) Attention has been paid to the new measures to prevent corrosion.

8) Computer algorithms are used to make the comparisons and verify identity.

9) Rapid condensation is accomplished by means of condenser.

10) Polonium is used to set off a nuclear boom.

3.3.3 Negative vs. Affirmative

Full negative: no, not, none, never, nothing, nobody, nowhere, neither...nor

Semi negative: hardly, scarcely, seldom, barely, few, little ...

Partial negative: not every, not all, not both, not much, not many, not always...

Words with negative implication: fail, without, beyond, until, unless, lest, ignorant, refrain, refuse, neglect, absent, instead of, other than, except, rather than...

Special negative expressions:

not...because 并非因为……而

cannot ... too 怎么……也不

all/every ... not 并非……都

both...not 并非两者……都

Exercise: Translate the following sentences.

1) All of the heat supplied to the engine is not converted into useful work.

2) Every one cannot do these tests.

3) Both instruments are not precise.

4) This plant does not always make such machine tools.

5) The engine didn't stop because the fuel was finished.

6) All that glitters is not gold.

3.3.4 Long Sentence Translation

Long sentence translation is also a headache for the translator in Chinese-English translation. Since there is a great disparity between Chinese and English sentence structures, we should learn to tackle them discriminatingly. The usual method adopted in translating long Chinese sentences is cutting, namely, cutting the long sentences into several sections regardless of the punctuation marks. Of course, before cutting a long Chinese sentence, the most urgent task for a translator is to discern its main idea and the layout of the structure. After a careful analysis, he may cut the sentence into separate sections and then translate them one by one. This technique may contribute a lot when we are going to translate the long sentences which have the similar narrative structures as Chinese. From this perspective, the long sentences are constructed chronologically or logically in the same way just as what English and Chinese do.

长句的大量使用使科技英语显得正式、严谨,只要把握原文的脉络,层层译出其含义就可以了。翻译科技英语长句,首先要通过句法分析弄清句中各部分之间的语法关系、时间先后和逻辑顺序。在正确分析和理解原文的基础上,可以采用不同的方法,运用恰当的汉语表达,使译文达意、流畅。

Sequential

e. g.

During the high energy period of a physical biorhythm we are more resistant to illness, better coordinated and more energetic; during the low energy period we are less resistant to illness, less well coordinated and tired more easily.

【译文】当身体的生理节奏处于高能期的时候,抗病力较强,身体各部分更加协调一致,精力更旺盛;处于低能期的时候,抗病力较弱,身体各部分不太协调一致,而且更容易疲劳。

分析:原文为并列句,各分句意思的表达顺序和汉语的逻辑顺序基本一致,按原文的语法结构顺序翻译成的汉语应符合汉语的表达习惯,语句顺畅,又能清楚、准确地传达出原文的信息。

Reversing

Opposite to the sequential translation method, the sequential reversing translation method reads that when we are going to translate the EST which possesses the opposite logic compared to Chinese, it is advisable for us to reverse the order of the long sentence.

Adverbial clauses of condition, purpose, concession or cause, and so on in English may stand either before or after a principal clause, however, when translated into Chinese, they are normally placed before the principal clause.

e. g.

Scientists are learning a great deal about how the large plates in the earth's crust move, the stresses between plates, how earthquakes work, and the general probability that the given place will have an earthquake, although they still cannot predict earthquakes.

【译文】尽管科学家仍不能预测地震，但对地壳中的大板块如何运动、板块间的压力大小、地震如何发生、特定地区发生地震的概率为多少，了解得越来越多。

Aluminum, the richest metallic element in nature, remained unknown until the nineteenth century, because nowhere in nature it is found free, owing to its always being combined with other elements, most commonly with oxygen, for which it has a strong affinity.

【译文】铝是自然界储藏量最丰富的元素，它总是和其他元素化合。与氧化合的情况最为普遍，因为这种元素对氧具有很强的亲和力。由于这个原因，在自然界任何地方都找不到处于游离状态的铝，所以它直到 19 世纪才被人们知道。

Recasting

实际上在翻译长句过程中并不只是单纯地用一种方法,需要把各种方法综合使用。在一些情况下,某些英语长句的翻译单纯地使用一种方法并不方便,这就需要仔细分析,按时间顺序或逻辑顺序,顺逆结合、主次分明地对全文进行综合处理,以便把全文翻译成通顺、忠实的汉语句子。

e. g.

Plastics is made from water which is a natural resource inexhaustible and available everywhere, coal which can be mined through automatic and mechanical processes at less cost and lime which can be obtained from the calcinations of limestone widely present in nature.

【译文】塑料是由水、煤和石灰制成的。水是取之不尽的、到处都可以获得的天然资源;煤是用自动化和机械化的方法开采的,成本较低;石灰是由自然界中广泛存在的石灰石得来的。

3.4 Semantic Features of EST

The most conspicuous semantic feature of EST is the use of a language in which most of the words are in their conceptual meaning. In other words, rhetorical devices and figures of speech can hardly find their places here, since the main purpose of EST is to give information, not to show feelings.

Clarity and factuality are more important in EST than in other varieties, which may result in the frequent use of connectives, including the repetitions of nouns; the demonstrative reference of ***this*** and ***that***, the transitive of ***thus***, ***therefore***, ***as a result*** to show logical sequence; the nominal substitution of ***one*** as well as many time relaters, place relaters and space relaters.

3.4.1 Nominalization of EST

As defined by linguistics in *Oxford Dictionary*, nominalization is any process by which either a noun or a syntactic unit functions as a noun phrase which is derived from any other kind of unit such as a verb or an adjective. Nominalized language can be more concise, objective and formal. Nominalization is one of the most typical features of EST writing, which is more formal than its counterpart. By nominalizing, a large number of nominalized structures are used in the texts to represent the semantic meaning of a verb and a noun or of an adjective and a noun simultaneously.

科技英语的名词化是从体现“过程”的动词或体现“特征”的形容词转换而来的,因而兼有双重语义特征。所以,在翻译时必须对名词化结构进行解构,弄清其内在的语义关系,避免错译。同时,英语和汉语的一个差异是“静态”和“动态”之别。连淑能在《英汉对比研究》中指出:“英语倾向于多用名词,因而叙述呈静态;汉语倾向于多用动词,因而叙述呈动态。”名词化使用得越多,语篇的技术性越强。

不同语篇类型名词化情况统计

语篇类型	科技	法律	新闻	小说	童话、寓言
小句总数	197	79	236	250	418
名词化总数	143	66	95	68	3
名词化比例	72.6%	83.5%	40.3%	27.8%	0.7%

Exercise: Translate the following sentences.

1) All substances will permit the passage of some electric currents, provided that the potential difference is high enough.

2) The heat loss can be considerably reduced by the use of firebricks round the walls of the boiler.

3) Television is the transmission and reception of images of moving objects by radio waves.

4) The accumulation of new data during the past decade has brought a refinement of some earlier views and concepts.

5) The shrinkage of the sun to this state would transform our oceans into ice and our atmosphere into liquid air.

3.4.2 Metaphoric Translation in EST

Metaphor plays an important role in the evolution of English technical vocabulary, giving rise to rich association. Metaphor makes EST texts comprehensible, informative, and attractive. Probing into the translation of metaphor in EST can deepen our understanding of it and contribute to the popularization of scientific knowledge.

第二章综合练习

【汉译英】

1）钢制的工具箱放在仓库里。箱里除了一些标准工具以外，还有下列工具：一把12英寸长的卷尺、铜线、一些10公分长的铁钉、两脚插头、保险丝和一个油壶。如发现工具丢失，请务必通知车间主任。（复合名词的使用）

2）由于物体反射光线，我们才能看到颜色。能把大部分红色的光反射出来的东西看上去是红的。同样，一个绿色的物体反射出来的绝大多数是绿色的光。白色的东西能把所有颜色的光都反射出来。而黑色的东西对任何颜色的光都不反射。（中英文句式特点）

3）工业用途金刚石的价值在于它的硬度，而不在于它是否美观。其价值还在于它具有千百种用途。（中插结构的合理使用）

4）科学是讲求实际的。科学是老老实实的学问，来不得半点虚假，需要付出艰苦的劳动。同时，科学也需要创造，需要幻想，有幻想才能打破传统的束缚，才能发展科学。（合并零散小句）

5）既能提高单位工作效率同时又省时、省钱的办法是什么？电视会议目前就是一个几乎可供所有单位选择的可行办法。其性能之先进、价格之便宜、局域网之便利以及数字电话网之优势，使研究、发展与采购各界看到了电视会议所具有的竞争优势和威力。（技巧综合运用）

【英译汉】

1）This means that traditional programming could thus be called single thread because the program is responsible for managing only a single thread during its careful journey from one instruction to the next.

2）If a window freezes on your screen, press Ctrl + Alt + Del (all three keys at the same time).

3）The latest finding will fuel the debate over the environmental safety of those crops by giving both sides more ammunition.

4）We are living in the middle of a revolution in consciousness. Over the past few decades, geneticists, neuroscientists, psychologists, sociologists, economists, and others have made great strides in understanding the inner working of the human mind. Far from being dryly materialistic, their work illuminates the rich underwater world where character is formed and wisdom grows. They are giving us a better grasp of emotions, intuitions, biases, longings, predispositions, character traits, and social bonding, precisely those things about which our culture has least to say.

5）In actual practice, however, several variations have crept into high-level languages so that no high-level language is totally portable to all the computer systems with a complier for the language in question.

6) Reusability can be a mixed blessing for users, as a programmer has to be able to find the object he needs.

7) This brief tour will get your feet wet. By the time you acquaint yourself with Window 95 here, you will be prepared for the everyday tasks.

8) In effect, the network can end "tyranny of geography".

9) Today, it can be said that wheels run America. The four rubber tires of the automobile move America through work and play.

10) This telemetry streamed back to earth, a torrent of computer data updated 1,000 times a second.

Passage One

Britain: No Privacy in the Privy

It is another first for Britain industry and design: urinals with screens. They are called "Viewrinals", and they feature a small screen at eye level displaying adverts which, one hopes, are not too distracting. Already positioned in roughly 100 nightclubs and bars, their makers, a firm called *Digital View*, hope to see them adopted everywhere.

Viewrinals are just the latest (and most peculiar) example of how moving pictures are replacing conventional advertising. Screens can now be found in supermarkets, corner shops, service-station forecourts, and so on. They can either generate revenue for the shop owners or promote specific products within the store.

Liquid-crystal display technology is partly responsible for this new intrusion. The price of LCD screens has been falling, and their advantages are many. Unlike a cathode ray monitor, an LCD screen is thin and so can fit in tight spaces and on walls. It also needs less power and is easier to protect from vandalism.

Furthermore, the Viewrinal's screen can now be plugged straight into the Internet, and thus be fed with commercials from anywhere in the world, which are in turn transmitted with the latest video compression techniques. The Viewrinal is thus at the cutting-edge of modern technology.

Digital View has introduced advertising screens in shops, buses and trains, as well as in more unusual places. A few nightclubs now sport Digital View's cigarette machines with built-in televisions, to advertise different parts of the venue. The company also has plans for screens in taxis and on cash registers, and for tiny ones on the side of beer pumps to promote each drink.

Will Viewrinals catch on? Advertisers can keep a tab on how many times each advertisement is seen. On the other hand, a loo sophisticated enough to be at risk of computer hackers is not necessarily in progress. And, although Digital View also makes Viewloo-screens placed tastefully by the basin, it has no plans for a female equivalent to the Viewrinal. Thank God.

Passage Two

A Leading Stem-cell Researcher Found Guilty

According to a report published on December 29th by Seoul National University in South Korea, its erstwhile employee Hwang Woo-suk, who had tendered his resignation six days earlier, deliberately falsified his data in the paper on human embryonic stem cells that he and 24 colleagues published in *Science* in May 2005.

In particular, Dr. Hwang claimed he had created 11 colonies of human embryonic stem cells genetically matched to specific patients. He had already admitted that nine of these were bogus, but had said that this was the result of an honest mistake, and that the other two were still the real McCoy. A panel of experts appointed by the university to investigate the matter, however, disagreed. They found that DNA fingerprint traces conducted on the stem-cell lines reported in paper had been manipulated to make it seem as if all 11 lines were tailored to specific patients. In fact, none of them matched the volunteers with spinal-cord injures and diabetes who had donated skin cells for the work. To obtain his promising "result", Dr. Hwang had sent for testing two samples from each donor, rather than a sample from the donor and a sample of the cells into which the donor's DNA had supposedly been transplanted.

The panel also found that a second claim in the paper—that only 185 eggs were used to create the 11 stem-cell lines—was false. The investigators said the actual number of eggs used was far larger, in the thousands, although they were unable to determine exact figure.

The reason why this double fraud is such a blow is that human embryonic stem-cell research has great expectations. Stem cells, which have not yet been programmed to specialise and can thus, in principle, grow into any tissue or organ, could be used to treat illnesses ranging from diabetes to Parkinson's disease. They might even be able to fix spinal-cord injuries. And stem cells cloned from a patient would not be rejected as foreign by immune system.

Dr. Hwang's reputation, of course, is in tatters. The university is now investigating two other groundbreaking experiments he claimed to have conducted—the creation of the world's first cloned human embryo and the extraction of stem cells from it, and the creation of the world's first cloned dog. He is also in trouble for breaching ethical guidelines by using eggs donated by members of his research team.

Passage Three

The Age of Spiritual Machines

Since its beginnings in the work of Alan Turing, the British mathematical genius who conceived of the computer, artificial intelligence has been overly anthropocentric. It's traditional—some would say misguided—aim has been to build machines that are like humans. For example, the Turing test for machine intelligence holds that computer is a genuine thinker if it resembles a human being to the degree that someone interviewing both the computer and a human by teletype cannot tell which is which. Against this background, it is not surprising that researchers in artificial intelligence often make believe that their inventions possess human qualities. Turing himself described a simple computational mechanism as a "child-machine". To be "rewarded", "punished", and "taught" by a process intended to produce "discipline" and "initiative", Turing's child-machine was a "creature" that was taught by an inspector of schools but could not be sent to school without "the other children making excessive fun of it".

In a contemporary example, Daniel Dennett states that Cog, a robot under construction at the MIT Artificial Intelligence Lab, is to have an "infancy and childhood". Cog has "hips" and a "waist", and will have skin and a face. Cog is to be "as human as possible in its wants and learning, abhor error, strive for novelty, recognize progress".

Ray Kurzwell is another who anthropomorphizes machines: nanomachines (devices built on an atomic scale) have "brains", "bodies", "arms", "hands", and "little fingers". His new book, *The Age of Spiritual Machines*, is an excellent example of the blurring of fact and fiction so common in discussions of artificial intelligence. He blends together present day technologies, such as artificial legs and breast implants, with those he foresees, such as computers that store "migrated" human brains.

附录:科技英语常用词缀

科技英语常用普通前缀

前 缀	意 义	例 词
an-	无,不,缺少	anelectric 不起电的,anhydrous 无水的
cyber-	电脑的,网络的	cyberspace 电脑空间,cyberworld 网络世界

续表

前缀	意义	例词
de-	相反,除去,向下	despin 反自旋,dehydration 脱水,defluent 向下流的
demi-	半,一半	demilune 半月,新月,demirelief 半浮雕
dia-	贯通,透过	diagonal 对角线,diagnosis 诊断
dis-	不,除去,分离,相反动作	diseconomy 不经济,disroot 拔根,disarm 解除武装,dissolve 分解,disseminate 散布,distort 歪曲
dys-	反常的,不良的	dysfunction 机能失调,dysgenesis 生殖力不良
ec-	外,向外,自……出	eccentric 离心的,eclipse 日食,月食
ef-	出,外,离去	effluence 流出, effulge 放出光芒,efface 消除
en-	置内,用作	enclose 封入, encage 关入笼中, enring 用环装饰
infra-	下部	infrastructure 基础设施,infrasonic 次声的
inter-	在……之间,相互	intermolecular 分子间的, interface 界面
intra-	在内,内部	intranuclear 原子核内的,intracellular 细胞内部的,intravenous 静脉内的
intro-	在内,向内,内侧	introflection 向内弯曲
mal-/male-	恶,不良	malformation 畸形, malnutrition 营养不良, malefactor 罪犯
meso-	中央,中间	mesoblast 中胚叶,mesozoic 中生代的,mesotron 介子
met-/meta-	变换,超过	metamorphic 变形的, metaphysic 超自然的, metonym 转喻
mis-	误,恶,否定	misprint 误印,misconduct 行为不正
multi-	多	multicoloured 多色的,multimeter 万用表
neo-	新的	neolithic 新石器时代的,neonatal 新生的
non-	不,无,非	nonmetal 非金属,nonhuman 不属于人类的
ob-/oc-/ of-/og-/op-	越过,接近,封,反	oblong 拉长的, oblique 斜的, occlude 阻塞, offend 触犯,oppose 反对,ogre 妖魔
omni-	完全,完整	omnipotent 全能,omniscience 无所不知
ortho-	直,正	orthogonal 直角的,orthoptera 直翅类
over-	越过,过度	overexposure 感光过度,overweight 超重
pan-	全,总,泛	panchromatic 全色的,pancosmism 泛宇宙论

续表

前缀	意义	例词
para-	侧,副,伪,隔离	parabola 抛物线,paraxial 偏轴的,paramarginal 临边界的,paramagnetic 偏磁的,paratyphoid 副伤寒
peri-	周围,环绕	perimeter 周长, perigee 近地点,perihelion 近日点
post-	后	postnatal 产后的,post-depositional 沉积作用后的
pre-	前	preamplifier 前置放大器,precontinent 大陆架
proto-	第一,原始	prototype 原型,protopetroleum 原油
pseudo-	伪,类似	pseudoscience 伪科学,pseudosymmetry 假对称
quasi-	准,似,半	quasi-static 准静态的,quasi-cholera 似霍乱
re-	再,后,反	regression 退化,resistance 阻抗,revolve 旋转
retro-	后,回,反	retroflex 反曲的,retrospect 回顾,retrogress 倒退
semi-	半	semiconductor 半导体,semicircle 半圆
sub-	下,接近,亚	subtropics 亚热带, subarctic 近北极圈的, subway 地铁
super-/supra-	在……上	supermarine 海面的,supravasal 导管上的
syn-	一起,共同	syntonic 谐振的,synchrotron 同步加速器
tele-	远离	teleseism 远震,telephotometer 远距离照相术
tra-/trans-	超过,转移	traverse 横过,traject 传导,transplant 移植
ultra-	超	ultrasonics 超声波学,ultrared 红外线的

Chapter Three
Translation of Advertising
广告文体翻译

Cultural Shift (文化转向)

Mary Snell-Horby suggested that culture, rather than text, should be regarded as the unit of translation and that cultural studies should be introduced into translation theories. This idea was taken as epoch-making by Andre Lefevere and Susan Bassnet and thus was named "cultural shift". Cultural school puts great emphasis on the role culture plays in translation and the influence of translation on culture. It maintains that the unit of translation is not word, or sentence, or even discourse, but culture. The purpose of translation is to achieve the identical effect between translation in target literature and source text in source literature. Susan Bassnet maintains that translation is by no means a pure language behavior. Actually, it is deeply rooted in the culture where language lies in. So, the equivalence of translation is the equivalence of cultural function between source text and target text.

关键词:文化转向;文化作用;巴斯奈特;文化对等

About Advertising

In the information age, the advertisements, as one of the ways to spread information, are pervasive in every corner of our daily life. We are confronted with advertisements all the time. Advertising has become, willy-nilly, a kind of purchasing guide for consumers. The very purpose of advertisements is to persuade consumers to purchase the products; improve the notability and promote sales of products. As a special text, advertising has its unique stylistic features, in which many kinds of rhetorical devices are used in advertisements such as metaphor, metonymy, personification, hyperbole, parallelism, repetition, pun, parody. Usually an ad consists of the headline, the body copy, the illustration, the slogan, and the standing details.

1. Definition, Function and Classification of Ads

1.1 Definition

The word "advertise" originates from the Latin word "advertere"（引人注意）, which means "to make known to the public ". According to *Webster's Dictionary*, advertising is a kind of activity which draws the public's attention to something, especially by means of paid announcements. Advertising is mass and non-personal selling, makes use of various media to deliver information to the consumer, such as newspapers, magazines, television, radio, mails, films, books, telephone directory, sports, art, performance, the Internet, and even the human body.

1.2 Function

There are two main functions of advertising: informing and persuading, of which the latter is also called the primary and influencing function. As a market promoting tool, advertising aims mainly to provide the public with the information about new products and to build brand preference and loyalty, and more importantly, to stimulate their action of buying the products. We can put advertising functions in detailed categories as follows:

(1) Providing information: Advertisements may convey basic information of the advertised products or services to the customer;

(2) Demand-creation function: Advertisements need to arouse the customer's curiosity and desire for the products;

(3) Persuading: Advertisements need to persuade the customer to buy new products in all means for the customer may hesitate to try them though he is interested in;

(4) Get-action function: Advertisements need to make the customer buy the products after he is persuaded. So "Attention, Interest, Desire, Action (AIDA)" is the slogan of advertisements.

1.3 Classification

Classified by the Media

Advertisements can be classified into newspaper ads, magazine ads, television ads, radio ads, mail ads, outdoor ads, human body ads, Internet ads and ads that reach us through advanced equipment such as telex, fax and computer.

Classified by Ultimate Purpose

All the ads can be divided into two categories: profit-oriented ads and non-commercial ads. Ads about products, services, ideas and so on belong to the former category. Non-commercial ads are usually sponsored by charity organization, civic associations, religious or political organizations, with the expectation of informing, or reminding the public of some particular ideas and causes.

Classified by Advertising Strategies

Hard-sell ads: promote sales forcefully and aggressively by providing the readers with detailed information about the characteristics and the advantages of the products as well as other information such as price, limited availability and guaranteed reliability. The language used here is serious, factual, accurate and objective, similar to journalistic and scientific English. Soft-sell ads: the language used in this kind of ads is typical of the variety—appealing to the emotion.

广告又分为“硬卖”和“软卖”两种。“硬卖”以介绍商品特性或优点的信息来说服消费者,使用了具有信息功能的语言。“软卖”侧重于唤起一种热烈的好感或美感,通过鼓动人们的情感来达到推销的目的,其语言表达追求形式美。

下面为两则软、硬广告的例子:软卖类广告注重情感的激发,硬卖类广告侧重信息的传递。许多软卖型商业广告经常借用文学语言中通用的各种修辞手法增加广告语言的生动和美感。

Soft Sell(软卖)

【原文】

Tomorrow Will Be a Reflection of Tonight

Nighttime is a special time, a time of rest and renewal. Your body begins to relax to unwind from the activity of the day and to slip into the softer rhythm of the night. It is the time when your body turns the energy needed for the smiles and laughter of the day into the magical replenishment of the night. This is the time your skin needs special care.

Night of Olay is special night care cream, created to make the most of magic of the night. It is greaseless and remarkably light to touch, a sheer pleasure on your skin, allowing it to breathe naturally while it absorbs this special nighttime nourishment.

"Hour after quiet hour all through the night." Night of Olay enhances your skin's own natural renewal by bathing it in continuous moisture, easing tiny dry wrinkle lines and encouraging the regeneration of softer younger looking skin.

Night of Olay tonight will be reflected in your youthful radiance tomorrow.

Night of Olay.

【译文】

明天是今夜的映像

夜晚是一段特别的时间——休息和更新的时间。您的身体开始放松,由白天的紧张活动松弛下来,转入夜晚轻柔的旋律。白天您的笑容和笑声所消耗的精力要由夜晚魔术般地来补充。这时您的皮肤需要特别护理。

Olay 晚霜是一种夜晚使用的特别护肤霜,能充分发挥夜晚的魔力。无油脂、轻柔、舒适,让皮肤一面自然呼吸,一面吸收 Olay 晚霜的特殊营养。

"一夜之中,每时每刻",Olay 晚霜使您的皮肤始终保持湿润,增强皮肤的自然再生能力,舒展细微的皱纹,让您的皮肤显得更柔软,更年轻。

今夜擦的 Olay 晚霜明天变成您青春的明艳。

Olay 晚霜。

【解析】

This is an advertisement for a brand of cosmetics (Olay). The first sentence seems to have no direct connection with its subject—special night care cream, yet this recollection of "relax", "rest", and "renewal" functions as an initiator and a bridge. Actually, this recall just indicates the unique feature of the product. The words "special", "naturally" and "natural" have been used several times to highlight the product which is different and accommodates the customers' flavor of getting closer to nature. At the same time words such as "magic", "magical", "softer rhythm", "remarkably light", "sheer pleasure"... have strong persuasive function.

Hard Sell(硬卖)

【原文】

SINGER

Presses out the Iron Age

The Magic Steam Press Reduces Ironing Time

By as much as 50%

The Singer Magic Steam Press will give your garments an instant, fresh-from-the-cleaners look.

An innovation in household ironing, it has a pressing surface ten times the size of most handheld irons and pressure over 100lbs. The Magic Steam Press provides exactly what you want—ease speed and professional results.

Burst of steam features for stubborn wrinkles;

Easy one-hand operation, either sitting or standing;

Variable temperature control adjusts temperature according to fabric selected;

Portable and easy to store;

Protects fine fabric;

Huge ironing pad surface;

Non-stick ironing pad surface;

100lbs, of even ironing pressure;

Automatic safety shut-off.

140 Years of Innovation

SINGER

Singer's worldwide retail and distribution system covers 100 countries.

【译文】

胜家熨斗

——神奇熨斗,开创熨斗新时代

神奇的蒸汽熨斗使您的衣服笔挺,犹如刚从洗衣店取回一样。

这是家用熨斗的一次创新。它的熨烫面是其他大多数家用熨斗的 10 倍,具有 100 余磅压力。神奇的蒸汽熨斗给予您所期盼的效果——时间短,操作简便,效果好。

喷出的水蒸气可熨平任何顽固的皱褶;

一只手操作,操作时可坐着,也可站着;

设有温度调制器,可根据不同的衣料调整温度;

携带、存放两便;

自动保护精细面料;

熨烫板宽大;

熨烫板表面不粘连;

熨烫压力为 100 磅,压力均匀;

自动安全开关。

胜家公司

140 年的创新历史

批发零售网点遍及 100 个国家和地区

【解析】

This piece of information belongs to the hard-sell advertisement. Originally, the language is brief and concise and the structure is short, and the number, such as 100lbs, sounds very scientific. The brand name "SINGER" has been translated into "胜家", which is very persuasive and focuses on the brilliant quality of the product itself. But some of the other translation needs to be modified in order to adjust to the idiomatic way of the Chinese expression. For example, "protects fine fabric" can be put into "不伤精细面料" instead of "自动保护精细面料"。

2. Language Features of Ads

2.1 Lexical Features

Frequent Use of Adjectives

The most conspicuous lexical feature of ads is the frequent use of active, favorable adjectives, which can impress the potential buyers with the good quality of the product and service. The following is only a short list of this kind of adjectives:

new, better, best, beautiful, big, fine, free, fresh, great, natural, special, superb, sure, good, real, lovely, bright, clean, extra, safe, full, rich, super, nice, extraordinary, latest, luxurious, fashionable, modern, original, flawless, outstanding, perfect, simple, splendid, unique, universal, valuable, economical, advanced, absolute, incredible...

e. g.

For the first time, there's a *remarkable* gel that can give your hair any look you want—sleeker, fuller, straighter, curlier, more *natural*, even wet—without a drop of alcohol or oil.

【译文】一种不同寻常的发胶问世了,它可以使您的头发随心所欲——更光滑,更丰茂,更平直,更卷曲,更自然,保湿——不含一滴酒精、油脂。

Use of Neologisms

e. g.

In Miami, it's *nonewelty*. (new + novelty)旅行广告

【译文】在迈阿密,这不新鲜。

Come to our *fruice*. (fruit + juice)果汁广告

【译文】来喝我们的果汁吧。

The *orangemostest* drink in the world. (orange + most + est)

【译文】世界上最浓的橘汁饮料。

2.2 Grammatical Features

Generally speaking, sentences used in English advertisement are quite brief, powerful and remarkable enough to attract the consumers' attention. It has its unique merits in syntax.

Preference for Short Sentences

In order to meet the commercial need and to reduce the ad cost, the ads must be used with the least page layouts and the most concise language to transmit the most information and stimulate the readers' or audiences' purchasing desire effectively.

Frequent Use of Elliptical Sentences

Because the restrictions of so many things such as space, fees, ellipsis used in advertisement can also produce brief and compact sentences. The omission has the power of letting you feel what you want.

e. g.

Sensuously smooth. Mysteriously mellow. Gloriously golden. Who can resist the magic of Camus XO Congnac?

This is an advertisement for XO which uses only a series of adverbs and adjectives in the first three sentences.

Use of Imperative Sentences

According to some linguists, above 1/4 of independent sentences are imperative sentences or commands in English advertising. Notice that *look*, *see*, and *watch* are common in commercials of demonstration type, where they call the consumers' attention to what is happening before the consumers' eyes.

Frequent Use of Interrogative Sentences

Interrogative sentences or questions are also commonly employed in advertising. They usually arouse the readers' curiosity and tempt to seek for the answer. The interrogative sentence is used to attract the readers to think and search for the answer.

e. g.

How can a magazine be strong regionally if it is not strong locally? (《亚洲周刊》推销广告)

3. *Rhetorical Features in Advertising English*

The frequent use of different figures of speech perhaps is the most conspicuous semantic feature of ads. In order to persuade the potential consumer to buy the product, the advertiser tries every means to manipulate the language, to make the language more persuasive and effective.

Rhetorical devices have been used because of their advantages of enriching the expressiveness and effect of language, enforcing the vividness and artistic beauty of language and in this way arousing people's free imagination and association. The most commonly used rhetorical devices are: simile, metaphor, pun, parallelism, rhetorical question, parody and rhyme.

3.1 Simile

The word simile comes from Latin word similis, meaning "like". A simile is a figure of speech which makes a comparison between two unlike elements having at least one quality or characteristic in common. Simile is always introduced by the following words: like, as, as...as, as it were, as if, as though, be something of, similar to, etc. A simile is usually made up of three parts, the tenor (the thing described), the vehicle (the thing compared to) and words used to show the relationship of comparison (as/like). The use of simile in adverts can create a vivid and clear image of the advertised product or service in consumers' interest.

Exercise: Discuss the following ad translation.

1) Light as breeze, soft as cloud. (服饰广告)
轻如风,柔如云。
2) Today, Sakura Bank is like a thriving Sakura. (樱花银行广告)
如今,樱花银行就如一棵茂盛的樱花树。
3) Breakfast without orange juice is like a day without sunshine. (橙汁广告)
早餐没有了橙汁就像一天没有了阳光。

3.2 Metaphor

A metaphor is a figure of speech where comparison is implied. It is also a comparison between two unlike elements with similar quality. But unlike a simile, this comparison is implied, not expressed with the word as or like. Metaphor in English adverts contributes to promoting the sales.

Exercise: Discuss the following ad translation.

1) The most sensational place to wear satin on your lips. (口红广告)
擦上此口红好似穿上了柔顺光滑、细薄透亮的丝绸一般。
(把口红喻为绸缎,这样的暗喻浑然无迹,可谓妙思偶得。)
2) You're better off under the Umbrella. (一家保险公司的广告)
购买本保险,远行自在又安全。
(把该保险公司比喻成一个 umbrella(保护伞),"better off "有"较自在、较幸福"之意,此广告达到了良好的产品宣传效果。)

3.3 Personification

Personification is a metaphorical attention of personal nature or character to inanimate objects or abstract notions. It is a representation of a thing or abstraction in the form of a person. Personification is employed in an advert to personify the advertised product so that it possesses human qualities or feelings. The use of it can achieve the effect of vitality and vividness.

Exercise: Discuss the following ad translation.

1) Poetry in motion, dancing close to me. (TOYOTA)
动态的诗,向我靠近。
2) The Global brings you the world in a single day. (《环球杂志》)
环球在手,纵览全球。
3) Unlike me, my Rolex never needs a rest. (Rolex)
昼夜不停,废寝忘食。

3.4 Antithesis

Antithesis, originated from the Greek *antithenai*, means "opposition". In fact antithesis is a rhetorical device in which "the writer deliberately uses opposite of different words, phrases or clauses in parallel structure so as to disclose and emphasize the contrast or contradiction between two things." With rhythmical sound, concise wording and well-balanced structure, antithesis describes abstract logic in a clear and effective form, which makes the sounds and rhymes of the advert full of melodiousness, leaving a strong impression on consumers.

e. g.

Cancer is often curable. The fear of cancer is often fatal.

【译文】癌症不可怕,恐癌才可怕。

3.5 Repetition / Parallelism

Repeating something can cause different effects on speed, rhythm and atmosphere. The forms of repetition can be various. We will confine our discussion here mainly to lexical repetition and syntactical repetition. The recurrence of a linguistic unit in an advertisement may help attract consumer's attention and be easy to remember.

Exercise: Translate the following sentences.

1) Give a Timex to all, and to all good time.
2) Castoria (成药,小儿轻泻剂广告)
When baby was sick, we gave her Castoria
When she was a child, she cried for Castoria
When she became MISS, she clung to Castoria

When she had Children, she gave them Castoria

(This advert of drug forcefully uses four simple parallel sentences to describe a girl's constant affection with Castoria, at her three growth stages: childhood, teenager and adult. By using parallelism, it proves the long history of the brand.)

3.6 Parody

Parody is a humorous or satirical imitation of idioms, proverbs, sayings, songs and so on. Parody is the deliberate imitation of them with some words changed to express a new idea. Parody is concise and implicative. The employment of parody in adverts brings the reader a sense of familiarity as well as originality. Especially, it is a creative way to create affective and impressive advertising headlines and slogans.

仿拟(parody)是语言中一种常见的修辞格，它以某一特定的文本如名言、警句、谚语、俗话、诗词或歌曲等为参照，对其进行词句、篇章、局部或整体的改写，从而构成一种奇特的表达形式，其创意新颖、语言生动、内涵丰富。广告中的仿拟可分为三种：仿词、仿句和仿篇。

e. g. We take no pride in prejudice.

【译文】对于您的偏见，我们没有傲慢。

这是《泰晤士报》为自己做广告时用的一句妙语，它源于奥斯汀的一部传世名著《傲慢与偏见》，报社援引该书名做广告，以标榜自己不偏不倚，主持公道。

Exercise: Translate the following sentences.

1) Lose ounces, save pounds. (Goldenlay 牌鸡蛋广告)

2) To smoke or not to smoke, that is a question. (香烟广告)

3) Quality breeds success. (福特汽车广告)

4) Where there is a road, there is a Toyota. (日本丰田车广告)

5) 苹果电脑，不同凡"想"。(苹果电脑广告)

6) 谁跑到最后，谁笑得最好。(轮胎广告)

7) 城乡万里路，路路有航天。(航天牌汽车广告)

8) A Mars a day keeps you work, rest and play. (巧克力广告)

9) 与其道听途说，不如亲自体验。(碧丽牌健美苗条霜广告)

10) Pepsi-cola hits the spot;
Twelve full ounces, that's a lot;
Twice as much for a nickel, too;
Pepsi-cola is the drink for you. (Pepsi 广告)

11) One man's disaster is another man's delight! The sale is now on. (促销广告)

12) 人带梅花，准时乐道。(梅花牌手表)

3.7 Hyperbole

Hyperbole is also one of the most frequently used figures of speech that deliberately use exaggeration in order to give emphasis on writing. Hyperbole as a figure of speech is so powerful and widely-employed that it stretches its antenna to the field of English advertising.

e. g.

If you're looking for the place that has everything, there's only one place to visit. And that's New York. It's a whole world in a city.

【**译文**】不游世界不死心,不到纽约非好汉。

3.8 Pun

Pun is a play on words, which involves an amusing use of expressions with double meanings or the same sound but different meanings. The nature of puns in adverts is to enforce an ambiguity and make readers pay attention to the dormant meaning but not the sentence meaning. English pun and Chinese pun, by using certain terms of semantic or voice in a particular environment, have a dual meaning.

双关语不仅能增加广告的趣味性和幽默感,更重要的是使品牌名称更能吸引人们的注意,便于记忆,增加宣传效果,以此达到宣传产品的目的。

e. g.

Make your every hello a real good-buy.

【**译文**】让您的每一次通话都货真价实。

这是一家电话运营商的广告,利用"good-buy"的谐音,以引起消费者的充分注意。作者利用 Good-buy 和 Goodbye 谐音这一特点,使同一发音暗含两层意思:一是指划算的好买卖;二是道别。一箭双雕,旨意深远,耐人寻味。英语中的双关语可以分为以下几类。

谐音双关(Homophonic Pun)

谐音双关是由拼写相似、发音相同或相近的词构成的。此类双关具有风趣、幽默、俏皮、滑稽的语言风格。

语义双关(Homographic Pun)

语义双关是利用词语或句子的多义性在特定环境下形成的双关。

语法双关(Pun on Grammar /Grammar-based Pun)

语法双关是指由于语法方面的问题产生的双关,如省略结构、词或词组具有两种以上语法功能等。

成语双关(Pun on Idioms)

广告语言特别善于引用一些人们耳熟能详的成语或俗语,既增强了广告的吸引力,又体现了广告语言的艺术性,更使广告具有令人回味的弦外之音。

Exercise: Translate the following sentences.

1) More sun and air for your son and heir.(某海滨浴场的宣传广告)

2) Trust us, over 5,000 ears of experience.(助听器广告)

3) Money doesn't grow on the trees. But it blossoms at our branches.(英国劳埃德银行的户外广告)

4) Spoil yourself and not your figure.(Weight-Watcher 冰淇淋广告)

5) Which lager can claim to be truly German? This can.(罐啤酒广告)

6) You'll go nuts for the nuts you get in Nux.(纳克斯牌坚果)

7) Try our sweet corn. You'll smile from ear to ear.(甜玉米的商业广告)

8) A Mars a day keeps you work, rest and play.(玛斯牌巧克力)

4. Translation of Advertising Texts

A complete advertising text usually consists of five elements: brand name(商标); slogan(口号); headline(标题); body text(正文)and illustration(插图). However, not every advertisement includes all the five elements, among which body text, slogan and brand name play important roles. Domestication of advertising texts can be perceived through the deliberate arrangement of the body text, brand name and slogan apparently different from the original.

4.1 Translation of Brand Names/Trade Marks

A brand name is a symbol of a product, which is used to identify one product from another. A brand name generally plays an important part in influencing consumer's decision. A decision of purchase is usually determined by whether the brand name of the product appeals to the consumer or not. Look at some typical examples of brand name translation.

e.g.

Coca-Cola——可口可乐

This is the most recognized trademark of the world most popular drinks. The Chinese version of the brand"可口可乐" does not only reach a close phonetic iconicity(语音相似性)but matches the original in almost every aspect. "可口" does not only mean something for drinking or eating, but also refers to "pleasant to the taste", or "delicious", while "可乐" tells the possible effect of this product—enjoyable and bringing you a feeling of happiness. Integrated, the brand conveys the meaning of "the drink is tasty, delicious and makes you happy".

4.1.1 Transliteration

Transliteration is translating the name according to its pronunciation; transliteration is the habitual practice when we translate foreign trade names. If we use the transliteration skill properly, sometimes it will make an ordinary trade name become distinctive suddenly. For example, the sports shoes "Peak" is translated as "匹克". It has made full use of the similar pronunciation of English and Chinese, and it also makes people associate the name with Olympic Games. Here are more examples of that:

Kodak (American film)——柯达
Casio (Japanese watch)——卡西欧
Motorola——摩托罗拉
Nissan (Japanese car)——尼桑
Mercedes-Benz——奔驰

4.1.2 Homophone Translation

Homophone translation gives consideration to both the pronunciation and word meaning, and the word meaning is not the original meaning, but recreated one without breaking away from the category. The first and the most successful example of homophone translation is an American beverage Coca-Cola. The trade name of this kind of black beverage is formed by two words "coca" and "cola": "coca" was firstly translated into "古柯" which is a plant growing in south America and translated into "古拉" which is another kind of plant growing in Africa. Now, the translation "可口可乐", makes the consumer feel sweet and happy. Firstly, it has the same form of original brand name because they all have four words. Second, it has the same function as the original brand name as they all give the customer a feeling of happiness.

The tooth paste "Colgate" is translated into "高露洁", which gives consideration to two similar pronunciations and the word "洁" gives prominence to the characteristic of the product, and reveals the theme.

4.1.3 Free Translation

Free translation is well adopted in translating brand names to carry the products' message about its quality and function and a kind of national preference. For example, the cigarette named "Good Company" from America was translated into "古德·康帕涅" (transliteration) when it was imported into Chinese market. We feel no phonetic charm, and no favorable association from the translated name. The free translation "良友" does not only have the same form as "Good Company" but also gives us a kind of comfort and care.

4.1.4 Combination of Transliteration and Free Translation

Some brand names have to be translated both transliterally and freely. This method preserves the phonetic rhythm and the characteristics of culture contained in the product name.

For example, "Head & Shoulders" with the translated Chinese name"海飞丝", head and "海" are similar in pronunciation, and at the same time a picture comes into our mind: the shining and elegant long hair is flowing down the shoulders.

It is the same as "Revlon", the brand name of American cosmetics, which was translated into "露华浓"。The Chinese translation originates from Li Bai's poem describing the beauty of Yang Yuhuan: "云想衣裳花想容,春风拂槛露华浓。" The translation is similar in pronunciation to the original one. Moreover, it arouses people's association of Li Bai's poem as well as the beauty of Yang Yuhuan. It reminds the Chinese reader of the reflection of sunlight in the "dew drops in the morning" (朝露) or fresh and cool feeling of the dew-like cream.

4.1.5 Transformation

Sometimes, we have to break away from the binding of the literal meaning of the original trade name, and open up a new train of thought to recreate an excellent trade name, which is called transformation.

Another good example of equivalent effect is "Goldlion" which enjoys a good reputation in China. It is a well-known brand of neckties. The literal translation of "goldlion" can be "金狮", which is a good combination of gold, a symbol of wealth, and lion, the king of the animal world. But the problem is in Chinese "金狮" and "金失" sound the same with each other. "金利来" effectively avoids such defect in pronunciation. "利" equals to profit, benefit or interest in English.

4.2 Translation of Slogans

The purpose of the slogans, when used in ads, is to impress the readers deeply. They are simple, brief and easy to understand and remember. A slogan is mainly aimed at maintaining the continuity of an advertising campaign and holding consumers' interest and promoting sales. An advertising slogan consists of just a few words, which are smooth to read and easy to remember. That is to say, an ideal slogan should be simple, clear, attractive, memorable and persuasive. In a successful piece of translating work, the essence of the source text can be melted harmoniously into the target language. Some of the slogans are popular among the public and cause favorable responses, and are deeply rooted in people's minds.

4.3 Illustration

Illustrations: an illustration is the non-verbal part of an advertisement and indispensable part to various kinds of ads as well. It can be categorized as painting, photograph, etc.

e. g.

The earth is heating up.

【译文】变暖让整个地球脱去了外套。

You can lose more than your patience.

【译文】因为失去耐心而打孩子,你会失去比耐心更多的东西。

5. Cultural Factors in Selecting Translation Strategies

5.1 Authorities vs. Facts

Chinese and English advertisements are quite different in choosing proofs. Traditionally the Chinese show great respect to authorities, so the advertisements are frequently quoted from all levels of authorities to prove their product qualities.

汉语广告中常用的套话,如:"省优部优"(Awarded the superior quality produced by the provincial government and the Ministry concerned);"信誉第一,顾客至上"(Reputation first and customers the utmost);"在有关部门的领导下,取得了很大进步"(It makes great improvement under the leadership of the sectors concerned);"获得质量金奖"(Awarded Gold Cup for quality)等旨在说明产品的优质和公司形象,以示产品的权威性。有的产品广告则以某专家、教授作为承诺,如由……发明(invented by...)。此类内容结构松散,不符合广告英语翻译原则,而且还会让国外消费者感到莫名其妙,翻译中也应删除。

If these phrases are translated into English literally, the western consumers will be confused. On the other hand, ads in the West focus on the fact obtained by experimental data through numerous tests and surveys. While doing the translation work you have to understand the differences and make certain changes.

Exercise: Compare the following translation versions.

2002 年,国家税务总局和中华全国工商联合会授予劲牌“诚信纳税企业”;2003 年,国家工商行政管理总局评定劲牌为“全国守合同重信用企业”;2003 年 12 月,劲牌公司被湖北文明委评为“湖北文明单位”;2007 年 9 月,劲牌保健酒被食品工业联合会评为“中国名牌产品”。

【译文 1】In 2002, Chinese *Jin* Wine was conferred “honest Taxpayer” by the State Administration of Taxation and the All-China Federation of Commerce and Industry; in 2003, “Enterprise honoring the contract and keeping the promise” by SAIC; in December of 2003, “The Best Civilized Unit of Hubei province” by Hubei Civilization Commission; in September of 2007, the products of *Jin* Brand are considered “Food quality reaching a set standard nationally” by Chinese Food and Industry Association.

【译文 2】Chinese *Jin* Wine has won many honors, which guarantees its high quality and good service. And we believe that's what you concern about.

5.2 Group Orientation vs. Individual Orientation

Group orientation, or collectivism, puts greater emphasis on the views, need, goals and experience of the in-group rather than oneself. A “We” consciousness prevails. Many examples which stress group behavior can be found in Chinese ads: “我们都喝”、“深受大众喜爱”。

On the contrary individual orientation, or individualism, fixates on the uniqueness of each individual. As a result, words such as “independence”, “uniqueness”, or “you” are usually found in the English ads, while when put into Chinese you may have different choice.

中英文广告的诉求点不同。英语以“个性”作为诉求点或主题,对消费者进行说服,因而往往采用第二人称“you”,表示诚恳的提议(暗含引导),以缩短厂家和消费者之间的距离。中国文化中强调“集体、整体观”,推崇“男女老少皆宜”,鼓动“大家都在用”、“大家可以用”或“大家都喜欢用”。翻译时可以适当增添第二人称,加强亲切感或者删减那些难被外国消费者理解的套语。

6. Flexibility in Choosing Translation Strategies

6.1 Over-translation

It can be regarded that ad is a specialized translation. In brief, the translator of advertising or tourist material will always try to make the text better than the original.

汉语中有大量的结构工整、押韵、对仗而又通俗易懂的成语典故,这为超额翻译以及通常优于原文的创译提供语言便利。

e. g.

Trust us for life. (American International Assurance)

【译文】财务稳健,信守一生

Straight talk smart deals. (BEA)

【译文】直言实干,称心方案

Your future is our future. (HSBC)

【译文】与您并肩,迈向明天

6.2 Condensed Translation

若将译文与原文进行对比研究,常可发现超额翻译(over-translation)和欠额翻译(under-translation)在广告翻译中屡见不鲜,而欠额翻译作为一种翻译策略可以在原文写得不够精练、信息过剩的时候使用。下例中画线部分的信息已经过浓缩。

e. g.

一电通减价热浪迫人而来,让你在炎炎夏日以炽热价每分钟 \$0.1 致电中国、美国、澳大利亚及加拿大。如此热烘烘之优惠,定能令您完全熔化。快快投入一电通之炽热旋涡,以独一无二之姿态横扫各大热点。(香港一电通公司的电讯广告)

【译文】IDD hot wave is now coming to town. Call your favorite spots: China, USA, Australia and Canada at just \$ 0.1 per minute. It's one. Tel Summer IDD fever that you never gonna miss.

译文中除了一些作为传递有效商品信息的硬信息(hard information),如公司名、地名、价格、优惠期限等,其他过剩信息可以省略。

第三章综合练习

1)山海关啤酒厂坐落在风景优美的避暑胜地、历史名城——山海关。素有“龙头”之称的万里长城的东部起端,由此伸向大海。该厂始建于 1982 年,后经两次扩建和技术改造,如今已形成了具有年产 8 万吨啤酒和 9 千吨麦芽的生产能力,是我国啤酒行业的重点骨干企业之一。

2) You will notice how kind new Sanara is to your hair. See it, Feel it. Sanara's naturally derived formulations bring out the shine and smoothness in your hair, leaving it manageable and healthy. You won't actually see how kind Sanara is to the environment, but it's nice to know that the whole range is biodegradable. So it doesn't pollute water or soil. And naturally, packaging is recyclable.

3)太子精品礼盒是精品之组合,是礼品市场之需求,是对各界人士一份诚意的贡献。

4)该厂生产的各种类型钻头均符合 API 标准,工艺先进、结构新颖、钢材优质、制造精致、质检严格,均已达到国内同类钻头的先进水平。

5)我厂生产的 112 型和 145 型电冰箱,造型美观,质量可靠,噪声小,耗电少,使用方便、安全。

6)本厂已有 35 年生产丝绸服装的历史,产品远销全球 50 多个国家和地区。完全真丝,质量上乘,做工精细,款式新颖,光滑柔和,耐洗耐晒,永不褪色,舒适高雅,女士必备,如欲购买,尽快联系。

7)天津工艺品进出口公司(Tianjin Arts & Crafts Import & Export Company)成立于1965年7月,是中国北方经营工艺品最大的专业公司(the leading specialized exporters)之一。凭借地处沿海,交通便利,工业发达,城市繁荣等天时地利之优,本着多年来遵循的平等互利、广交朋友、优质服务、信誉至上的宗旨,竭诚同世界各国发展贸易关系。

8)所有顾客凭本券享受打折优惠,购买50瓶矿泉水可享7折优惠。凭此券每户限购一份。

9)华夏公司始建于1949年5月,至今已有40多年悠久历史,业务关系遍及世界,是一个具有丰富经验,享有良好信誉,以航运为主的综合性运输公司。

10)上海国际展览中心拥有国际标准的展览空间,优良的设施和高质量的服务,自从1992年3月成立以来,该中心成功地举办了大规模的国际展览,赢得了来自世界各地的主办者、展商和广大观众的一致好评。

11)对比下面两则英汉营养品广告并说明差异,同时在译文中凸显中英文广告的特点。

<table>
<tr>
<td>

科学减肥新概念

"国民全营养素"把调节脂肪代谢,补充全面营养的独到理论应用于控制体重,以便达到拥有苗条身材,保持充沛精力的目的。相信曾为肥胖困扰的你,因为服用了全新口味的"国民全营养素"不久也能体态轻盈,充满活力。

"国民全营养素"是著名营养学家国敏元教授从中国传统调养理论出发,针对多数肥胖者的基本成因,以调节体内营养平衡,改变脂肪代谢能力为目的,精心配制的富含蛋白质、维生素、多种氨基酸及微量元素的全天然、全营养食品,充分调动体内多种酶的活性,迅速分解体内多余脂肪,使体态恢复健康苗条。

"国民理论"以其科学性、实效性在减肥领域开创了一条新路,"国民全营养素"被中国女子体操队指定为控制体重营养品。减肥的同时,轻松愉快,精力充沛,体重正常之后,不会轻易反弹。所以,更多的体操运动员,都钟情于"国民全营养素"。

</td>
<td>

Cholesterol Has Natural Enemies

In the battle against cholesterol, it seems man has a natural ally.

Deep-sea, cold-water fish contain special oil called Omega-3. An oil that recent studies indicate helps control cholesterol.

Now Squibb brings you Omega-3 in a dietary supplement.

Introducing Proto-chol.

A natural oil from only deep-sea, cold-water fish rich in Omega-3, and it's concentrated in an easy-to-swallow sealed gelcap, so there is no fishy taste or smell.

Of course, proto-chol should be part of a complete cholesterol control program, which includes regular exercise, foods low in saturated fats and regular medical checkups.

So start your cholesterol control program today.

Cholesterol is one enemy you should fight everyday.

E. R. Squibb & Sons, Inc.
Princeton, N.J.

</td>
</tr>
</table>

12）比较下列译文并指出如何译出商业广告的“诱”性。

Your body is beautiful
It's your jeans that are out of proportion.

Even the most beautiful body can get lost under the wrong pair of jeans.

That's why it's important to wear jeans that let you look your best, jeans that make that most of what you've got like our Relaxed Riders.

When we make Relaxed Riders, we cut our material on a curve to conform to the natural contours of your body. So where your proportions change, the proportions of your Lee's Relaxed Riders jeans change too.

If you've been thinking that something is wrong with you just because your jeans don't fit, try Relaxed Riders. You'll see it's not a better body you need. It's better jeans.

【译文1】	【译文2】
你的身材美极了 是你的牛仔裤不成比例 穿上不合身的牛仔裤，再美的身材也无法展现。 因此，重要的是，要穿就穿最能体现你风采的牛仔裤，要穿就穿最能展示你自身有利条件的牛仔裤，就像我们的“轻松骑士”。 在生产“轻松骑士”时，我们将布料裁剪出一定的弧度，以顺应人体的自然曲线。所以，你的身材比例若有变化，你所穿的李氏“轻松骑士”牛仔裤的比例也会随之而变。 如果你因为牛仔裤不合身而正觉得有什么不对劲时，试试我们的“轻松骑士”吧！你会发现，你所需要的并非是更好的身材，而是更好的牛仔裤。	你身材美妙， 但不合体的牛仔裤 会使美的身材黯然失色。 “李氏”休闲牛仔裤 体现最佳风采，显露优美体态 剪裁得体，自然流畅， 随身所欲，调整体形， 好牛仔赛过好身材。

附录：经典广告用语

1. Just do it. 跟着感觉走。（耐克运动鞋）
2. Ask for more. 渴望无限。（百事流行鞋）
3. Obey your thirst. 服从你的渴望。（雪碧）
4. Feel the new space. 感受新境界。（三星电子）
5. Focus on life. 瞄准生活。（奥林巴斯相机）
6. Good to the last drop. 滴滴香浓，意犹未尽。（麦氏咖啡）

7. Share moments. Share life.（柯达胶卷）
8. Started Ahead. 成功之路，从头开始。（飘柔洗发水）
9. Make yourself heard. 理解就是沟通。（爱立信手机）
10. Intelligence everywhere. 智慧演绎，无处不在。（摩托罗拉手机）
11. The choice of a new generation. 新一代的选择。（百事可乐）
12. We integrate, you communicate. 我们集大成，您超越自我。（三菱电工）
13. The relentless pursuit of perfection. 不懈追求完美。（凌志轿车）
14. Poetry in motion, dancing close to me. 动态的诗，向我舞近。（丰田汽车）
15. Where there is a way, there is a Toyota。有路就有丰田车。（丰田汽车）
16. Good teeth, good health. 牙齿好，身体就好。（高露洁牙膏）
17. Can't beat the real thing. 挡不住的诱惑。（可口可乐）
18. Tide's in, dirt's out. 汰渍到，污垢逃。（汰渍洗衣粉）
19. Apple thinks different. 苹果电脑，不同凡"想"。（苹果电脑）
20. Not all cars are created equal. 并非所有的汽车都有相同的品质。（三菱汽车）
21. Anything is possible. 没有不可能的事。（东芝电子）
22. Our wheels are always turning. 我们的车轮常转不停。（五十铃汽车）
23. The world smiles with *Reader's Digest*. 《读者文摘》给全世界带来欢笑。
24. Nobody is perfect. 没有一个人的身材是十全十美的。（苗条健身器材）
25. New Beijing, Great Olympics. 新北京，新奥运。
26. Live well, snack well. 美好生活离不开香脆的饼干。（斯耐克威尔士饼干）
27. We're the dot. in. com. 我们就是网络。（太阳微系统公司）
28. No business too small, no problem too big. 没有不做的小生意，没有解决不了的大问题。（IBM 公司）
29. The new digital era. 数码新时代。（索尼影碟机）
30. We lead. Others copy. 我们领先，他人仿效。（理光复印机）
31. Impossible made possible. 使不可能变为可能。（佳能打印机）
32. Take time to indulge. 尽情享受吧！（雀巢冰激凌）
33. Come to where the flavor is, Marlboro Country. 光临风韵之境——万宝路世界。（万宝路香烟）
34. To me, the past is black and white, but the future is always color. 对我而言，过去平淡无奇；而未来，却是绚烂缤纷。（轩尼诗酒）
35. The taste is great. 味道好极了。（雀巢咖啡）
36. From Sharp minds, come sharp products. 来自智慧的结晶。（夏普产品）

37. Mosquito, bye, bye, bye. 蚊子,杀、杀、杀。(雷达牌驱虫剂)
38. Connecting People. 科技以人为本。(诺基亚)
39. Ideas for life. 为生活着想。(松下电子)
40. Time is what you make of it. 天长地久。(斯沃奇手表)

Chapter Four
News Translation
新闻文体翻译

Translators' Subjectivity (译者主体性)

For a long time, translators are deemed as "transparent", and they are expected to maintain as much information as they could. After "cultural turn", people's attention has been diverted to translators. Translator is the subjectivity of translation.

The so-called subjectivity refers to the essential characteristics reflected in activities by subject. To put it in detail, subjectivity is the externalization of its essential features in the activities by the subject. Subjects can initiatively transform, influence and control the objects, making the objects serve the subjects. In one word, subjectivity means initiative. But the initiative has to be restricted to play. When subjects exert influence on the objects, they will also face reaction; meanwhile, initiative is also to be restricted by objective conditions to play. Therefore, subjectivity also includes passivity within its definition. Based on the aforementioned analyses, translator's subjectivity can be defined as: translators, as the subject of translation, should show respect to the source text, on the other hand, fully display his initiative so as to realize the purpose of translation.

关键词:译者主体;创造性;主观能动性

On News Report

Freshness / Timeliness (新闻的时效性)

"News today is gold; tomorrow it is silver and the day after tomorrow, garbage".

Yesterday's newspaper is only good for wrapping fish. The all-important news element fades into history within 24 hours.

Prominence—Formula of News (新闻的显著性公式)

Ordinary persons + usual occurrences ≠ news

Ordinary persons + unusual occurrences = news

Extraordinary persons + usual occurrences = news

Extraordinary persons + unusual occurrences = big/good news

1. Characteristics of News Translation

News translation has its special characteristics, which distinguishes itself from other translation activities. First of all, news translation is always carried out under the pressure of time. Due to the timeliness of news report, translators have no choice but to struggle for minimizing the loss of time. Second, news translation should be uncompromisingly accurate. The pursuit of high speed usually results in translator's hasty mistakes, which should be particularly avoided in the work. Besides, translators need to focus primarily on the important information of news reports and employ brief and plain wording as possible as they can.

2. Classification of News

In terms of content: politics, business, law, health, education, military, science and technology, sports, entertainment, social life.

In terms of the place: international news, national news and local news.

In terms of time: unexpected news and sustained news. The unexpected news refers to those incidents which took place suddenly, such as car accident, air disaster, earthquake and snow storm. While thc sustained news reports things changing gradually, such as it is getting hotter, the price is getting lower, or the youth are gaining weight.

In terms of the nature of events: hard news and soft news. Hard news is of great importance and has direct influence on people's life, such as killings, city council meetings and speeches by leading government officials. Soft news generally provides people with entertainment, knowledge or just a good topic for conversation, such as a luncheon to honor a retiring school custodian or money raise for a classmate with cancer.

3. The Make-up of News Report

3.1 The Headline

Headline is usually regarded as the "eye" of news. A headline should not only be informative, but also be interesting and eye-catching. A headline is required to be accurate, brief and clear. Headlines have to contain a clear, succinct and, if possible, intriguing message to kindle a spark of interest in potential reader. A headline has functions of advertising the story, summarizing the story, and beautifying the newspaper page, etc. All these functions require more refined and vivid language embodied in the headline forms, punctuation, syntax, words and rhetoric.

一般来讲新闻标题通常有以下特点:简约、醒目、概括、风趣。然而,从词汇、语法、修辞三方面来看,英语新闻标题和汉语新闻标题各具不同。

3.1.1 Lexical Feature of English News Headlines

Since a headline is the shortest thesis of news, it possesses a diverse nature of vocabulary. The following are several lexical features in news headlines.

Nouns and Midgets Words

Midgets words refer to some simple-structured but actively functioning words, which enjoy wide popularity because news is believed to be "literature in a hurry", and "saying a lot in least space". No time is given to editors to consider the elegance or the wording. At the same time space is limited in the newspaper.

新闻中选取简短生动的日常词汇如"*Police Probe*"而不用"*Police Investigation*";用"*Ticket Sales Soar*"而不用"*Ticket Sales Increase Dramatically*"。下列两组收集了一些名词与动词的对照组。毫无疑问,其中短小、精练的词汇更会受到新闻用词的青睐。

Nouns with large information capacity:

aide—assistant aim—purpose drive—campaign talk—negotiation blast—explosion

body—committee crash—collision deal—transaction demos—democrats

fake—counterfeit pact—treaty probe—investigation job—mission ties—relations

chief—commander ok—approval

Lively midget verbs:

ask—inquire axe—reduce ban—prohibit bar—prevent drop—abandon

check—examine curb—control ease—lessen end—terminate map—formulate

mark—celebrate name—nominate opt—choose sway—influence vow—determine

Clipped Words

Clipped words are some incomplete words, which means that the edge (the front part or the back part) of the original word has been deliberately cut off. They are favored in news edition because of their mini size.

grad—graduate hosp—hospital cig—cigarette champ—champion con—convict

deli—delicatessen expo—exposition homo—homosexual pro—professional

com'l—commercial tech—technology vet—veteran stats—statistics

e.g.

Overseas co-ops to get boost(co-ops = co-operation)

【译文】政府将加强海外合作

Six charged in child porn ring(porn = pornography)

【译文】儿童色情犯罪团伙的6名成员被指控

Migration raises bird-flu worries(flu = influenza)

【译文】候鸟迁徙让人们对禽流感忧心忡忡

Initials and Acronyms

Acronyms are the initial letters of words that form a group of words used for denoting an object, institution or procedure. For instance:

AIM(*America Online's Instant Messenger*，美国在线即时对话软件)

TCM(*traditional Chinese medicine*，传统中药)

DJ(*disc jockey*，音乐节目主持人)

HIPCS(*heavily indebted poor countries*，负债累累的贫穷国家)

DINK(*dual income and no kids*，丁克家庭)

GLAM(*graying*, *leisured*, *affluent and married*，头发渐白,悠闲、富足的已婚者)

Exercise: Traslate the following sentences.

1) U. N. officials discuss early Iraq elections

2) PC, fax sales expected to soar

3) Rally calls for more black MPs

4) The NPC drafts new law to stem corruption

5) WB: Poverty Relief Efforts Impressive

Old Words with New Sense

dove—a person who advocates peace or negotiation in preference to confrontation or conflict

hawk—a person who favors military force or action in order to carry out foreign policy

mafia—an alleged international criminal organization

donkey—American Democratic Party

elephant American Republican Party

a big gun—a very important or influential person

Journalistic Coinages

Some news words in the headline are actually combinations of two or more than two words. They are called "Journalistic Coinages", making up a lot of neologisms in news headlines.

smog = smoke + fog

newscast = news + broadcast

sitcom = situation comedy

reaganomics = Reagan's economics

stagflation = stagnation + inflation

Euro mart = European + market

e. g.

Grain sale expected to fall at *Euromart*(Euro + mart)

【译文】欧洲市场谷物销量预计下跌

Governator Arnold Schwarzengger (governor + terminator)

【译文 1】"终结者"当州长

【译文 2】施瓦辛格今日走马上任

3.1.2 Grammatical / Syntactic Features of News Headlines

Tenses Used

"Time" is a key element in the 5 W and 1 H model of news report. In translating news headlines, the time conception in Chinese is demonstrated by auxiliary words and adverbs rather than transformation of predicate verbs. That is to say such auxiliary words of Chinese as "将，要，会" and "快" can be used to imply the Future Tense, while the auxiliary words like "正，越" and "一直" can be used to imply the Continuous Tense. The application of Chinese auxiliary words will get straight the time of news events without occupying much space in headlines. Tense in news headlines has the following main characteristics.

英语新闻标题时态用法独特，一般用现在时态，即使是过去发生的事情也不例外，如"*Famous Actor Dies*"，"Dies"可能发生在近期，也许是昨天，但没有关系，这样可以省略篇幅，还能给读者造成一种直接感。

一般现在时(sometimes present tense marks the time of past events)

Husband and Wife Team Unlocks New Gene Secrets 夫妻联手揭开新的基因奥秘

Bush Defends Decision of War 布什为伊战辩护

现在进行时(continuous tense is expressed by *be* + *Ving* and *be* is usually omitted)

Women Are Becoming Experts at Home Repairs 妇女正在成为家庭装修能手

Children Getting More Homework, Study Says 研究表明孩子们的功课愈加繁重

一般将来时(infinitive phrases can be used to indicate future tense)

U. S. Will Not Curb Arms for Israel 美国无意削减对以武器援助

Iraq to Suspend Anti-Kurdish Campaign 伊拉克将暂停镇压库尔德人

Exercise: Translate the following sentences.

1) G8 Summits Aims at Eliminating Poverty

2) Putin Faces Harsh Press Criticism over Terror

3) Olympics Begin in Style; Swimmer Takes 1st Gold

4) UK's Oldest Person Dies at 115

Block Language in Headlines

The block language is a type of minor sentence, which differs from the normal clause pattern in omitting function words of low information value such as the articles and the finite forms of verb BE. Look at the following examples: 37 Killed in Italian Plane Crash (37 killed in an Italian plane crash) that can be put into "意飞机失事,37 人遇难". In this sentence the article "an" is omitted.

e. g.

Nepal Royal Family Massacred = *The* Nepal Royal Family *is* Massacred

【译文】尼泊尔皇室遭屠戮

Moscow's Food Prices Soaring = Moscow's Food Prices *are* Soaring

【译文】莫斯科食物飞涨

EU, NATO Throw New Lifeline, to Macedonia Talks = EU *and* NATO Throw *a* New Lifeline to the Macedonia Talks

【译文】欧盟、北约为马其顿和谈寻求新路

3.1.3 Figures of Speech

Figures of speech are often applied to English news headlines to increase their appeal. Translators need to be equipped with not only excellent mastery of English and Chinese language but also rich knowledge about rhetoric.

此类新闻标题英译汉时可以发挥汉语的优势,适当采用对仗、押韵、成语,甚至文言用语,使标题的翻译更加出彩。

Big Crime*, *Small Cities (Antithesis) **小城,大案**

This English headline adopts Antithesis, which means sharply contrasting ideas are juxtaposed in a balanced or parallel phrase or grammatical structure. "Big" and "small" constitute a sharp contrast between size of cities and the criminal record. The Chinese version 大 and 小 effectively transfer the same feeling.

Can New York Rise Again (Personification) **纽约还能东山再起吗?**

Personification is used here, in which objects or abstractions are endowed with human qualities or are represented as possessing human form. The Chinese idiom "东山再起" means that one stages a comeback after failures, which refers to the recovery of New York City after the 9. 11 Attack.

Microsoft Opens a New Window (Pun)**微软又开“新窗”**

Pun is used here to plan on different senses of the same word and sometimes on the similar sense or sound of different words. “Window” means the PC Operation System produced by Microsoft, and to open a new “window” means launch a new Window product. “新窗” is used instead of “新视窗系统”. In this way, the feature of the original is saved.

World Cup Prelim Premiere(Alliteration)**世界杯预选赛初燃战火**

The repeated “P” sound (alliteration means the repetition of the same consonant sounds or of different vowel sounds at the beginning of words or in stressed syllables) increases the auditory effect of the headline and makes it easier for reader to remember. If it is hard to reproduce alliteration in the translation version, translator can shift their focus to visual impact. “初” matching “premiere” indicates that the football tournament just kicked off; “燃” and “战火” are in fact metaphors presenting a picture of flaming soccer games.

Pei's Pyramids Puzzle Paris(Alliteration)**贝式金字塔使巴黎困惑不解**

Four capitalized letters are in rhyme “P”. Pei refers to the famous architect “贝聿铭”.

Nixon's Odyssey to China(Historical Allusion)**尼克松访华的破冰之旅**

Here historical allusion is used. *Odyssey* is an ancient Greek epic written by Homer, in which Odysseus endured a long hardship during the collapse of TROY.

Exercise: Translate the following sentences.

1) Courage Knows No Gender (拟人)
2) After The Boom, Everything Is Gloom (押韵)
3) Soccer Kicks Off Violence (双关)
4) Liberty Mother Of Invention (借用典故)
5) Middle East: A Cradle Of Terror (比喻)
6) The World' s Toughest Car Rallies (对仗)
7) Saving Time for a Rainy Day (成语)
8) Stepping Up To The Firing Line (夸张，套用诗句)

9) German Ready, Fans Ready (尾韵)
10) The Old Man and The Economic Sea (仿拟)
11) To Buy or Not to Buy (仿拟)
12) Is Love for Labor Lost? (设问句式)
13) Five Steps to Invest in Real Estates
14) Too Busy to Read a Book, People Jump Online
15) Clinton Inauguration Most Expensive Ever
16) Bush Begins to Woo Democrats
17) Ex-aide to Blair says the British spied on Anna
18) Oil to hit $100 by end of year and keep rising
19) 人民币对美元汇率再创新高
20) 重庆“钉子户”挑战物权不公
21) 回首过去,展望未来
22) 他山之石,可以攻玉
23) 长沙遭遇罕见秋旱
24) 北京人口总量超过1 740万

3.2 The Lead 导语

The lead is also the most difficult part to write. The writer must try to engage reader's attention at once because by several seconds, the reader decides to read or turn to the next story. Journalists spend more time on the lead than on the body. It must be succinct, informative and intriguing. So the lead is called "the show-window" of the story.

3.2.1 Variants of Lead

Summary / Direct Lead (事实导语)

The so called "roundup" lead, as the earliest lead style, is employed by journalists. The direct lead concentrates all the essentials or elements of the report in the first paragraph. It is mainly for hard news stories, especially for "inverted pyramid" structure.

此类导语交代最重要的事实,有的甚至涵盖尽可能多的新闻要素,即五个W和一个H (when, where, who, why, what and how)。这类导语一般用于比较严肃的政治经济新闻和突发事件,即所谓“硬”新闻(hard news)。

e.g.

US President George W. Bush will be in China on a working visit from February 21 to 22 at the invitation of President Jiang Zemin. In Bush's three-nation Asia tour, he will visit Japan and the Republic of Korea before traveling to China.

这段导语交代了“谁”、“干什么”、“在哪里”和“什么时候”四个新闻要素,堪称综合提要式导语的典范。

The famous typical classical summary lead was written by an AP reporter on April 14, 1865, immediately after President Abraham Lincoln was assassinated:

WASHINGTON, FRIDAY, APRIL 14, 1865—

The President was shot in a theater tonight and perhaps mortally wounded.

This lead includes the following elements:

WHO—the president;

WHAT—was shot;

WHERE—in a theater;

WHEN—tonight;

HOW—perhaps mortally wounded.

Delayed / Interest / Descriptive(延缓型导语)

The delayed lead is often used on features and news features, the kind of stories that are not about developing or fast-breaking events. The delayed lead usually sets a scene or evokes a mood with an incident or anecdote. The purpose of the writing style is to arouse the reader's curiosity and to enhance the readability.

延缓型导语不遵循概括性导语或主要事实导语所必须做到的直截了当、开门见山的原则,而是采取一种带有文学色彩的写作手法,使导语更加生动活泼,情趣盎然。

e. g.

Under the brilliant, mellow early November sunshine, multi-colored chrysanthemums of over 500 varieties rioted in color and beauty at Shanghai's annual chrysanthemum show opened at the People's Park today.

【**译文**】11 月初的上海,阳光明媚,500 多种绚丽多姿的菊花竞相斗艳。每年一次的上海菊展今天在人民公园开幕。

Historical or Literary-allusion Lead (历史典故导语)

The historical or literary-allusion lead draws on some characters or events in history or literature in relation to a current event or person in the news. The event or literary reference selected should be familiar to the average reader, or it loses its impact. Allusions are phrases or expressions which originated from history, myths or legends, such as Trojan horse, tower of ivory, sour grapes, Sphinx's riddle. All allusions are part of western civilization, and they are rich in meaning and colorful in culture.

To translate allusions well, the translator should make careful examination of the connotations of allusions. Generally speaking, some of them can be translated literally because they have become acceptable by the Chinese people. For example, tower of ivory, sour grapes, crocodile tears can be translated directly into "象牙塔,酸葡萄,鳄鱼泪"。But some allusions are not familiar to the Chinese, and in this case, we'd better not translate their connotations directly. For instance, Trojan horse, Sphinx's riddle, The fifth column, a Judas' kiss, catch 22 can be separately translated into Chinese like "暗藏的敌人,难解之谜,间谍,背叛行为,左右为难,尴尬的". In the following version, the translation is completely dependent upon the acceptability of the version, such as the word "Rambosim" which has to add ***annotation*** (加注) for the target reader to understand.

e. g.

The Christmas decision to sent troops into Panama has gone down well at home. A *Newsweek* poll found that 80% of Americans approved of the invasion. Among democrats, normally suspicious of Republican Ramboism, 74% did so.

【**译文**】圣诞节做出的向巴拿马发兵的决定在国内颇受拥护。《新闻周刊》的一项民意调查表明,80%的美国人赞成入侵。通常对共和党的兰博式好战精神持怀疑态度的民主党人中也有74%赞成此举。(兰博(Rambo)是美国电影《第一滴血》中的好战形象。)

3.2.2 Different Textual Characteristics of News Lead and Translation

On News Source(新闻来源)

Generally, the English lead is shorter than the Chinese one. It is usually found that in the Chinese lead the news source is put at the beginning and English news lead is usually at the end of it. The following are two news reports on a wildfire in Los Angeles, and a careful comparison between them will find the differences.

中国政府向美飓风区提供500万美元援助

外交部发言人秦刚3日表示,中国政府已决定向美国飓风区人民提供500万美元救灾援助,并另提供一批救灾急需物资。

China to Offer $5 m to Katrina-hit US Regions

The Chinese government has decided to offer disaster relief up to 5 million US dollars alone with emergency supplies to the people in the United States victimized by Hurricane Katrina, a Foreign Ministry Spokesman said in Beijing Saturday.

Way of Showing Time(时间的表达方法)

英文报道中习惯用星期表示时间,而中文报道却习惯用日期来表示。下面汉英互译的两个例子中,可以观察中英文新闻报道中时间表达的不同。

MEXICO CITY (Reuters)—Spanish tenor Placido Domingo said *On Tuesday* his opera singing is likely to last only five more years, although he will continue to give concerts.

【路透社墨西哥城4月9日电】4月9日,西班牙著名男高音歌唱家普拉西多·多明戈宣布,自己的歌剧生涯将持续5年左右,不过音乐会还将照常进行。

Narrative Perspective（叙事角度）

The following example shows that the Chinese lead and its English translation are different in the way of accounting.

省中医院3月1号将举行百名专家大型义诊。医院所有专科、门诊均由副主任级以上的专家亲自坐诊。届时，将对所有前来就诊的患者免收挂号费和处方费。

People seeking medical care will be able to consult experienced doctors for free one day next week. Provincial Hospital of Chinese Traditional Medicine has set aside March the first for this activity. Its ranking physicians will diagnose patients without charging for registration or prescriptions.

On Textual Progressive Pattern（语篇推进模式）

It is believed that Chinese news leads sometimes are progressed from background information to the news, while their English counterparts are progressed the other way around.

中文导语的篇章推进方式是由新闻背景推向新闻事实，而英文导语则从新闻事实推向新闻背景。

2003年11月5日，两院院士、西南交通大学教授沈志云，中科院院士、北京科技大学教授葛昌纯，国家超导技术委员会首席专家赵忠贤院士以及杨叔子、熊有伦等全国14名院士，联名"上书"科技部和北京市政府，提议为奥运会修建一条世界第一的高温超导磁悬浮列车试运行线。

Version 1

On November 5, 2003, Shen Zhiyun, member of both the Chinese Academy of Science (CAS) and the Chinese Academy of Engineering (CAE) and Professor of Southwest Jiaotong University, Ge Changchun, member of CAS and Professor of the University of Science and Technology of Beijing, Zhao Zhongxian, Chief Expert of the National Committee on Superconducting Technology, Yang Shuzi and Xiong Youlun, these 14 people jointly wrote to the Ministry of Science and Technology and the Municipal Government of Beijing, urging the construction of an experimental high temperature superconducting (HTS) maglev line, the first of its kind in the world, for the 2008 Olympics.

Version 2

On November 5, 2003, 14 members of the Chinese Academy of Science (CAS) and the Chinese Academy of Engineering (CAE) jointly wrote to the Ministry of Science and Technology and the Municipal Government of Beijing, urging the construction of an experimental high temperature superconducting (HTS) maglev line, the first of its kind in the world, for the 2008 Olympics. Among the 14 academicians figured Shen Zhiyun, member of both CAS and CAE and Professor of Southwest Jiaotong University, Ge

Changchun, Professor of the University of Science and Technology of Beijing, Zhao Zhongxian, Chief Expert of the National Committee on Superconducting Technology, Yang Shuzi and Xiong Youlun.

Exercise: Translate the following sentences.

1) After five weeks of legal arguments that included the US Supreme Court, the US Electoral College voted on Monday for Republican Texas Governor George W. Bush to become the 43rd president of the United States.

2) The director of the World Health Organization, Mr. Halfdan Mahler, yesterday predicted that up to 100 million people world-wide may become infected with AIDS virus in the next four or five years and by that time it would cost at least $1. 5 billion a year to counteract the disease, when virus may vary as time goes and become harder to control.

3) 昨天上午,长江太昌段 7 号浮标附近发现一条特大中华鲟(a Chinese sturgeon),已经死亡。

4) 昨天上午,周恩来与邓颖超生平事迹图片展在南京梅园新村纪念馆拉开帷幕。

5) BEIJING, AUG. 19 (Reuter)—The president's visit has turned a new page in relations between the two countries, mass media here say.

6) LONGDON, OCT. 20 (Reuter via Xinhua)—London Markets closed mixed on profit taking after a higher opening in fairly active trading, it was announced here.

7) 公安部将在全国 36 个大、中城市实施的道路交通"畅通工程"今天下午在北京拉开帷幕。

8) 新华社电记者 7 日从民航总局获悉,今年两岸中秋包机航班已正式排定,两岸共有 12 家航空公司总计将执飞 24 个往返航班。

9) The efficiency of the vaccines is the Achilles' heel of India's anti-polio campaign.

10) "The Chinese market is a bottomless pit," said the visiting Nike CEO here in Shanghai.

11) E-mail is a pipeline to thousands of experts on virtually everything; it is a means of meeting people with similar interests or problems.

12) 救援队员在井下又发现了一名遇难者遗体。截至目前,孙家湾矿难遇难者人数上升到 211 人。

13) US Senator and former First Lady Hillary Rodham Clinton has collapsed during a public appearance in Buffalo, New York State.

14) LONDON, Oct. 16 (Reuter)—Winds up to 170 kilometers an hour lashed the streets and houses here today in the worst storm since records began, killing at least 13 people and bringing the southern half of the country to a virtual standstill, according to police.

3.3 The Body

Body is the biggest part of a news reporting, though it may not be the most important one. It contains more details and explanations of the headline and leads to a further development. The body of a piece of news usually begins with a lead. "The first paragraph of a news story is called the lead ".

3.3.1 Reversed/ Inverted Pyramid Structure

The structure of the whole story looks like an inverted pyramid whose head is big, while the end is small. Events are reported in the order of importance. The most important and latest events always appear at the beginning, that is, the lead paragraph.

Combined together, it has the following structure:

Lead;

Explanatory and amplifying material;

Background (if necessary);

Secondary(if necessary).

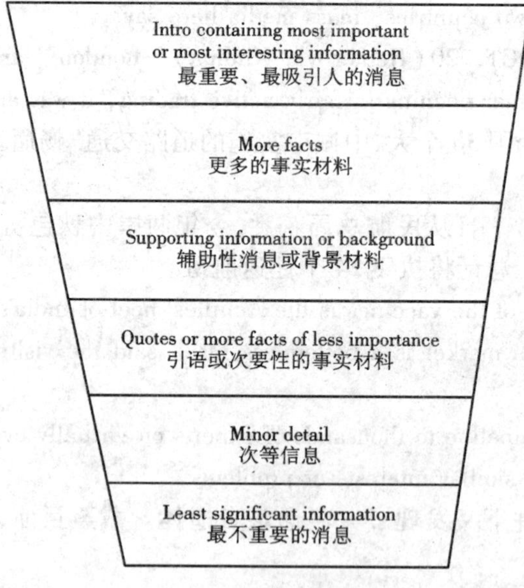

The Inverted Pyramid

Exercise: Traslate the following sentences.

1) Britain and Russia are to co-operate next year in sending an unmanned space probe to Phobos, one of the two moons of Mars, Mr. Blair and Mr. Putin agreed yesterday in Moscow.

The two leaders did not mention any technical details. Officials in Britain disclosed that the probe will hover for 15 minutes only 50 yards above the surface of Phobos, which is 12 miles in diameter, analyzing its composition.

The Anglo-Russia Mars plan has been in the making since last October, when Dr. Roy Gibson, director of Britain's National Space Center, paid a little-publicized visit to Moscow.

British scientists are to provide much of the electronic software for the mission, while Russia will provide the rocket and the spacecraft which will be launched in mid-2003 from earth orbit on its six-month mission. This mission, if successful, is to be followed by a later unmanned Anglo-Russian mission to the surface of Mars itself.

The first mission will fly by Mar's largest moon and not go to Mars itself, because of Phobo's very low gravity.

2) US grateful for recovery of missing pilot's remains

The visiting US Deputy Assistant Secretary of Defense on Friday expressed his sincere appreciation for Chinese efforts in recovering the remains of a missing American pilot believed to have been buried during a time of war.

Jerry D. Jennings, responsible for Prisoner of War Missing Personnel Affairs, said a DNA test showed that the body, which was exhumed last May with the help of the local government in Dandong in Northeast China's Liaoning Province, belonged to the missing pilot Troy G. Cope.

Jennings said he came to China to express thanks to the Chinese people and related government departments on behalf of the family of Captain Cope as well as the American people. He said that without the assistance of local people, the search would have been mission impossible.

Yang Peiyi, director of the foreign affairs office of the local government, said that searching for missing US pilots and the wreckage of their planes is just part of the friendly cooperation between the two countries.

(China Daily, Febl 26 – 27, 2005)

3.3.2 Chronological Structure

This structure is organized in time order. As the development of story goes on, the climax comes in the subsequent part.

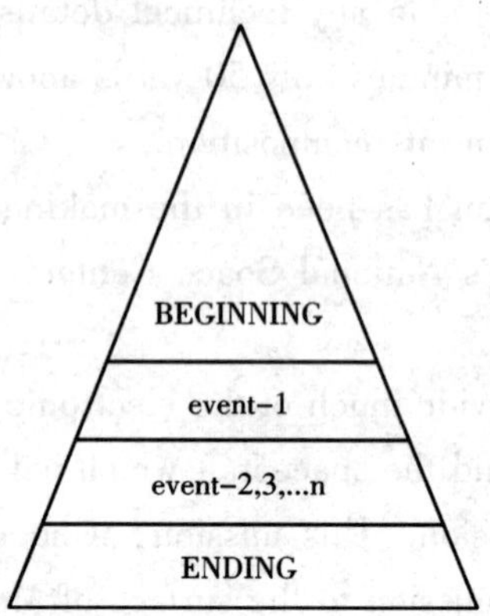

Events Ordered in Time Sequence

3.3.3 Interpreting Cultural Factors in NET Translation

To deal with cultural factors properly in NET translation, translators must locate and interpret its cultural intertextual factors. Cultural factors can be classified into six general categories.

Thought Culture

This kind of culture is based on the mode of thinking and habitual way of thinking. It shows that different nationalities recognize the world and ponder in different ways. For example, native speakers of English use "*black tea*" instead of "*red tea*" in China, because they identify tea in the light of the color of tea leaves while Chinese people distinguish tea according to the color of tea water. In fact, the differences in the ways of thinking between the West and the East are manifested in all respects. For instance, Westerners stress analytic principles and tend to think in a factual perspective, while Easterners emphasize the whole and prefer to think in scattered perspective; Westerners pursue reasoning, logic and abstract, while Chinese people accentuate concreteness, providing examples to illustrate things. English News is the very manifestation of thought culture in English speaking countries. Not only is it embodied in the use of words, but also in the whole configuration of NET and sentence structure.

Conventional Culture

This kind of culture is derived from daily social life and communicative activities, and it is reflected in all walks of life, such as greeting, making apology, showing gratitude, saying goodbye, telephoning, etc. For instance, when it comes to eating habits, Westerners like using words "*bread, milk, cheese, butter, coffee, salad, jam*", etc.; while Chinese people frequently adopt words like "*rice, noodle, cabbage, bean-curd, green pepper*", etc.

Historic Culture

It is formed in the development of particular history and the sediment of social legacy. For example, Chinese people regard "*pine, bamboo and plum*" as the symbol of good virtue; American and British people say "*he is green*" to mean that "*he is inexperienced or naive*"; *lemon* in the West is taken as "*disgusting fellow*".

Psychological Culture

This kind of culture has taken shape in peculiar ethnic psychology and ideology. It is mainly embodied in such aspects as value concept, moral and ethics, euphemism, modesty and courtesy. In recent years, newspapers are stuffed with all kinds of euphemisms to avoid taboos and vulgarity, to show respect or politeness, to or conceal the truth. For example, "*money problem*" is used to mean "*money shortage*"; "*Watergate thing*" refers to "*Watergate Scandal*": "*to pass away*" is used to take the place of "*to die*".

Geographic Culture

This kind of culture is related to the geographical condition. It demonstrates that different nationalities express the same things in different ways because of different geographical conditions. For example, "*to spring like mushroom*" is used by British people to mean that something develops or grows rapidly. But we Chinese people select "*to spring like bamboo shoots after rain*" to account for the phenomenon.

Religious Culture

This kind of culture is represented by Christianity which has a long history in the West. It has already penetrated all aspects of the social life, constituting one of the dominant cultural characteristics in the Western society. In terms of NET, religion-bound words such as *God*, *holy communion*, *pray*, *priest* and *clergyman* are often found.

第四章综合练习

【英译汉】

1) Coast guard: ship aground off Italy, bodies found

GIGLIO, Italy (AP) —The Italian Coast Guard says its divers have found two more bodies aboard the stricken Costa Concordia cruise ship.

The discovery of the bodies brings to five the number of known dead after the luxury ship ran aground with some 4,200 people aboard on Friday night.

The Coast Guard said Sunday the bodies of the two elderly people were found in the submerged restaurant.

A helicopter earlier airlifted a third survivor from the capsized hulk of the ship.

Authorities are holding the captain for suspected manslaughter among other possible charges.

2) France can overcome crisis with reforms: Sarkozy

(Reuters) —President Nicolas Sarkozy said on Sunday France could overcome its debt crisis as long as it was prepared to pull together to adopt economic reforms, two days after the country lost its prized triple-A credit rating.

Sarkozy said he would announce reforms at the end of the month and that he intends to implement them rapidly following talks with union leaders and employers this coming week.

" The crisis can be overcome provided we have the collective will and the strength to reform our country. "

Three months away from a presidential election, Sarkozy has turned his focus to growth, vowing to overhaul welfare financing, company labor charges and job flexibility, with plans for a so-called " Social VAT " to fund welfare and a tax on financial transactions.

3) Beijing receives 2012 first snow, flights delayed

BEIJING, Jan. 7 (Xinhua)—The first snow for 2012 falling down in China's capital late Friday night continued into Saturday morning, with roads slippery and some flights delayed.

By early Saturday morning, light snow has brought about more scraping traffic accidents in Beijing. But the traffic remained normal in all major highways as the snowfall was not heavy, said local traffic control authorities.

As of 9 a. m. , ten flights have been delayed in the Beijing Capital International Airport.

US trade deficit with China breaks the US 100b barrier

The United States' trade deficit with China has risen above the US $ 100 billion level. According to figures released yesterday by the Department of Commerce, the US trade deficit with China last year was US $ 103 billion. This accounted for almost one-fourth of America's total US $435 billion trade deficit for 2002, the largest imbalance in history, suppressing the US $379 billion mark set in 2000.

The monthly deficit with China for December reached US $9. 5 billion, up a remarkable 73 percent over December 2001. No reason was given for the year-on-year surge.

China overtook Japan three years ago as the country with which the US has its largest trade deficit, and has maintained that position ever since.

China posted a trade deficit with its global trading partner of US $1. 25 billion in January, attributing its first monthly trade deficit for at least five years to the rising of oil import.

Notes:

trade deficit	贸易逆差
monthly deficit	月度逆差
barrier	关口
surge	大幅度增长
Department of Commerce	商务部
to account for	占……
imbalance	失衡,不平衡
year-on-year	按年增长
to overtake	超过
trading partner	贸易伙伴
to surpass	超过
to attribute to	归之于

【汉译英】

1)(诺贝尔奖官方网站报道)授予中国作家莫言2012年诺贝尔文学奖,他的"魔幻现实主义作品将民间故事、历史和当代社会融合在一起"。莫言的作品将幻想与现实、历史和社会视角等融合在一起,他作品中营造的世界,会令人同时联想起美国作家威廉·福克纳和哥伦比亚作家加西亚·马尔克斯的作品,同时又从中国的古老文化和口头文学传统中寻找写作的出发点。

2)(美国《纽约时报》网站10月11日报道)多产且享有国际声誉的中国作家莫言今天获得2012年度诺贝尔文学奖。莫言在长篇和短篇小说中描绘了中国纷乱而复杂的农村生活,常常采用丰富的想象——动物叙事者、地下世界、神话故事元素——让人联想起南美魔幻现实主义的手法。

伦敦大学亚非学院中文教授贺麦晓说,莫言属于"文化大革命"后开始用新的眼光关注中国社会、尤其是农村社会的一代作家。贺麦晓说,莫言的作品没有描写社会主义超级英雄,而是充满了具有真正弱点的真实人物,与此同时他把中国农村描写成一个"发生奇妙事情的神奇的地方"。

3)北京暴雨致37人遇难。北京市政府周日晚间通报,周六持续时间达20小时的北京暴雨共造成37人死亡,其中溺水死亡25人,房屋倒塌致死6人。

4)红茶可能有助防癌。(印度时报网站6月19日报道)据研究人员说,喝茶对健康有一系列好处,现在又多了一个好处:一天一杯茶能大幅降低患癌症的风险,它可以使肿瘤缩小。

5）公共交通有利于锻炼和减肥。城市规划者和居民常常极力要求改善公共运输条件。他们声称，好的公交能减轻交通堵塞，同时较少私家车的尾气排放。现在，对公交的"狂热"又有了一个新的理由——它有助于人们的身材变得更苗条。发表在《美国预防医学杂志》(*American Journal of Preventive Medicine*)八月份期刊上的一项研究得出了上述结论。

附录1:世界主要通讯社——World News Agency Acronyms

国别	缩略语	原名全称	中文译名
俄罗斯	TASS	Telegraph Agency of the Soviet Union	塔斯社
英国	Reuter	Reuter's News Agency	路透社
德国	DPA	Deutsche Presse Agentur	德新社
法国	AFP	Agence Francaise de Presse	法新社
比利时	BNY	Belga News Agency	比利时通讯社
西班牙	EFE	La Agencia EFE	埃菲社
巴基斯坦	APP	Associated Press of Pakistan	巴联社/巴通社
印度	AIM	Agencia Information Mozambique	印度东北通讯社
伊朗	ATP	Agence Telegraphique Pars	波斯通讯社
日本	KNS	Kyodo News Service Kyodo Tsysgubsga	共同社
日本	TSJ	Tokyo Shimbun of Japan	东京新闻
韩国	KBS	Korea Broadcasting System	韩国广播公司
朝鲜	KCNA	Korean Central News Agency	朝中社
越南	VNA	Vietnam News Agency	越南通讯社
澳大利亚	AAP	Australian Associated Press	澳大利亚联合新闻社
新西兰	NZPA	New Zealand Press Association	新西兰报联社
埃及	MEN	Middle East News Agency	中东通讯社
美国	AAP	American Associated Press	美洲报联社
美国	UPI	United Press International	合众国际社
美国	USIS	US Information Service	美新社
美国	AP	Associated Press	美联社
加拿大	CP	Canada Press	加拿大通讯社

附录2:世界主要报刊

The Times《泰晤士报》

The Daily Telegraph《每日电讯报》

The Financial Times《金融时报》

The Guardians《卫报》

The Sun《太阳报》

The New York Times《纽约时报》

The Washington Post《华盛顿邮报》

Los Angeles Times《洛杉矶时报》

International Herald Tribune《国际先驱论坛报》

The Wall Street Journal《华尔街日报》

USA Today《今日美国》

《时代》Time

《财富》Fortune

《新闻周刊》News Week

《商业周刊》Business Week

附录3:消息来源常用套语

According to Analysts 据分析家称

AP reports 据美联社报道

authoritative sources 据权威人士称

commercial quarters 据商界称

the data made available 据此间获得的资料表明

diplomatic sources 据外交界人士称

informative sources 据消息灵通人士称

military sources 据军方人士称

neutral sources 据中立人士称

observers 据观察家称

official sources 据官方人士称

reliable sources 据可靠人士称

semi-official sources 据半官方人士称

the spokesman/spokeswoman 据发言人称

Chapter Five
Translation of Business English
商务英语翻译

Toury and Descriptive Translation Studies (DTS) (图里和描写翻译)

Descriptive Translation Studies, with its setting in the social culture of the target language, employ empirical methods to describe and explain the translation behavior and translation works so as to form the theoretical principle, i. e. to study translation within the social culture of the target language. Toury abandoned one-to-one notions of correspondence as well as the possibility of literature/linguistic equivalence. He involved literary tendencies within target cultural system in the production of any translated text and destabilized the notion of an original message with a fixed identity.

Additionally, both the original text and the translated text are integrated in the semiotic web of intersecting cultural systems.

描写性翻译理论就是"在研究翻译的过程、产物以及功能的时候,把翻译放在时代中去研究。广而言之,是把翻译放到政治、意识形态、经济、文化之中去研究"。

关键词:描写性翻译;实证研究;目标语文化;政治;意识形态

Introduction to Business English

Business English, as a language form, serves as the means of communication and carrier of rules and regulations governing the business activities in the world of business. English concerned with various fields of commercial activities such as the technology transfer, foreign trade, the introduction of foreign investment, international financing, transnational tourism, international transportation, is as a whole called business English. Business English letters, contracts, documents, advertisements, telexes and telegrams, all belong to this category. Business English is a branch of special English in use and an application of English in business occasion. It is classified by many linguists into English for Special Purposes (ESP).

1 Definition and Classification of Business English

Generally, business English refers to the English used in business correspondences and activities. Business English can be divided into Ordinary Business English and Specialized Business English.

1.1 Ordinary Business English

It covers any English book, magazine, news report and so on, which are related to business activities. They are closely related to the general English and share to a great degree the major linguistic features with general English.

1.2 Specialized Business English

It refers to documents, laws, regulations, specialized theories and practice in business activities. Without any specialized business knowledge and practice the translator can hardly guarantee a sufficient understanding and satisfactory translation.

2 The Principles of Business English Writing

2.1 Courtesy

To be polite is a basic principle for business writing. Every letter should be looked as a representative of the firm and as a messenger of goodwill. Adopting the right tone is also very important. The right tone arouses good will, warmth and the interest in your reader. Phrases like "If what you said is true...", "If... as you stated..." may make your reader think that you are suspicious of his integrity. "You neglected...", "You forget..." may risk your reader with accusation. Answer your customers promptly, for punctuality will please your customers who are waiting for days before they obtain reply to their questions. Whenever necessary, do not forget to say "Thank you...", "Would you please...", "We would appreciate it...".

Exercise: Compare each pair of writing work of the following sentences and tell which expression is more polite?

A1. We have received your letter of March 4, but we still do not understand what we should do.

A2. Thank you for your reply of March 4th. In order that we may be of the greatest possible help to you, would you please frankly tell us what you want us to do?

B1. You did not read the instruction for the new equipment.

B2. You enjoy the full benefits of the new equipment; you should follow the instruction carefully.

2.2 Conciseness

Conciseness is the expression of an idea in the fewest possible words without sacrificing clarity. In business correspondence, this means increased effectiveness and decreased cost. Wordy expressions and redundancies such as "in accordance with your request" should be "as you requested". Phrases like "repeat again" and "combined together" should be avoided.

2.3 Clarity

The message should convey exactly what you wish to say and is not liable to misunderstanding. Avoid vague and ambiguous expressions. Much confusion has been caused by unclear business communication.

Exercise: Please tell which expression is clearer than the other.

A1. These brakes stop a car within a short distance.

A2. These Type W31 power brakes stop a 2.5 ton car traveling 70 miles an hour, within 250 feet.

B1. He wanted a policy for his house that would cost US $ 50 every year.

B2. For his house he wanted a policy that would cost US $ 50 every year.

2.4 Completeness

A complete business document should contain whatever details that are needed to produce the response you want. If you leave out something the reader should know, it will be annoying and costly because it holds up business transitions and duplicates work. Even worse, it may cause costly lawsuits. For example, you should let the consumer know more than the terms of price, such as delivery time, mode of payment, packing, and even if you cannot supply the customer with your products, you could offer alternative to him.

2.5 Concreteness

Effective business communication is marked by concrete words. Make your message specific, definite and vivid. To express your intention clearly, you should not only use nouns with specific and concrete meaning, but also verbs that emphasize action.

Exercise: Make a comparison between the following sentences.

A1. We are interested in your vehicle.

A2. We are interested in your ZF100 Future Fighter motorcycle.

B1. There appears to be a tendency on the part of our customers to buy Green Food. (Weak verb)

B2. Our customers tend to buy Green Food now. (Action verb)

C1. It will be proposed at the board meeting by Mrs. Stewart that bonus be increased by the ABC Corporation. (Weak verb)

C2. Mrs. Stewart will propose at the board meeting that ABC Corporation increases its bonus. (Action verb)

2.6 Correctness

No business document should ever be permitted to go out with a misspelled word, or a typographical error, or an incorrectly or poorly constructed sentence. Poor grammar, misspelled words, lack of punctuation or improper use of it should be avoided. Carefully attention to details, conscientious proofreading, and use of reference books will be helpful to reduce errors in business translation.

2.7 Consideration

Business letters should develop good will. They should be made as personal and interesting as possible. Try to understand and respect your reader's point of view. If your reader think you are standing in his shoes, he will feel more comfortable.

Exercise: Tell the differences of the following sentences.

A1. We allow 2.5% discount for cash payment. ("I" or "we" attitude)

A2. You can earn 2.5% discount when you pay cash. ("you" attitude)

B1. As the fiscal year is coming to an end, would you please pay your overdue bill now? ("I" or "we" attitude)

B2. In order to maintain your excellent credit reputation, please remit $ 2,000. ("you" attitude)

3. Stylistic Features of Business English

3.1 Being Objective and Impersonal

Business English mainly belongs to expository writing, which involves giving explanation, illustration, classification, instruction, definition and presenting information, facts, figures, numbers, terms, etc.

A contract is an agreement whereby the parties establish, change or terminate their civil relationship.

合同是当事人之间设立、变更、终止民事关系的协议。(Definition)

Generally speaking, telegrams can be divided into two kinds: Plain Language Telegrams and Code Language Telegrams.

一般而言,电报可分为两种:明语电报和电码电报。(Classification)

3.2 Being Specialized

Business English is the combination of English and the knowledge of many branches of learning, such as marketing, economics, finance, accountancy and management, as a result of which there is a heavy use of related technical terms (including conversion of common words).

e.g.

an outstanding cheque	(未兑现支票)
default terms/value	(违约条款/默认值)
judgment by default	(缺席裁判)
futures /drugs/buy	(期货、滞销货、便宜货)
force majeure	(不可抗力)
draft at sight	(即期汇票)
letter of credit	(信用证)
bill of lading	(提单)
documents against acceptance	(承兑交单)
bill of exchange	(汇票)
fixed capital	(固定资本)

offer(发盘);a firm offer(实盘);counter offer(还盘)

offer(要约); offerer(要约人); offeree(受要约人);

accept(承诺);acceptor(承诺人);acceptee(接受承诺人)

3.3 Formal and Standard in Style

3.3.1 Complete, Long and Complicated in Sentence Structure

With a view to expand international economic cooperation and technological exchange, the People's Republic of China permits foreign companies, enterprises, and other economic organizations or individuals to establish joint ventures together with Chinese companies, enterprises, or other economic organizations within the territory of the People's Republic of China on the principle of equality and mutual benefit and subject to approval by the Chinese Government.

【译文】中华人民共和国为了扩大国际经济合作和技术交流,容许外国公司、企业和其他经济组织或个人,按照平等互利的原则,经中国政府批准,在中华人民共和国境内,同中国的公司、企业或其他经济组织共同举办合营企业。

3.3.2 Use of Formal Structures

The use of fixed sentence patterns

We hereby confirm...

兹确认……

Enclosed please find...

随函附上……,敬请查收……

Please be advised that...

兹通知……

For your reference, we are enclosing a few copies of leaflets, and will send you samples under separate cover.

兹随函附上几份说明书并另寄样品,供你方参考。

Please inform us what special offer you can make us.

请告知贵公司能给多少特价优惠。

In reply to your inquiry of May 10, we are pleased to quote as follows.

兹复贵公司5月10日之询价函,很高兴报价如下。

We should appreciate full particulars of your newly developed product.

如蒙赐寄贵公司新产品的详细资料,我们将深表感激。

Exercise: Practice the following expressions.

1) 本合同于合同签署之日生效,以此为证。

IN WITNESS WHEREOF, this contract has been executed by the parties as of the date first above written.

2) 由__与__同意按下列条款,签订本合同。

The Contract is made by and between __ and __ according to the terms and conditions below.

3) 根据__,本着__,经过__,双方同意__。兹订立本合同。

In accordance with ____, adhering to ____ and through ____, both parties agree ____. The Contract is worked out there under.

4) 我们已收到你们第A3481号信用证,非常感谢。

We are in receipt of/admit /acknowledge /receipt of/have received (with thanks) your L/C No. A3481 with thanks.

5) 我们很高兴收到你们第712号订单,再次订购电动打字机。

We are pleased to have received your Order No. 712 for a further purchase of electric typewriters.

6）随函附上发票和提单。

We are enclosing the invoice and the bill of lading.

7）一接到你们回信，我们即电报开出信用证。

Upon receipt of your reply we will open an L/C by cable.

8）根据《中华人民共和国合同法》及有关规定，为明确双方在项目承包建设过程中的权利、义务和经济责任，经双方协商同意签订本合同。双方达成协议如下：

In accordance with The Contract Law of the People's Republic of China and other regulations and rules concerned, and for ascertaining the rights, obligations and economic liabilities of parties in the process of contracting this project construction, both Parties have agreed to sign this contract with the terms and conditions stipulated as follows:

The use of phrases instead of subordinate clauses

e. g.

an agreement which has been approved / approved by/ under the approval of / subject to the approval by / subjected for the approval of the government

The use of formal words and expressions

Formal (Legal) Words	**Ordinary Words**
commit /perform	carry out /do
commence	begin
with regard to	about
anticipate	expect
terminate	end
surrender	give
certify	prove
notify	tell
complete	finish
abbreviate	shorten
category	class
participate	take part in
comply with	stick to
evidence	proof
illustrate /demonstrate	show
witness	see
utilize	use
residence	house

be of the opinion	think
encounter	meet

With rigid form and the use of refined words and expressions such as "request, pleasure, your company, R. S. V. P. ", the following example is standard and dignified.

e. g.

Mr. and Mrs. Fernando Smith
request the pleasure of your company at dinner
on Saturday, the fourth of July
at half past seven o'clock
Seabreez
Edgartown, Massachusetts
R. S. V. P
BOX636
Edgartown, Massachusetts02539
凡纳得·史密斯夫妇敬备小酌,恭请光临
7 月 4 日(星期六)下午七时半
麻省埃得加镇海风酒楼
恭候回音
636 信箱
埃得加镇,麻省 02539

The use of archaic words such as

hereafter = after this(自此,今后), *hereby = by this means*(特此,兹), *herein = in this*(此中,于此), *hereinafter = later in this Contract*(在下文中), *hereof = of this*(在本文中), *thereto = to that*(另外,随附), *thereof = of that*(其中,它的), *whereas = since*(鉴于), *whereby = according to which*(凭借), *whereupon = hence*(因此,于是)

The use of prepositional phrases such as

with a view to(*with the aim of*), *with respect to*(*concerning*), *in line with*(*according to*), *with reference to*(*about*; *in connection with*), *for the purpose of*(*for*), *in the event of*(*if*), *in case of*(*if*)

e. g. ***In case of*** any divergence of interpretation, the Chinese text shall prevail.
若对解释产生异议,以中文文本为准。

3. 4 The Use of Plain, Accurate Language

Words in commercial correspondence should be common and easy to understand. The language should be clear and concise, avoiding redundancy.

3.5 Some Useful Expressions

付款方式

L/C——信用证 D/A——承兑交单 B/L——提单
COD——交货付款 T/T——电汇 L/G——保函
D/P——付款交单

运输业务

ETA——预抵期 CIF——到岸价 ETD——预离期
C&F——成本加运费价 ETFD——预计卸毕时间
AFRA——平均运费率指数 FOB——离岸价

A Firm Offer from the Seller
卖方报实盘

Dear Sirs,

As requested in your letter of April 18th, we offer your firm as follows, subject to your reply reaching us by the end of this month:

根据贵方 4 月 18 日来函要求,我们报实盘如下,以贵方在本月底复到有效:

1,000 dozen cotton shirts at U. S. $ 60 per dozen CIF New York. The shipment is to be made during June. We require ***payment by confirmed irrevocable letter of credit payable by draft at sight***.

棉衬衫 1 000 打,每打 CIF60 美元纽约价。6 月装运。我们要求**以保兑的不可撤销即期信用证支付**。

This is the best offer we can make at present and we trust that you will accept this offer without lose of time as the demand for our cotton is heavy.

这是我们目前能报的最低价,由于对我们棉衬衫的需求甚殷,我们相信贵方会立即接受这项报盘。

For your reference, we are sending some samples separately.

我们将另邮一些样品供贵方参考。

Yours very truly
您真诚的

As business English involves ironed-hard facts, data, clear duties or obligations or definite stipulations, it admits no vague language so as to avoid any misunderstanding to the parties concerned.

3.6 Heavy Use of Abbreviations

Abbreviations are words usually formed from the initial letters of words that make up a descriptive phrases or proper names. In common English, abbreviations are not necessary and thus are used not much. However, as trade has developed rapidly with the invention of telegram, telephone and telex, telephone talk and telex sending between buyers and sellers overseas need to be concise and brief, convenient for memory and record. Therefore, a great many abbreviations are created and the types of them are various, which include the following aspects.

Abbreviations in Names

OPEC—The Organization of Petroleum Exporting Countries 石油输出国家组织

EEC—European Economic Community 欧洲经济共同体

APEC—Asia-Pacific Economic Cooperation 亚太经贸合作组织

ITT—International Telephone and Telegraph 美国国际电话电信公司

WTO—World Trade Organization 世界贸易组织

ISO—International Organization for Standardization 国际标准化组织

CN(=China) 中国

PEK(=Peking)北京

WAS (=Washington) 华盛顿

In Currencies, Weights and Measures

$ —the US Dollar

RMB—Ren Min Bi

Gal—gallon

CNY—China Yan

USD—United States Dollar

GBP—Great Britain Pound

Varieties of Technical Terms

B/L—bill of lading 提单

COD—cash on delivery 发货付款

L/C—letter of credit 信用证

L/G—letter of guarantee 保证函

PCT—percent 百分比

B/C—bill for collection 托收发票

C. B. S. —cash before shipment 现金交易

DOC—document 单据

SPEC—shipment 装运

ASAP—as soon as possible 尽快

BTWN—between 在……之间

In Telex

NLT—not later than

DOC NT RCVD PLS CHCK N RPL—The documents have not been received. Please check and reply.

YTLX 918 N 936 WL RVRT NX MON—We will revert your telex 918 and 936 next Monday.

3.7 Employment of Polite Formula

Common English pays no attention to intimacy and pleasure in social contact, so it needs little polite formula. But in order to achieve high efficiency of business contact in business English, courtesy and caring should be required, and also excessive intimacy should be avoided. Therefore, "Business English forms a set of formulated language acceptable in the international—polite formula."

➢ ***Polite Formula for Expressing Acknowledgement***

We shall appreciate your... 我们将甚为感谢……

Please accept my sincere appreciation for you. 请接受我方对您的真挚谢意。

➢ ***Polite Formula for Expressing Regret***

With much regret 十分遗憾

I owe you an apology. 我应该向你道歉。

➢ **Polite Formula Formation**

use of simple past tense such as "could / would you...? I wondered..."

Could you reduce the price?

您可以把价格降一降吗?

use of passive voice

It was considered a mistake to put off shipment wantonly.

任意拖延装运时间是错误的。

use of subjunctive mood

Were it not for your manager, we shouldn't have missed the first vessel.

要不是你们经理,我们不会错过第一条船。

use of "not always / quite / really / particularly..."

The question was not always with you.

你不会总碰到这种问题的。

3.8 Frequent Use of Archaic Words

Frequent use of archaic words is another stylistic feature of business English, especially in the legal documents. Archaic words and phrases mean the words or phrases are now not used in ordinary language but retained in some literary, biblical and legal language, a few of which are showed in the following table:

Hereby*: *in this way or this letter（以此,以此方式,特此）
Herein*: *in this document（此中,于此,在此批文中）
Here from*: *from this fact or statement（由此,从此）
Thereby*: *by that（按此）
There from*: *from that（从此）
There with*: *with that（与那）
Therein*: *in which（在那方面）
Whereof（关于那个）

3.9 Words Acquiring Different Meaning in a Business Text

action	诉讼
hand	签名
instrument	文件
said	上述
serve	送达
consideration	对价
counterpart	同等效力的副本
avoid	废除
alienation	转让
limitation	时效
negligence	过失
prejudice	损害
satisfaction	清偿
offer	要约,出价
prayer	请求书
specialty	盖印契约

4. Translation of Business Contracts

4.1 What is a Contract?

A contract is a written certificate made for the purpose of smooth cooperation between the parties concerned, which involves such problems as business, technology, law, etc. Linguistically, it is characterized as formal and rigorous, elaborate and exact, pedantic and stereotyped, complicated and abstruse.

4.2 The Stylistic Characteristics of the Contract

4.2.1 Orientation of the Content

A contract is made for a particular matter, subject, project or situation, which is relevant only to parties concerned, and which, therefore, covers only a limited number of readers.

4.2.2 Standardization of Format

A contract is usually made up of three parts: the preamble (前言), the body, and the final clauses (最后条款) or witness clauses (结尾条款).

The preamble states the names of the parties concerned, aiming at concluding the treaty and the underlying principle.

The body stipulates the concrete rights and duties of the relevant parties, reparation (compensation) for breaking the contract, settlement of disputes and laws applicable.

The witness clause includes the legal site, the range of effects (效力范围), the effective terms and conditions stipulated in the contract, and the signatures by the parties concerned.

4.2.3 Syntactic Complexity

Sentences in a contract are normally long, with many modifying elements, which are just for the sake of precise and exact expression and avoiding negligence and omission. It is quite normal that a sentence constitutes a paragraph.

e.g.

Technical Documentation means the technical literatures, drawings, pictures, tapes, etc. that Party B possesses and has applied or developed for its own production as well as in its current manufacture during the validity term of the contract for designing, calculating, manufacturing, quality control, assembling, installations, maintaining and testing of the contract Products (hereinafter referred to as Documentation)...

【译文】技术文件指的是乙方所持有的并在生产中加以应用和开发的技术文献、图纸、照片、磁带等,在合同有效期内仍在当前的制作过程中,用于对合同的产品进行设计、计算、制造、质量控制、安装、维护、测试等(以下称"文件")……

4.2.4 Indirect Reference

Expressions for indirect reference are used throughout the text of a contract, just for the aim of showing that the terms and provisions in the contract are equal and fair to all parties concerned.

e.g.

Both *Party A* and *Party B* agree that a technology transfer agreement shall be signed between the joint venture company and *Party X* (or *a third party*).

甲、乙双方同意,由合营公司与X方(或第三方)签订技术转让协议。

Other expressions for indirect reference: the Seller, the Buyer, the Recipient Party (受方), the Supplying (供方), the Transferor (转让方), the Transferee (受让方), etc.

4.2.5 Itemized Expression

A contract normally contains outlines, clauses and sub-clauses, which requires well-knitted arrangement both logically and linguistically. Clarity in expression and arrangement is the most typical characteristic of the contract, which distinguishes itself from both academic writing and descriptive articles.

4.2.6 Legal Character in Wording

The rights and duties stipulated for parties concerned in a contract are legally binding. In order to avoid any misunderstanding and ambiguity, a contract must be precisely and exactly worded throughout the text, to achieve the solemnity of legal writing. For example, archaic words such as ***thereof***, ***aforesaid*** and ***herein*** are often used in a contract. ***Shall*** as a specific legal term is also used to indicate the situations to be mentioned are legally binding.

4.3 Structure of Contract

____________________有限公司

公司地址:________________

电话:________________

传真:________________

合　　同

合同编号________________　　　　　　日期________________

________________(买方)和________________(卖方)按下

列规定条款达成协议,据此,买方同意购买,卖方同意出售下列商品:

品名:

规格:

数量:

单价:

总金额:

包装:

交货日期:

目的地:

保险:

付款条件:

备注:

(买方签字)＿＿＿＿＿＿＿＿ (卖方签字)＿＿＿＿＿＿＿＿

日期＿＿＿＿＿＿＿＿ 日期＿＿＿＿＿＿＿＿

＿＿＿＿＿＿＿＿ Ltd.

Address:＿＿＿＿＿＿＿＿

Tel:＿＿＿＿＿＿＿＿

Telex:＿＿＿＿＿＿＿＿

CONTRACT

Contract No. ＿＿＿＿＿＿＿＿ Date ＿＿＿＿＿＿＿＿

＿＿＿＿＿＿＿＿(the Buyers) and ＿＿＿＿＿＿＿＿(the Sellers) have reached an agreement, whereby it is agreed that the buyers undertake to buy and the sellers undertake to sell the following goods on terms and conditions as stipulated here below:

Name of Commodity:

Specification:

Quantity:

Unit Price:

Total Amount:

Packing:

Shipment:

Destination:

Insurance:

Terms of Payment:

Remarks:

Buyer's Signature ____________________

Seller's Signature ____________________

Date ____________________ Date ____________________

4.4 Translation Tips for Business Contracts

4.4.1 Selection of Ambiguous Words

英译商务合同时,常常由于选词不当而导致词不达意或者意思模棱两可,有时甚至表达的是完全不同的含义。

shipping advice 与 shipping instructions

shipping advice: 装运通知,是由出口商发给进口商的。

shipping instructions: 装运须知,是进口商发给出口商的。

vendor & vendee: 卖主 & 买主

consignor & consignee: 发货人 & 收货人

abide by 与 comply with

abide by: 遵守,主语须是"人"。

comply with: 遵守,主语是非人称。

e. g.

Both parties shall abide by/All the activities of both parties shall comply with the contractual stipulations.

双方都应遵守/双方的一切活动都应遵守合同规定。

change A to B 与 change A into B

change A to B: 把 A 改为 B。

change A into B: 把 A 折合成/兑换成 B。

e. g.

Both parties agree that change the time of shipment to August and change US dollar into RMB.

双方同意将交货期改为 8 月,并将美元折合成人民币。

ex 与 per

ex: 由某轮船"运来"的货物

per: 由某轮船"运走"的货物

by: 由某轮船"承运"

e. g.

The last batch per /ex / by S. S. "Victoria" will arrive in London on October 1st.

由"维多利亚"轮运走 / 运来 / 承运的最后一批货将于 10 月 1 日抵达伦敦。

in 与 after

in: "多少天之后"的确切的一天

after："多少天之后"的不确切的任何的一天

e. g.

The goods shall be shipped per M. V. "Dong Feng" on November 10 and are due to arrive at Rotterdam in 41 days.

该货于 11 月 10 日由"东风"轮运出，41 天后抵达鹿特丹港。

on/upon 与 after

on/upon：……到后，就……

after："……之后"的时间不明确

e. g.

The invoice value is to be paid on / upon arrival.

发票货值必须货到付给。

by 与 before

by：在翻译终止时间时，比如在"某月某日之前"，如果包括所写日期，就用 by。

before：如果不包括所写日期，即指到所写日期的前一天为止，就用 before。

e. g.

The vendor shall deliver the goods to the vendee by June 15 (before June 16)

卖方须在 6 月 15 日前将货交给买方。

4.4.2 Dealing with the Details of Contract

限定责任

and/or

e. g.

如果上述货物对船舶和（或）船上其他货物造成任何损害，托运人应负全责。

The shipper shall be liable for all damage caused by such goods to the ship and /or cargo on board.

by and between

e. g.

买卖双方同意按照下述条款购买、出售下列商品并签订本合同。

This Contract is made by and between the Buyer and the Seller, whereby the Buyer agrees to buy and the Seller agrees to sell under mentioned commodity subject to the terms and conditions stipulated below.

限定时间

on and after/on or before

e. g.

自 9 月 20 日起，甲方已无权接受任何订单或收据。

Party A shall be unauthorized to accept any orders or to collect any account on and after September 20.

not（no）later than

e. g.

本合同签字之日起一个月内,即不迟于 12 月 15 日,你方须将货物装船。

Party B shall ship the goods within one month of the date of signing this Contract, i. e., not later than December 15.

include 的相应形式:inclusive; including; included

e. g.

本证在北京议付,有效期至 1 月 1 日。

This credit expires till January 1st（inclusive）/ till and including January 1st for negotiation in Beijing.

如果不包含 1 月 1 日,则翻译为 till and not including January 1st。

限定金额

大写文字重复金额

e. g.

聘方每月付给受聘方 500 美元整。

Party A shall pay Party B a monthly salary of US $500（SAY FIVE HUNDRED US DOLLARS ONLY）.

正确使用货币符号, $ 既可以代表"美元"也可以代表其他地方的货币。

金额数字必须紧靠货币符号,例如:US $400。此外,还要注意小数点和逗号,务必看清楚。

4.4.3 Conversion of Sentence Structures

➢主语的转换

主语转换为谓语

原文的主语为动作性的名词,且采用被动语态。译成汉语时,须将英语的被动语态调整为汉语的主动语态,进行翻译转换。

e. g.

Delivery must be effected within the time stated on the purchase order, otherwise the Buyer may at his option cancel the order without cost to him, and charge the Seller for any loss incurred as a result of the latter's failure to make such delivery.

卖方必须在购货订单规定的时间内交货,否则,买方可取消合同,而不承担任何损失,并要求卖方赔偿由不交货所造成的一切损失。

主语转换为宾语

原文的主语往往为普通名词,且常常采用被动语态。译成汉语时,将英语的被动语态改译成汉语的主动语态,主语转换为宾语。

e. g.

Should ***all or part of the Contract and its appendices*** be unable to be fulfilled owing to the fault of one party, the breaching party shall bear the responsibilities thus caused.

由于一方过失,致使不能履行或不能完全履行**本合同及其附件**时,由过失方承担违约责任。

主语转换为定语

如果主语和宾语之间的关系密切,或宾语本身就是主语的一部分,译成汉语时,为使译文符合汉语的表达习惯,往往把原文的主语转换为定语。

e. g.

Each Party is liable to the Joint Venture Company only up to the limit of the capital subscribed by it.

各方对合资公司的责任以**各自**认缴的出资额为限。

➢宾语的转换

宾语转换为主语

合同英语中的某些动词宾语,在逻辑上是应说明的主体,为使其突出醒目,翻译时一般将其转换为汉语的主语。

e. g.

Party A shall send twice ***its technical personnel*** to Party B's factory for training, and the total number of the participants shall not exceed 320 (excluding the interpreter).

甲方的技术人员将分两批赴乙方接受培训,参加培训人员不超过 320 人(翻译人员除外)。

宾语转换为谓语

如果原文的谓语动词不易处理成汉语的谓语,而原文中的宾语又是含有动作意义的名词,那么在汉译时可以将原文中的宾语转换成汉语的谓语,或与原文动词一起合译为汉语的谓语。

e. g.

The Licenser will, at its own cost, take ***such actions*** to eliminate infringement of the Licensed Patents as may be reasonably necessary and proper in its own opinion.

许可方应在其认为有必要的时候,以适当的方式,自费**采取行动**,消除对特许专利的侵权。

➢表语的转换

表语转换为主语

在英语中,当用名词作表语时,主语和表语所表达内容往往是一致的。在译成汉语时,为使上下文连贯,或突出表语所述内容,可将原文句中的表语转换为汉语的主语。

e. g.

This is ***the final arbitration award*** and binding on both Contracting Parties.

这一仲裁是最终的,对双方均有约束力。

表语转换为谓语

当介词和名词构成短语作表语时，其功能类似于汉语的谓语部分，一般可选择一个适当的汉语动词作为谓语来处理译文。

e. g.

In the course of arbitration, the Contract shall be continuously executed by both parties except the part of the Contract which is ***under arbitration.***

在仲裁过程中，除了**正在仲裁**的部分条款外，合同的其他条款应继续执行。

➢定语的转换

在汉语中，形容词是可以作谓语的。因此，当英语的形容词作前置定语时，很难将其译成通顺的汉语。此时，如果将定语转换为汉语的谓语，使之和所修饰的名词一起构成汉语的主谓词组，则可使译文流畅规范。

e. g.

The sample of the machine submitted by the Seller is featured by ***novel*** shape, ***easy*** operation, ***high*** calorific efficiency and ***low*** fuel consumption.

卖方提交的样机的特点是造型**新颖**、操作**简便**、热效率**高**、油耗**低**。

5. Translation of Business Letters

5. 1 Layout of a Business Letter

There are several acceptable styles for business letter writing. The most popular forms are full block (完全齐头式), indented block (缩进式), modified block (修正齐头式), semi-block style with indented paragraphs(混合式).

Full Block Style

Every line in the full block begins at the left margin, and the open style of punctuation has been adopted.

使用开放式标点符号——除了非用不可的标点以及缩略语中使用的句点外，地址行末不用标点符号。

February 4, 1967

T B Gartside 15 Normanshire Court Southport

Dear Sirs

Yours faithfully

Indented Block

The main feature of this style is that each line of the " inside name and address" should be indented 2 to 3 spaces, and the first line of each paragraph should be indented 3 to 8 spaces.

5.2 Normally English Letter Consists of Six Parts

Letter head(信头): telling the reader the name of the firm and often what it makes or sells.

Inside name & address(信内名字及地址): giving the full name, the title and address of reader.

Salutation(称呼): The greeting of business letter is salutation.

Body(正文): The body of the letter is the most important part of any business letter and contains the essential information.

Complimentary close(结束语): The complimentary close ends the letter in a polite way, consequently making a good impression on the reader.

Signature(签名): Every business letter must be signed by its writer, thus telling the reader who writes the letter.

the heading	信头
the reference line	编号
the date	日期
the inside address	收信人地址
the salutation	称呼语
the body of the letter	正文
the complimentary close	结束敬语
the signature	签名
enclosure	附件
carbon copy	抄送副本
postscript	附加遗漏内容

6. Case Study

6.1 Order Letter

August 13, 2003

Vemeer Manufacturing Company

P. O. Box 200/3804 New Sharon Road

Pella, Iowa 50219

U. S. A

Gentlemen,

From the samples sent to us on June 5, we have made selections, and have the pleasure of handing you the following order, which we commend to your immediate and best attention, viz:

500 chests Ceylon Black Tea,

500 sacks of Brazilian Coffee, not ground.

Kindly forward these by fast freight. Enclosed please find a draft as per memorandum bill you sent us.

Yours Truly

F. McFARLAND E CO. (Signature) President

尊敬的阁下:

贵公司6月5日寄来的样品已收悉。经我方选择,现向贵公司订货如下:

锡兰红茶500箱,

巴西咖啡(免滚平)500袋,

以上订货请速备货并尽快发运。按贵公司寄达我公司的价格单,随函寄上汇票一份,请查收。

总经理　麦克法兰　敬上

2003年8月13日

6.2 General Letter

Nov. 20, 2000

Dear Sirs,

We received, on Nov. 11, 2000, with thanks, your Check No. 006869 for RMB 36,000, in payment of our commission. The amount has been placed to your credit.

Manager John

尊敬的阁下:

我方已于2000年11月11日收到贵方第006869号支票一张,金额计人民币36 000元,用以支付我方佣金。该笔款项已入账,谢谢。

总经理　约翰

2000年11月20日

6.3 Business Letter

1117 The High Road

Austin TX 78703

6 June 2006

MR. David Patricks

... Road, Yiwu

Zhejiang Province, China (PRC)

Dear buyer,

It is good to hear from you again. You inquired about my bamboo baskets on September 15, 1998. I sent you a company catalog at that time. I can send you a second catalog if you need.

You are not the only importer in Brazil that has asked us about bamboo baskets. I have also received inquires from ABC company, Universal Co., Ltd in Brazil, but they always inquired another kind of baskets. I will introduce this kind of basket for you if you need. Would you like me to help you by making a special sample for your Brazil market?

We are a professional bamboo products manufacture with 14 years experiences in China, offering over 1,500 various kinds of bamboo products and monthly output up to 5 million pieces. We are the best manufacturer that you can trust in China. The details for the product (as the attached photo) you inquired as following: FOB XXX, Min. Order: 2,000, Price: USD1.80/pc, Delivery Time: 30 days after the receipt of deposit. If you provide us with your express accounts, we will send you a sample with a catalog.

I look forward to your reply!

买家您好,

很高兴再次收到您的查询:您在去年9月15日曾向我们查询过竹篮,那时我们曾寄过公司目录给您,如您需要我可再寄一次给您。

您并不是巴西唯一向我们查询过竹篮的进口商,我们也曾收到来自巴西ABC、Universal等进口商的查询,但他们总是查询另一种竹篮,如您有需要,我可以向您介绍那一类的竹篮,您是否希望我为您的巴西市场做些特别的样品给您?

我们是有十四年专业竹制品经验的中国制造商,提供超过1 500种多样的竹制品,月产量达五百万个,是您最值得信赖的中国竹制品供应商。您询问的产品如附图资料如后:离岸价:XXX;最小订单量:2 000;价格:USD1.80/pc;交货期:收到预付款后30天之内交货。我明天会寄一份目录给您,若您能提供您的快递账号,我们将把样品一同寄给您!

期待您的回复!

第五章综合练习

1)如果贵方能把尿素报价降低至每吨1 200美元,我们可订购150吨至180吨。

2)As to direct and indirect exporting, which approach is best depends on such factors as the company's size, its export volum, the number of foreign countries involved, investment required to support the operation, the profit potential, the risk present, and ...ires of the overseas buyers.

3) All disputes in connection with or in the execution of this Contract shall be settled through friendly negotiations. Where no settlement can be reached, the disputes shall be submitted for arbitration.

4) After the seller receives the relative documents issued by the shipping company, the seller shall pay to buyer within 20 days.

5) We wish to cover the goods against All Risks.

6) Engineering services are often handled through turn-key operations, contracts for the construction of operating facilities that are transferred to the owner when the facilities are ready to begin operations.

7) Multinational banker's services include issuing letter of credit, buying and selling foreign exchange, issuing bank's acceptances, accepting Eurocurrency deposits, making Eurocurrency loads, and assisting in the marketing of Eurobonds.

8) There are quantities of this item here, in different weights and sizes, with varied colors and shapes. The price is very reasonable and the quotations will be given upon request.

9) Our prices already make full allowance for large orders, and, as I am sure you know, we operate in a highly competitive market in which we have been forced to cut our prices to the minimum.

10) Unless the Contractor's Representative is named in the Contract, the Contractor shall, *prior to the Commencement Date*, submit to the Employer for consent of the name and particulars of the person the Contractor proposes to appoint as Contractor's Representative.

11) *Time for Completion* means the time for completing the Works or a Section (as the case may be) under Sub-Clause 8.2 [Time for Completion], as stated in the Particular Conditions, calculated *from* the Commencement Date.

12) The Contractor's obligations of inspection, care, custody and control shall not relieve the Employer of liability for any shortage, defect or default not apparent from a visual inspection.

13) Nothing herein contained shall prevent a carrier or a shipper from entering into any agreement, stipulation, condition, reservation or exemption as to the responsibility and liability of the carrier or the ship for the loss or damage to, or in connection with, the custody and care and handling of the goods prior to the loading on, and subsequent to, the discharge from the ship on which the goods are carried by sea.

14) No party or anyone acting on its behalf shall have any ex parte communication relating to the case with any candidate for presiding arbitrator. (Ex parte 单方的，片面的)

15) This agreement is made by and entered into between China National Import & Export Corporation (hereinafter referred to as Party A) and American Smith Wells Corporation (Hereinafter referred to as Party B), whereby Party A agrees to appoint Party B to act as its sole distributor for the under-mentioned commodity (ies) in the designated territory on the terms and conditions set forth below.

Chapter Six
Tourist Text Translation
旅游文体翻译

Schleiermacher & Hermeneutics

Hermeneutics is the study of interpretation theory, and can be either the art of interpretation, or the theory and practice of interpretation.

According to Schleiermacher, hermeneutics is divided into Grammatical Interpretation and Psychological Interpretation. The former studies how a work is composed from general ideas while the latter considers the peculiar combinations that characterize the work as a whole. Schleiermacher said that every problem of interpretation is a problem of understanding. He even defined hermeneutics as the art of avoiding misunderstanding.

关键词:阐释学;解释学;施赖尔马赫;理解

Tourist Text

Tourist text may appear in various forms including brochures, pamphlets, guidebooks, picture albums, tour maps, etc. Generally speaking, tourist texts could be classified into four categories, namely publicity of place of interests, publicity of cities, publicity of countries, and publicity of tourist operations. The language in these tourist information texts is appropriate written English, not too colloquial or too formal, and can be well understood by tourists of different classes and with different educational backgrounds. The vocabulary employed is expected to be brief, appealing and non-stereotyped. Some typical features in the language of English tourism publications can be summarized as follows: (1) concise and readable, (2) vivid, non-stereotyped and appealing, (3) figurative use of language.

1. Definition and Scope of Tourism English

Tourism English, as it is so called, is the English language used for tourism and is a particular variety of English in terms of linguistics. It appears with the development of tourism industry, especially international tourism. When people make a visit to some place, they will be provided with all kinds of services needed during the tour.

According to *Oxford Advanced Learner's English-Chinese Dictionary*, tourism is "the business activity connected with providing accommodation, services and entertainment for people who are visiting a place for pleasure." The services refer to transportation service, hotel service and tourist spot services. Therefore, tourism English is widely used in transportation (including airplane, train and bus), hotel (including restaurant) and tourist spot, both spoken and written in forms.

2. *Functions of Tourism English*

As a particular variety of English language, tourism English has its own language functions, which are mainly informative, directive and evocative functions.

2.1 The Informative Function

Language serves an informative function when it is used to tell what the speaker believes, to give information about facts, or to reason things out. Tourists need to acquire all kinds of information when they start a tour to a new place.

Such information includes: what kind of place they will visit; what they will see or do at that place; what kind of entertainment they will enjoy in that place; where they will stay if needed; how they can get there, by air, train or bus...

2.2 The Directive Function

Generally, tourism English is directed at helping tourists arrange their tours and make it effective. When they are informed the details of their tours, they receive the directions or guidance from the tourism organizations. As an effective medium, English performs a directive function in the process. In most cases, guides make full use of this language function of tourism English.

2.3 The Vocative Function

As a typical vocative text, being appealing is a predominant element in tourist publicity material. Publicizing effect and readers' response are stressed in this kind of text. Readership is always considered as the core of publicity materials. "Calling upon the readership to act, to think or feel, to react in the way intended by the text". (Newmark)

3. Linguistic Features of Tourist Texts

3.1 Lexical Feature

Like other varieties of English, such as legal English or journalism English, tourism English has its own lexical features besides the very general use of English vocabulary.

3.1.1 Translation of Names of Scenic Spots

Names of scenic spots give the initial information upon tourist's mind. Translation of names of scenic spots is of great significance, since the good first impression of scenic spots may trigger tourists to make their tours. Some of them derive from historical allusions, some of them come from myth and legend, some of them are closely related to religion and some of them are poetic charmingly or named after animals or plants. When translating names of scenic spots some scholars advocate the principle of transliteration-centered, supplemented with liberal translation or explanation. The cultural connotation of the names should be focused on.

e. g.

Sites with historical allusion: 故宫(the Imperial Palace), 颐和园(the Summer Palace), 长城(the Great Wall)

Sites with myth and legend: 龙宫(Dragon Palace),水晶宫(the Crystal Palace)

Sites with religion: 开元寺(Kaiyuan Temple),大雁塔(Dayan Pagoda/Wild Goose Pagoda)

Sites with animals: 象鼻山(Xiang Bi Shan/the Elephant Hill), 骆驼峰(the Camel *Peak*)

Sites with poetic charm: 三潭印月 (Three Pools Mirroring the Moon)

Sites with plants: 桃花溪(Peach Blossom Stream), 仙桃山(Peach Mountain)

3.1.2 Translation of Chinese Poetry and Couplets

Translation of Chinese poetry and couplets will highlight the tourist attractions and promote China's culture. Since poetry features pleasant rhythm and succinct language, the flavor and its spirits are needed to transfer to the foreigner.

e. g.

海水朝朝朝朝朝朝朝落
浮云长长长长长长长消 (山海关)
Sea water tide, day to day tide, every day tide and every day ebb,
Floating clouds appear, often appear, often appear and often go.

e. g.

西湖犹如西子,无论晴雨,无论四季更迭,都有着美丽的容颜。正如苏东坡所写的:"欲把西湖比西子,淡妆浓抹总相宜。"

West Lake is often likened to Xizi, one of the four ancient beauties in China. No matter whether it is sunny or rainy, or no matter in what season it is, she is always so pretty. It is just as Su Dongpo, a great Northern Song poet, wrote, "West Lake may be compared to Beauty Xizi at her best,/it becomes her to be richly adorned or plainly dressed."

3.2 Grammatical Feature

3.2.1 The Tenses

As mentioned above, one of the language functions of tourism English is to deliver information. Since the information delivered is mostly told as the fact or truth, the present tense is often used in tourism English. Sometimes past tense is also adopted to explain the cultural background information; usually some historical stories or events happened in the tourist-spot. For instance:

鹿回头公园

位于三亚市区以南3公里处,关于这个公园,有一个美丽动人的爱情故事。相传很久以前一位黎族猎人追逐一头山鹿,从五指山一直追到南中国海。当山鹿面对大海,无路可逃时,回头一望,突然变成一位美丽的少女。以此传说建成的壮观雕塑"鹿回头"已成为浪漫爱情的见证。鹿回头公园也是登高鸟瞰三亚市和三亚湾全景的首选之地。

The Turn-round Deer Park

Located three kilometers south of Sanya City, the park is known for a beautiful and moving love story related to it. A long, long time ago, there was a young hunter from the Li nationality who once chased after a deer from the Five Finger Mountain all the way to the South China Sea. Unable to flee any more, the deer could do nothing but turn its head and into a beautiful girl in no time. Hence the stone statue of the turn-round deer is known as Luhuitou in Chinese. It bears witness to the romantic love between them. The park named after the story is the best place for enjoying a panoramic view of Sanya and the Sanya Bay.

3.2.2 The Voices

Tourism English tends to use the active voice instead of the passive. Generally speaking, the active voice is more subjective and flexible in communication, and can easily express the speakers' or writers' feelings. Active voice serves for the function of directive or evocative. In the following example, the writer uses active voice throughout the whole paragraph to describe Beijing's scenery, which makes a vivid and delightful impression on tourists.

e. g.

Today's Beijing is not only famous for its long history, but also for its rapid economic and social development. Tian'anmen Square, the Forbidden City, Jingshan Mountain and Beihai Park situated in its center symbolize a profound traditional culture, whereas modern skyscrapers represent the openness and fast tempo of the modern lifestyle. Visitors to Beijing should learn about its past and its present, so let's have a look at modern Beijing.

3.3 Contrasted Analysis between CTT and ETT

鉴于英汉旅游文体特征和表达风格上的差异,在翻译的理解和表达过程中,译者必须准确理解原文实质,把握原文与译文间的社会、文化差异,结合考虑各种语境因素,对原文信息和内容进行判断和取舍,做到虚实互化、各展其长,用符合译语规范和文化标准的语言准确传达旅游翻译的功能,让各自读者喜闻乐见。

Tourism texts translation bears an important task to transfer unique features of one culture to tourists of another culture. The cultural features of tourism texts are indicated by particular choices of language use. Both CTT and ETT are classified as the non-literary text type for practical application. Both writings employ the techniques of narration, argumentation and exposition. So there are a lot of stylistic features that are in common in both CTT and ETT, such as preference for figurative use of language, prominent use of adjectives and adverbs. But they also show a lot of differences.

3.3.1 Different Preference in the View of Narration

Most CTT are narrated in the view point of "third person" or no person while most ETT are written in the viewpoint of "first" and "second person". In CTT the subjects and objects are often covered by "人们", "地方", "人民", "朋友们", which make the CTT sound rather polite and formal in style and imply respect for potential readers. Also, it sounds as official as administrative reports Comparatively, the frequent use of "I" and "you" carries a friendly tone, which makes the ETT less formal and more intimate and psychologically shortens the distance between the tourist attraction and the tourist. That is why ETT have a strong persuasive power. Most foreign tourists are accustomed to the informal and intimate style of tourism texts. When translating CTT into English, the translator must consider the narrative perspective of the text which can be accepted by the foreign tourist.

CTT：桂林山水甲天下。桂林具有典型的喀斯特和丹霞地貌，山清、水秀、洞奇、石美为世间传诵，宜人的自然环境再加上大规模城市改造，形成了"城在景中、城景交融、相映成趣"，"千峰环野立，一水抱城流"的绝世景观。桂林山水是我国自然风光的典型代表和经典品牌。桂林人民以他们最大的热情欢迎全世界的朋友。

ETT：The Hawaii of Your Imagination Still Exists：And it's available right now... in Hawaii. For most of us, Hawaii begins to weave her spell with some little glimmer of awareness. A friend describes a sunset off Waikiki. We hear the Twang of steel guitar. Or we open a magazine and there it is... Golden beaches and golden people. Sun, sand, sea and surf. And somewhere between the blue skies and the palm trees... we're hooked.

3.3.2 Different Preference for Diction

CTT prefers literary words or archaic words, most prominently, a lot of four-character clichés, fixed phrases and idioms.

西湖在杭州市区的中部，面积约 6.03 平方公里。沿湖四周，花木繁茂；群山之中，溪泉竞流；亭台楼阁，交相辉映；湖光山色，千古风情，令多少人流连忘返。上有天堂，下有苏杭的赞语真是恰如其分。

Situated to the west of Hangzhou, the West Lake area covers 6.03 square kilometers. The causeways, bridges, pavilions, springs, trees and flowers in and around the West Lake make it a paradise on earth, where one cannot tear himself away.

译者将原文的四字成语用 causeways, bridges, pavilions, springs, trees, flowers 等一系列名词短语所代替。

3.3.3 Different Discourse Structure

Discourse structure, also called rhetorical structure or macro-structure, refers to "the underlying structure which accounts for the organization of a text or discourse".

Different texts are distinguished by the way in which the topic and other information are linked together to form a unit. The general structures of CTT and ETT are illustrated as the following.

Discourse Structure of CTT

General introduction (*social status and social influence*)

Specific introduction and description of scenic spots (cultural characteristics, historic background, historic records, folktales, legends, anecdotes, allusions, *relevant poems, quoted literature works or celebrities' commends*)

Discourse Structure of ETT

General introduction (brief description of scenery)

Culture characteristics (historic background, folktales, legends, anecdotes, allusions, evolution)

Local facilities (transportations and services tips)

Notices to tourists (advantages and disadvantages of local environment and facilities)

3.3.4 Hypotactic vs. Paratactic

旅游文体是书面语与口语的结合，是为了传达信息，争取顾客，所以一般来说，旅游英语的句子比较简短易懂，但有时为了体现景点的形象性、特色和美感，也会出现简单句与复合句、长句与短句/小句并用的情况，这就使文章显得错落有致。下例中英文文本表面看是4句，但却包含了6句（含从句等）。汉语文本里其实有8个小句，虽然只有3个句号。英文重形合，句子长短不一，错落有致，句型灵活多样；而汉语则重意合，呈流水句，松散、自如，逐步展开。

e.g.

南宋的杭州还是全国文化中心。杭州在北宋时已经是全国印刷业的四大中心之一，南宋时雕版印刷得到进一步的发展，杭刻书籍成为全国宋版书的精华。南宋最高学府——太学也设立于此，此外还有算学、书学、医学等专门学校，教育得到普及，文化传承的脉络即使经过战争的洗礼也从未终止过。

Hangzhou in the Southern Song Dynasty remained China's cultural center after the Northern Song Dynasty, during which it had been one of the country's four centers of printing industry. Block printing developed further in the Southern Song, and books printed in Hangzhou became known as the best Song edition nationwide at that time. Taixue or Imperial College (the supreme institution of higher learning) in the Dynasty was also founded here, in addition to math, calligraphy, and medical schools. Thus, education was popularized and culture handed down despite repeated wars.

4. Special Translation Methods of Tourist Materials

Rewriting

The strategy of rewriting refers to rearranging the contents or the structure of the source text. It is desirable in cases where the source texts are badly written or unsuitable for translation. Though the Chinese versions of most tourism publications, intended for domestic tourists, are not badly written, sometimes, they don't conform to the expectations of foreign tourists. In this case, rewriting works more effectively than literal translation as displayed in the following examples.

改译实例

雷峰塔

——西湖边的另类风景

西湖多塔。塔是佛教用来藏舍利和经卷的地方，每一座塔都有它自己的历史、它独特的形态以及其特殊的故事。六和塔壮丽挺拔，白塔小巧玲珑，保俶塔端庄秀美。而以塔列为西湖十景的，只有雷峰塔，即雷峰夕照。

雷峰塔，位于西湖南面，在净慈寺前的夕照山上。西湖是秀美的，而雷峰塔却十分敦厚；西湖是浪漫的，而雷峰塔是浪漫故事中另类的插曲；西湖的历史是持续的，而雷峰塔的经历却一波三折。

雷峰塔建于吴越国时期(975)，吴越国王钱弘俶因为黄妃生得一子，对佛心生感激，所以修建此塔以谢佛的恩德。塔初名“黄妃塔”，是一座八面砖木结构的楼阁式塔，塔心是砖砌的，塔檐、游廊、栏杆等为木结构。南宋以后，雷峰塔木构檐廊屡毁屡修。当时的《雷峰夕照》图中，斜阳的余晖照耀在塔身上，成了西湖边静穆的图画。明代嘉靖时期，雷峰塔被毁，仅存塔心。杭州诸塔中，其他的塔都是随毁随修的，只有雷峰塔自那时起便不曾修葺过，以残缺的姿态在湖畔耸峙了四百余年。

【译文 1】

Leifeng Pagoda with Its Special Stories

The West Lake has many pagodas. The pagoda is the place where Buddhism uses to reserve relics and texts. Each one has its own history; each has its unique form and special legend. Six Harmonies Pagoda is magnificent, tall and handsome; White Tower is petite and pretty; Baochu Pagoda is elegant and graceful. However, it is Leifeng Pagoda that is listed as one of the West Lake's Top Ten Views, namely Leifeng Pagoda in Evening Glow.

Leifeng Pagoda, to the south of the West Lake, is on the Xizhao Hill in front of Jingci Temple. While the West Lake is beautiful, Leifeng Pagoda is lenient; while the West Lake is romantic, Leifeng Pagoda is the peculiar interlude of the romantic story; while the history of the West Lake is lasting, the experience of Leifeng Pagoda is full of twists and turns.

Leifeng Pagoda was constructed during Wuyue Period (975). It is said that Qian Hongchu, the king of Wuyue State, wanted to express his thanks to Buddha because his wife, Princess Huang, gave birth to a son. So he donated to build the pagoda. The initial name of the pagoda was Princess Huang Pagoda and it was a building with brick timber structure of eight sides. The core was built of brick, but the eaves, veranda, railing, etc. were timber structures. Since Southern Song Dynasty, the eaves corridor of timber of Leifeng Pagoda had been repeatedly destroyed and repaired. In the picture of "Leifeng Pagoda in Evening Glow" at that time, the sunshine of the setting sun glows on the pagoda, forming the solemn and quiet picture by the West Lake. Leifeng Pagoda was destroyed in Jiaqing of Ming Dynasty, only left a brick core. All pagodas in Hangzhou except Leifeng Pagoda are rebuilt instantly after being destroyed. However, Leifeng

Pagoda since then had not been rebuilt. The ruin has been standing by the West Lake with the incomplete posture for more than 400 years.

（吴渝等译）

【译文 2】

West Lake boasts numerous pagodas. The pagoda is the place where sarira (Buddhist relics) and Buddhist scriptures are preserved. Each one has its own history, its unique form and its special story. Pagoda of Six Harmonies stands lofty and majestic, while White Pagoda appears much smaller yet attractive. Baochu Pagoda looks elegant and graceful. Of all the local pagodas, however, it is only Leifeng Pagoda that ranks among the West Lake's Traditional Top Ten Views, namely, Leifeng Pagoda in Evening Glow.

Leifeng Pagoda is situated south of the lake on Xizhao Hill in front of Jingci Temple. It is said that West Lake is like a pretty girl, but Leifeng Pagoda is like a simple and sincere man; West Lake is known for her romantic stories, but Leifeng Pagoda features different ones; West Lake grows without stop, but Leifeng Pagoda has undergone many ups and downs.

Leifeng Pagoda can be traced back to 975 during the Kingdom of Wuyue, in which King Qian Hongchu was so happy to have his concubine give birth to a son that he erected a pagoda to express his gratitude to Buddha and named it after the concubine Huang Fei. This pagoda was an octagonal brick-and-wood structure of storied-pavilion type. The core part was built of brick, but the eaves, veranda, railing, etc. were of a wooden structure. Since the Southern Song Dynasty, the eaves and veranda had been damaged and repaired repeatedly. In the painting of "Leifeng Pagoda in Evening Glow" at that time, the pagoda was bathed in sunset glow, forming a solemn and quiet picture by West Lake. It was destroyed in the mid 1500 during the Ming Dynasty, with the only brick core remaining. Historically, all pagodas in Hangzhou were rebuilt after destruction, except Leifeng Pagoda that had been left in disrepair for more than 400 years.

（编者重译）

【解析】

这一篇文章的翻译实则应为改写(rewriting),这也是旅游翻译(尤其是汉译英)的常用方法,使译文更加符合目标读者的语言习惯,更容易被接受。译文 1 错误过多,译语过"直",过于"机械",对一些历史事件和不少词语的理解不够准确,甚至完全错误,难以再现原文的意义、内涵及情趣。总体译文的可读性较差,很难算是一篇合格的旅游介绍文章。译文 2 就采取了**"改写"**的方法,感觉完全不同。第一段起着总领全篇的作用,先是总体介绍了"西湖多塔",以及一些名塔的概况,然后突出只有雷峰塔属于西湖十景这一事实,显示出其出众之处。其中,第二句话的定语部分,由于有动词和并列结构,较为复杂,所以在英译时把它转化为 where 引导的定语从句。

第三句用了 each one 来代替“每一座塔”以使上下文更加连贯，并避免重复。就选词的准确性和生动性以及对原文理解的正确性而言，译文 2 显然高于译文 1。接下去的段落、篇章基本上是脱离中文语言形式的英文重写，可用**“得意忘形”**来描述。为了比较好地领略改写的所谓“真谛”，读者不妨根据自己对中文的理解，先进行自译，然后对照译文 1，最后对照译文 2。这里需要从研究的角度来审读中文和译文，若能通过理论结合实际，写一篇有学术性的翻译实践小论文，相信一定会印象深刻，受益匪浅。

第六章综合练习

1）上有天堂，下有苏杭。

2）太湖明珠无锡，位于江苏省南部，地处美丽富饶的长江三角洲中心地带。这里气候宜人，物产丰富，风景优美，是中国重点风景旅游城市。与万里长城齐名的古京杭大运河纵贯市区。

3）崂山，林木苍翠，繁花似锦，到处生机盎然，春天绿芽红花，夏天浓荫蔽日，秋天遍谷金黄，严冬则玉树琼花。其中，更不乏古树名木。景区内，古树名木有近 300 株，50% 以上为国家一类保护植物，著名的有银杏，桧柏等。

4）贵重物品、现金请交服务台保管，否则后果自负。

5）东方明珠广播电视塔位于黄浦江畔、浦东陆家嘴尖上，塔高 468 米，三面环水，与外滩的万国建筑博览群隔江相望，是亚洲第一，世界第三的高塔。

6）游客必须遵守景区的规章制度，服从工作人员的管理，爱护公共财物。

7）中国之旅简介——十日游的“重头戏”（特别套餐）

长城漫步

品尝闻名遐迩的“北京烤鸭”

参观秦始皇兵马俑

观看精彩绝伦的杂技表演

日程安排如下：

第一天：抵达北京，下榻国际宾馆（地处市中心）

第二天：游览紫禁城、天坛，观赏京剧

第三天：登长城，游明十三陵，体验茶馆文化

第四天：游览颐和园、动物园，品尝北京烤鸭

……

第十天：旅行结束

10 人以上的旅游团体价目

每人：690 美元，798 加拿大元

8）Blessed with excellent transportation facilities, it takes only ten minutes by car to get to the renowned scenic spot named Splendid China from Luomazhou Post. The spot is easy of access both by China Travel Service (Hong Kong) Limited (CTS) direct tourist coach between Hong Kong and Shenzhen and by buses or light buses through Shen-Nan Highway, Guang-Shen Highway and Beihuan Freeway.

Welcome to Splendid China.

9) Dear Guest:

The hotel does not subscribe to credit cards. As a registered guest, you may settle your account by cash, traveler's checks or personal checks. For your convenience, counter checks are available.

When settling your account, please remind the cashier of recent charges such as room service or gratuities which may not have reached her counter. This will avoid a later charge billing after your departure. Thanks.

ROBERT H. BUTTERFIELD
Vice President and
General Manager

10) Hawaii

For most of us, Hawaii begins to weave her spell with some little glimmer of awareness. Golden beaches and golden people. Sun, sand, sea, and surf... And somewhere between the blue skies and the palm trees... we're hooked. The Hawaiian Islands are one of the most beautiful places on earth. The weather is friendly. The temperature ranges from 60—90 degrees all year long. It's a little warmer in summer, and a little cooler in winter, but every day is a beach day for somebody. There are no strangers in Paradise. Perhaps the most beautiful part of Hawaii is the genuine warmth of people. We call it the spirit of Aloha. It has allowed a melting pot of cultures from all over the world to find common ground, and a new home, in this most gentle of places.

附录 1:常用旅游翻译词语中英对照

旅游景点 tourist attraction; tourist destination; scenic spot; places of tourist attraction

自然景观 natural splendor/attraction

避暑胜地 summer resort

国家公园 national park

出土文物 unearthed cultural relics

古建筑群 ancient architectural complex

陵墓 emperor's mausoleum/tomb

古墓 ancient tomb

洞穴 cave

石笋 stalagmite

钟乳石　stalactite

石窟　grotto

坛　altar

亭　pavilion

台　terrace

廊　corridor

楼　tower; mansion

庵　Buddhist nunnery

江河湖泊　rivers and lakes

池潭　ponds and pools

堤　causeway

舫　boat

榭　pavilion; house on a terrace

水榭　waterside pavilion/house

琉璃瓦　glazed tile

城堡　castle

教堂　church; cathedral

宫殿　palace; hall; chamber

皇城　imperial city

行宫　temporary imperial palace for brief stays

御花园　imperial garden

皇太后　empress dowager

四大金刚　the Four Guardians

十八罗汉　the Eighteen Disciples of the Buddha

甲骨文　inscription on oracle bones

青铜器　bronze ware

景泰蓝　cloisonné enamel

手工艺品　artifact; handicrafts

苏绣　Suzhou embroidery

唐三彩　tricolor-glazed pottery; ceramics of the Tang Dynasty

字画卷轴　scroll of calligraphy and painting

国画　traditional Chinese painting

文房四宝　the four stationery treasures of the Chinese study including writing brushes, ink sticks, ink stones and paper

工艺精湛,独具匠心　exquisite workmanship with an original/ingenious design

湖光山色　landscape of lakes and hills

依山傍水 enclosed/surrounded by the hills on one side and waters on the other
景色如画 picturesque views
湖石假山 lakeside rocks and rockeries
山清水秀 beautiful mountains and clear waters
诱人景色 inviting views
园林建筑 garden architecture
佛教名山 famous Buddhist mountain
丝绸之路 the Silk Road/Route
寺 temple
塔 pagoda
宫 palace
庙 temple
陵 tomb
祠 shrine
园 garden
山庄 villa
阁 hall;pavilion
斋 house;study room
故居 former residence
园林 gardens

附录2:杭州十景(老十景)

1. 苏堤春晓 Spring Dawn at Su Causeway
2. 曲院风荷 Breeze-ruffled Lotus at Quyuan Garden
3. 平湖秋月 Autumn Moon Over the Calm Lake
4. 断桥残雪 Lingering Snow on the Broken Bridge
5. 柳浪闻莺 Orioles Singing in the Willows
6. 花港观鱼 Viewing Fish at Flower Pond
7. 三潭印月 Three Pools Mirroring the Moon
8. 双峰插云 Twin Peaks Piercing the Cloud
9. 南屏晚钟 Evening Bell Ringing at Nanping Hill
10. 雷峰夕照 Leifeng Pagoda in Evening Glow

Chapter Seven
Translation of Literary Writings—Prose
散文翻译

Peter Newmark

Peter Newmark, the famous translation theorist, now is still teaching in Surrey University. His masterpiece *Approaches to Translation* which was published in 1981 contains two important theories: semantic translation and communicative translation.

Compared to the traditional faithful translation, semantic translation takes more account of the aesthetic value of the source language text. While in communicative translation, the translator attempts to produce the same effect on the target language readers as one that was produced by the original on the source language readers. This means that in communicative translation the emphasis should be on conveying the message of the original in a form which conforms to the linguistic, cultural and pragmatic conventions of target language than mirroring the actual words of source language as closely as possible without infringing the target language norms.

关键词:纽马克;语义翻译;交际翻译

On Literal Translation

Different kinds of translated texts have different criteria. For example the translation of scientific text gives the top priority to the accuracy of the source text because its main purpose is to introduce the scientific information whereas the translation of poetry gives more values to the artistic conception of the poem. Since the main purpose of essay translation is to express to target readers both the message and the aesthetic value of the source text so as to make the readers ideologically inspired and aesthetically entertained, the author proposes that the criteria of essay translation may be summarized as faithfulness, expressiveness and beauty.

Any translation between languages is first of all the transference of language structures and ideational contents. But literary translation is much more than that and it needs much higher level of representation. It differentiated from any other forms of translation. The most prominent characteristics of literary translation are the artistic aestheticism and artistic reproduction. Besides transmission of information and realization of communication, literary translation should keep aesthetic and educational functions of the original while convey the overtones and implications behind the tangible words.

文学翻译除了要传达出“思维内容”外，还着重强调了“风格特色”。没有风格的作品必然显得苍白无血，毫无生气，正如人缺少了个性一样。而作品有了风格，人物的音容笑貌便会跃然纸上，意趣横生。因此，作为文学翻译，它必然也要力求传达出原著的这种精神风貌，否则这种翻译是毫无意义的。

另一方面，文学翻译也强调“忠实、准确”——这可是文学翻译的难点所在。翻译毕竟不是创作，其性质决定了它必须忠实准确地传达出原著的精神风貌，而不得随心所欲，自由发挥。但是由于两种语言特点不同，规律不同，就需要进行调整，在保持“神韵”的准则下语言上作些变通——这便是文学翻译的“再创作”。否则，翻译出来的东西看似忠实，实则成了死译、硬译，违背了原作的精神风貌。

1. Definition and Characteristics of Prose

Prose can be defined both in a broad sense and a narrow sense. In its broadest sense, the term is applied to all forms of written or spoken expression which do not have a regularly rhythmic pattern. In a narrow sense, it refers to a literary genre as opposed to three other genres, namely, poetry, fiction and drama. It doesn't portray characters or tell stories as intricately and carefully as fiction, nor does it have dramatic conflicts as drama and differs from poetry or verse in that it is not restricted in rhythm.

散文是“集诸美于一身”的文学体裁，具有很高的审美价值，散文语言不受韵律的限制，是最自由的文体表达方式，杂文、短评、小品、随笔、速写、特写、游记、通讯、书信、回忆录等都属于散文。散文是与诗歌、小说、戏剧并称的一种文学体裁。通常一篇散文具有一个或多个中心思想，可将抒情、议论、记叙、论理等方式表达融为一体，形散而神不散。散文短小优美，生动有趣。在长期流传过程中，它浇灌了各个时代的文学园地，也灌溉了历代文人，至今仍使人们受益。通常来说，小说、诗歌、戏剧无论是在结构上，或是格律、剪裁、对话等安排布局上，都有很严格的要求。而散文，却可以自由些，看来只是不经意地抒写着一己的经历和感受，所表现的多是零星杂碎的片段人生。

The characteristic of essays is loose in form but focused in soul, in other words, essay in the final analysis is the beauty of wholeness; the characteristics of essays decide that a good translation of essays should be a combination of form and soul, which can well be approached from the perspective of aesthetics. In contrast with other genres, prose writing enjoys the freedom in expression, that is, it is a kind of style in the least consideration of formulation, rules and patterns. Prose writer's pen can go where his or her consciousness flows. Prose writing can reveal the style of the writer not only through the diction and rhetorical devices but also through the textual structure. So in translation of prose, writing an "equivalent effect" is expected to achieve. Translating an essay is a systematic project; it entails high craftsmanship and creativity of the translator.

2. *Aesthetic Comparison between English and Chinese Prose*

As a genre of literature, English prose gained acknowledgement in the family of literature between the late 16th century and early 17th century. A fresh literature style characterized with familiar language and flexible patterns emerged with the economic, political and cultural changes. The first British essayist, Francis Bacon published his collections *The Essays* about his life and study experience. From then on, this literary form is prosperous. Bacon is introduced to China, which exerts great influence on Chinese Sanwen. Sanwen has experienced a long evolving history in China before the May Fourth Movement in 1919. From the definition above, prose is rather a general term which is used to define all kinds of writings that do not fit a recognized poetical form. Essay is "composition, usually in prose, which may be of only a few hundred words or of book length and which discusses, formally or informally, a topic or a variety of topics. It is one of the most flexible and adaptable of all literary forms" (Cuddon). So it can be concluded that essay belongs to prose, which can also draw support from the fact that essay is always rendered into "随笔","小品文",etc.

It is found that there are much more nouns in English than those in Chinese, especially abstract nouns. According to statistics made by Prof. Curme, nine kinds of prepositions in English are powerful in indicating positions and directions when used together with nouns or verbs. There are more verbs and classifiers in Chinese. When combined, they become numeral-classifier compounds which can be used to depict not only people and things but also actions and movements.

English prose has main feature of being real and objective, due to the tendency towards imitation and representation, which emphasize three-dimensional construction in scenery depiction. However, Chinese people put emphasis on expression which tends to be one dimensional and Chinese Sanwen is featured by its trueness in subjective feelings.

English prose is in linear structure, and you can get a feeling of water flowing. While some linguists hold that the Chinese texts are developed in an inductive way while the English ones are developed in a deductive way. The structure of Chinese prose is not as clear as that of English, and metaphorically speaking, it is a screw-type.

3. Aesthetic Process of Literary Translation

According to the process of aesthetic evaluation, literary translation can be divided into four steps: the understanding of aesthetic object (aesthetic comprehension), the transformation of the understood object (aesthetic transformation), the improvement of the transformed object (aesthetic improvement) and the final representation of the improved object (aesthetic representation). (刘宓庆)

Aesthetic comprehension: a free coordination with the sentiments of aesthetic subject. Aesthetic evaluation can generally be divided into formal level and non-formal level. The formal level is largely embodied in phonetic, lexical and syntactic levels whereas the non-informal one is largely embodied in artistic conception, stylistic features, writing technique and cultural level.

Aesthetic transformation: the basic mechanism of aesthetic transformation is "empathy", which means the translator shall transform the feeling and beauty of aesthetic object and shift it from quantitative change into qualitative change.

Aesthetic improvement: the refinement of the translated text at various levels of language such as variety, genre, subject and syntax.

Aesthetic representation: the translator shall put all his result of aesthetic evaluation into translated text, so it is the last but hardest step in translation. It is the materialization of improved aesthetic experience.

3.1 Liu Shicong's Artistic Flavor—Rhythm, Mood and Style

著名教授刘士聪先生在其所著的《汉英·英汉美文翻译》中提出，散文的“情致”或“韵味”主要表现在以下三个方面：第一个方面是声响与节奏；第二个方面是意境和氛围；第三个方面是个性化的话语方式。

Many translation enthusiasts and practitioners show great interest in prose translation. However, their translations can't live up to expectations because of the lack of scientific theories and insufficient practice. So how should they improve the quality of their translations? Professor Liu Shicong proposes the theory of "artistic flavor" on the basis of decades of research. He points out that rhythm, mood and style should be put into consideration in order to reproduce the artistic flavor of a prose. This theory serves as a good guidance in prose translation. By applying this theory, one can reproduce the artistic flavor of a prose in full.

Exercise: Discuss the following translation.

1）荷塘四面，长着许多树，蓊蓊郁郁的。路的一旁，是些杨柳，和一些不知道名字的树。

All around the pond grow many trees, lush and dense, while on one side of the path there are some willows and other trees whose names are unknown to me.

2)我爱热闹,也爱冷静;爱群住,也爱独处。

I like excitement, and also like calm; I love to be in crowds, and also love to be on my own.

3)这是独处的妙处;我且受用这无边的荷香月色好了。

This was the beauty of solitude. I resolved to make the best of this abundance of lotus and moonlight.

4)荷塘的四面,远远近近,高高低低都是树,而杨柳最多。

On all sides of the pond, near and far, high and low, were trees, the majority being willows.

5)在南方每年到了秋天,总要想起陶然亭的芦花,钓鱼台的柳影,西山的虫唱,玉泉的夜月,潭柘寺的钟声。

When I am in the South, the arrival of each autumn will put me in mind of Peiping's Tao Ran Ting with its reed catkins, Diao Yu Tai with its shady willow trees, Western Hills with their chirping insects, Yu Quan Shan Mountain on a moonlight evening and Tan Zhe Si with its reverberating bell.

3.2 Reproduction of Images in Translation

Image can be defined as follows: it means any piece of descriptive writing that can evoke mental pictures through visual imagination. In literary works, an image means a word, phrase, or figure of speech (especially a simile or a metaphor) that addresses the senses, suggesting mental pictures, sights, sounds, smells, feelings and actions. Image is an indispensable component of artistic conception essays translation. Due to the great differences between Chinese and English in language and in culture such as thinking pattern, aesthetic psychology and historical allusion, the translation of image is no easy task in the reconstruction of artistic conception. The literal translation is considered to be the major strategy in translating these images. The literal translation gives readers a much wider space for imagination, conforms to readers' reading aim and aesthetic expectation, and is helpful to achieve the translation goal of spreading the Chinese culture.

Exercise: Translate the following sentences.

1)美国人在北平、在天津、在上海都洒了些救济粉,看一看什么人愿意弯下腰来,太公钓鱼,愿者上钩。嗟来之食,愿者上钩。嗟来之食,吃下去肚子要疼的。(《毛泽东选集》)

2)"三个臭皮匠,合成个诸葛亮",这就是说,群众有伟大的创造力。(《毛泽东选

集》)

3)他以为这回阿Q可遭了瘟。(鲁迅:《阿Q正传》)

4) Men sent flowers, love notes, offers of fortune. And still her dreams ran riot. The one hundred and fifty! The one hundred and fifty! What a door of an Aladdin's cave it seemed to be. (Dreiser: *Sister Carrie*)

4. Aesthetic Character of Prose—Stylistic Feature of Prose

4.1 Phonological Rhetoric—Musical Sound and Rhythm

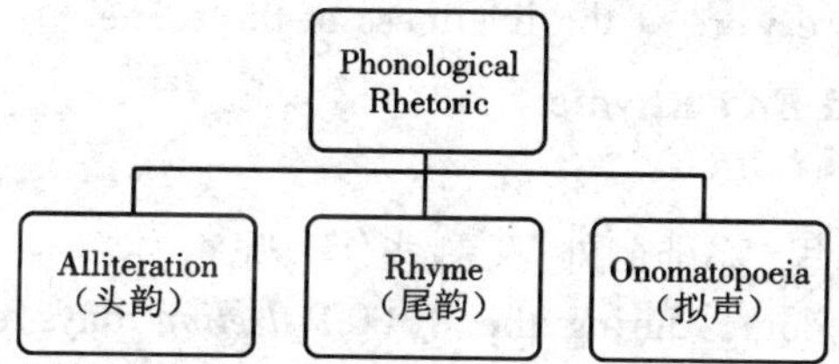

The phonetic characteristics of essays are not so prominent like that of poem and verse, but essayists sometimes will adopt some devices at phonetic level to add more appeal to it. Zhu Guangqian (朱光潜) once wrote that: "I strongly believe that the sound and rhythm should be the first concern of prose writing." Rhythm in prose mainly refers to the sentence structures and pauses. As to the sentence structures, long sentences and paragraphs move much more slowly than shorter ones. "Pause" can be created through grammatical method—using punctuation marks, such as comma, semi-colon, colon, full stop, etc.

The following translation is from Gaojian (高健). His translation sounds strong in rhythm and succinct, with his good handling at pauses and good adjusting of the order of the original sentence to seek rhythmical effect. For instance, in the first sentence, "我/平生/最喜/游览/新境,考察/种种/异地/人物/及其/风习", in which the series of two-character words make the whole passage flow regularly.

e. g.

I was always fond of visiting new scenes, and observing strange characters and manners. Even when a mere child I began my travels, and made many tours of discovery into foreign parts and unknown regions of my native city, to the frequent alarm of my parents and the emolument of the town-crier. As I grew into boyhood, I extended the range of my observations. My holiday afternoons were spent in rambles about the surrounding country. (*The Author's Account of Himself* by Washington Irving)

高健译:我平生最喜游览新境,考察种种异地人物及其风习。早在童稚时期,我的旅行即已开始,观察区域之广,遍及我出生城镇的各个偏僻之所与罕至之地;此事固曾使我的父母饱受虚惊,市镇报讯人却也赖以沾益颇丰。及长,我观察的范围继续扩大。无数假日下午尽行消磨在郊垌的漫游之中。(作者自叙)

4.1.1 Onomatopoeia

The use of this rhetoric device can make the description more vivid and life-like, and so more audibly appealing to the readers.

e. g.

母鸡们咯咯咯地叫起来,鸡雏们也啁啁地争起食来了。 张培基《夕暮》

At the *clucking* of the hens, the chicks scrambled for the feed, *chirping*. Onomatopoeias as clucking and chirping indicate the continuous sound of hens and chicks, as a result we feel as if we were at the liveliness of the scene.

4.1.2 Alliteration and End Rhyme

e. g.

在八千多日的匆匆里,除徘徊外,又剩些什么呢? 张培基《匆匆》

What have I been doing during the 8,000 *fleeting* days except of *wavering* and *wandering*?

The word "徘徊" is a disyllabic binding word (连绵字) sharing the same vowel /ai/ which is pleasing to the ears.

4.2 Semantic Rhetoric—Beauty of Lexis

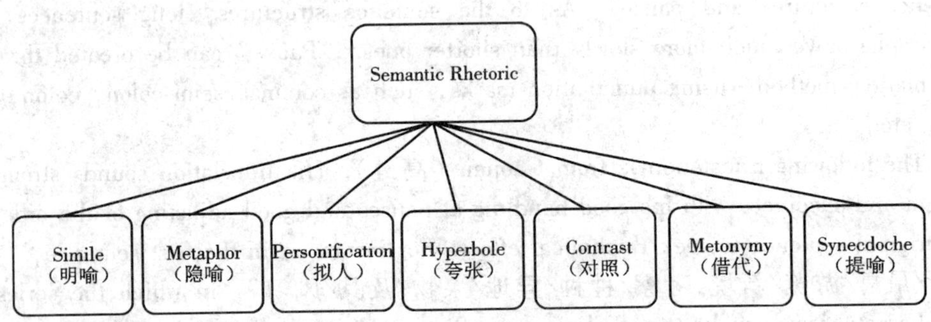

Semantic Rhetoric Structure

Aesthetic evaluation at the lexical level involves choices of words, register and collocation. Chinese characters bear formal and structural traits which easily appeal to reader's vision. Comparatively speaking, Chinese characters have more advantages in carrying aesthetic information than English letters because they are graphical and ideographical. The most common method adopted by writers is to use duplication of characters (叠字), which can intensify the visual image as well as the audio strength. For example: the following is extracted from the prose *Moonlight over the Lotus Pond*(《荷塘月

色》). There are eight duplications of characters not only bringing audio enjoyment but also forming a poetic visual image to readers. In order to reproduce original sound effect and image, 朱纯深 employs the method alliteration in the first and the second sentences.

①**曲曲折折**的荷塘上面,弥望的是②**田田**的叶子。叶子出水很高,像③**亭亭**的舞女的裙。④**层层**的叶子中间,零星地点缀着些白花,有袅娜地开着的,有羞涩地打着朵儿的;正如一⑤**粒粒**的明珠,又如碧天里的星星,又如刚出浴的美人。微风过处,送来⑥**缕缕**清香,仿佛远处高楼上渺茫的歌声似的。这时候叶子与花也有一丝的颤动,像闪电般,霎时传过荷塘的那边去了。叶子本是肩并肩⑦**密密**地挨着,这便宛然有了一道凝碧的波痕。叶子底下是⑧**脉脉**的流水,遮住了,不能见一些颜色;而叶子却更见风致了。

朱纯深译:All over this ***winding*** stretch of water, what meets the eye is ***a silken field of*** leaves, reaching rather high above the surface, like the skirt of dancing girls in all their grace. Here and there, ***layers of*** leaves are dotted with white lotus blossoms, some in demure bloom, others in shy bud, like ***scattering*** pearls, or twinkling stars, or beauties just out of the bath. A breeze stirs, sending over ***breaths*** of fragrance, like faint singing drifting from a distant building. At this moment, a tiny thrill shoots through the leaves and flowers, like a streak of lightening, straight across the forest of lotuses. The leaves, which have been standing ***shoulder to shoulder***, are caught trembling in an emerald heave of the pond. Underneath, the ***exquisite*** water is covered from view, and none can tell its color.

Simile (明喻)

The word simile comes from Latin word similis, meaning like. A simile is a figure of speech which makes a comparison between two unlike elements having at least one quality or characteristic in common. Simile is almost always introduced by the following words: like, as, as... as, as it were, as if, as though, be something of, similar to, etc.

e. g.

弓儿似的新月,挂在树梢。 张培基《笑》

The crescent new moon looked as if hanging on the tips of the trees.

e. g.

木匠老陈那时不过四十岁光景,脸长得像驴子脸。 张培基《木匠老陈》

Carpenter Lao Chen was then only about forty years old, with a longish face like that of a donkey.

Metaphor (隐喻)

A metaphor is a figure of speech where comparison is implied. It is also a comparison between two unlike elements with similar quality. But unlike a simile, this comparison is implied, not expressed with the word "as" or "like".

e. g.

骆驼的峰就是一座拱桥,它沟通了东方和西方的文化,骆铃是最可靠的信使,最动人的信息…… 张培基《耐力》

The camel's hump symbolized an arch bridge linking up the cultures of East and West. Armed with a jingling bell, it is a most reliable courier delivering most exciting message...

Personification(拟人)

Personification is a figure of speech in which inanimate objects or abstractions are endowed with human qualities or are represented as possessing human form, as in "Hunger sat shivering on the road" or "Flowers danced about the lawn". In Zhang Peiji's translation of essays, he tries his best to retain the personified image of the original in an effort to represent the aesthetic value of the original.

e. g.

贫穷剥夺了我童年的幸福,把我关在学校大门的外面,是书本敞开它宽大的胸脯,接纳了我,给我以慷慨的哺育。 张培基《书的抒情》

When I was deprived of happiness and schooling by poverty in my childhood, books took me to their large bosoms and nurtured me generally.

By personifying the inanimate object "books", Zhang reproduced the aesthetic value of the original.

Metonymy(借代)

Metonymy is a figure of speech in which one word or phrase is substituted for another, with which it is closely associated. Metonymy is not directly used to say the original name of things, but switches to another name or another way.

e. g.

我不知道他们给了我多少日子;但我的手确乎是渐渐空虚了。

I do not know how many days I have been given to spend, but I do feel my hands are getting empty.

"我的手"是一个以局部代替整体的借代。译文保持了原文借代(喻体)使得译文与原文具有一样的意象美和含蓄美。

Color Words(颜色词)

Color words are frequently used in essays to "add color" to the works. Due to the different perception in color system between E and C, it often presents problems to translators. Zhang's skillful handling of color words offers us a good example in *Selected Modern Chinese Essays*.

e. g.

蔷薇的花色还是鲜色的,一朵紫红,一朵嫩红,一朵是病黄的象牙色中带点血晕。

张培基《路畔的蔷薇》

They are still fresh in color. One was purplish-red, another pink, still another a sickly ivory-yellow, slightly tinged with blood-red.

The use of the word "sickly" instead of "unhealthy" is to express affection towards the rose.

5. Beauty at Syntactic Level

English sentences are usually more complex with embedded structures, whereas Chinese sentences are normally shorter, looser and more elliptical. In Chinese, there is a special kind of grammatical unit at syntactic level, which is the clause. While doing translation, it is often necessary for translators to turn short and loose Chinese sentences into long and complex English sentences so as to make the version conform to the syntactic conventions of the English language.

5.1 Syntactical Rhetoric Structure

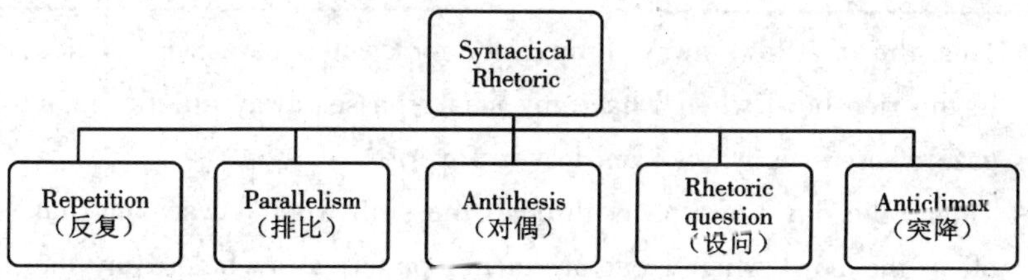

以下以朱自清的散文《匆匆》为例讨论句法修辞。

标题:**匆匆**

译文 1 Transient Days
译文 2 Rush
译文 3 Days Gone By

原文中还有 3 处直接使用了"匆匆"这两个字眼,其他处也以"一去不复返"、"转眼间"、"逃走"、"飞去"、"溜去"、"跨过"、"闪过"等与"匆匆"这个语义呼应。译文 2 以与原文相同的一个简略词 Rush 直译,突出了原文"匆忙"或"快"的意象,保留了原文的神秘与悬念,贴近原文语境。

Parallelism(排比)

In parallelism, the aesthetic information is mainly represented in the frequent reoccurrence of a certain structure. The use of identical or equivalent syntactic constructions in corresponding clauses or sentences is for emphasis and emotional coloring.

（汉语整句与英语"parallelism"有一些对应项）

e. g.

燕子去了，有再来的时候；杨柳枯了，有再青的时候；桃花谢了，有再开的时候。

译文 1　If swallows go away, they will come back again. If willows wither, they will turn green again. If peach blossoms fade, they will flower again.

译文 2　Swallows may have gone, but there is a time to return; willow trees may have died back, but there is a time of regreening; peach blossoms may have fallen, but they will bloom again.

译文 3　When the swallows have gone, there is still time to return; when the poplar and willow trees have become withered, there is still time to see green; when the peach flowers have already faded, there is still time to blossom.

e. g.

于是——洗手的时候，日子从水盆里过去；吃饭的时候，日子从饭碗里过去；默默时，便从凝然的双眼前过去。

译文 1　Thus the day flows away through the sink when I wash my hands; vanishes in the rice bowl when I have my meal; passes away quietly before the fixed gaze of my eyes when I am lost in reverie.

译文 2　Thus—the day flows away through the sink when I wash my hands, wears off in the bowl when I eat my meal, passes away before my day-dreaming gaze as I reflect in silence.

译文 3　When I wash my hands, my days wash off into my basin; when I am eating, the days vanish from my bowl and when I am sitting silently, my days pass by my gazing eyes.

Rhetoric Questions（反问）

Rhetorical question is a figure of speech in the form of a question posed for its persuasive effect without the expectation of a reply. It is often used by the speaker to assert or deny something and encourage the listener to reflect on what the implied answer to the question must be. In the original text, the author adopts a series of rhetoric questions to strongly reveal the author's emotion that time is so transient that we shall try to find out the true meaning of time and life. All the rhetoric questions in this text are put in parallel and used one after another to further increase the negative tone and emotional coloring of the author.

e. g.

在逃去如飞的日子里，在千门万户的世界里的我能做些什么呢？只有徘徊罢了，只有匆匆罢了；在八千多日的匆匆里，除徘徊外，又剩些什么呢？过去的日子如轻烟，被微风吹散了，如薄雾，被初阳蒸融了；我留着些什么痕迹呢？我何曾留着像游丝样的痕迹呢？我赤裸裸来到这世界，转眼间也将赤裸裸地回去罢？但不能平的，为什么偏要白白走这一遭啊？

译文1 Living in this world with its fleeting days and teeming millions, what can I do but waver and wander and live a transient life? What have I been doing during the 8,000 fleeting days except wavering and wandering? The bygone days, like wisps of smoke, have been dispersed by gentle winds, and, like thin mists, have been evaporated by the rising sun. What traces have I left behind? No, nothing, not even gossamer-like traces. I have come to this world stark naked, and in the twinkling of an eye, I am to go back as stark naked as ever. However, I am taking it very much to heart: why should I be made to pass through this world for nothing at all?

译文2 What can I do, in this bustling world, with my days flying in their escape? Nothing but to hesitate, to rush. What have I been doing in that eight-thousand-day rush, apart from hesitating? Those bygone days have been dispersed as smoke by a light wind, or evaporated as mist by the morning sun. What traces have I left behind me? Have I ever left behind any gossamer traces at all? I have come to this world, stark naked; am I to go back, in a blink, in the same stark nakedness? It is not fair though: why should I have made such a trip for nothing!

Repetition（重复）

Repetition is a kind of rhetoric device in which words or sentences are used for more than once within a sentence or paragraph to emphasize the idea or express some kind of emotion. Repetition depends on the high frequency of a certain grammatical phenomenon in syntactic level to reproduce the aesthetic value. This rhetorical device is often adopted in essays to intensify the author's emotion. In the original text, the sentence "你是一个活着的死人，朋友，你自已知道吗" is repeated for three times which expresses the idea that you are a walking corpse because of "the restriction on your life". The author's eagerness for freedom is fully reflected in the SL.

e. g.

生命的急流

张闻天

朋友，你做了家庭、社会与学校的奴隶，你失却了一切表现你自己的机会，你就是活尸,虽是每天吃着饭,做着事或是读着书,但是你还是一个活着的死人!

你是一个活着的死人,朋友,你自己知道吗?

朋友,你不是想有一个男朋友或是女朋友吗?你不是希望现社会能够社交公开吗?但是,朋友,你的家庭早不问你愿意不愿意,已经替你订了一个素不相识的女子或是已经把你放给什么小政客、小官僚或是什么其他不相识的男子了。学校、社会也不问你愿意不愿意已经把规则道德与法律来限制你的自由行动了。你们要想一同出去耍吗?他们说这是“野合”,就要把你捉到警察局里去。你们要想互相通讯吗?他们说这是有伤校风,就要把你驱逐出校。

哟,朋友,你是一个活着的死人,你自己知道吗?

朋友,你不是想有一点新鲜的思想拿来发表或拿来实现吗?但是,朋友,你的家庭,不就因为这一点要停止你的学费吗?你的社会,不就因为这一点要说你是“过激党”或“危险分子”,把你关进牢里或“推出斩之”吗?你的学校不也因为这一点要说你“有损学校名誉”或“犯校规第几十条”,把你记过或挂牌开除吗?

哟,朋友,你的“人权”在哪里,你能有一点思想的自由与行动的自由,努力去做一个人的权利吗?

不能,不能!

哟,朋友,你是一个活着的死人,你自己知道吗?

【译文】

The Torrent of Life

Friends, now that you've become a slave to family, society and school; you are deprived of any opportunity to assert yourself. You are a walking corpse, even though you eat, work or study every day!

You are a walking corpse, friends. Are you aware of it?

Friends, aren't you eager to have a boyfriend or girlfriend? Don't you hope that the present society will allow free contacts between boys and girls? But, friends, without your consent, your parents have already engaged you to a girl you don't know at all or arranged your marriage to a petty politician, official or any man who is a complete stranger to you. And, whether you are willing or not, schools and society have imposed restrictions on your free activities in the name of law, rules or morality. Don't you want to go on a date? But they will call this "illicit sex" and take you to the police station. Don't you want to correspond with a schoolmate of the opposite sex? But they will call this an immoral act in violation of school discipline and kick you out.

O friends, you are a walking corpse. Are you aware of it?

Friends, don't you intend to have some fresh ideas expressed or put into practice? But your family will, just because of this, discontinue financing your schooling. Society will, just because of this, have you put into prison or even "beheaded" on a charge of being an "extremist" or "dangerous element". And your school will, just because of this, give you a demerit, discredit you in public or dismiss you—all on a charge of "damaging the school reputation" or "violating this or that school rule".

O friends, do you have any "civil rights" to speak of? Do you have any freedom of thought and behavior, or the right of being a man?

No, none at all!

O friends, you are a walking corpse. Are you aware of it?

6. Reproduction of Prose Style from English to Chinese

6.1 The Plain Style

It is not easy to write a plain style, since it requires the precision and purity of language. Many English prose writers are distinguished for their plain style, such as Joseph Addison, William Cobbett, George Bernard Shaw, George Orwell, etc.

The following one is from Huxley's *At Sea*. His style is plain and natural. He uses easy, unaffected and lucid phrasing. Pedantry and eccentricity are eschewed in favor of the conversation style. Readers of the article feel they are being talked to. The first sentence is a parody.

e. g.

Familiarity blunts astonishment. Fishes do no marvel at water; They are too busy swimming in it. It is the same with us. We take our Western civilization for granted and find nothing intrinsically odd or incongruous in it. Before we can realize the strangeness of our surroundings, we must deliberately stop and think. (Aldous Huxley, *At Sea*)

多见则少怪。鱼类并不觉得水有何可怪;忙着游水,它们顾不上别的。我们自身也正是这样。我们往往把我们的西方文明视为当然,而不觉得其中有半点古怪或失调之处。要想认识我们周围环境的这种异常现象,我们就得坐下来着实思索一番。(高健译)

6.2 The Ornate Style

The ornate style makes a display of rich and rare phraseology, and occasionally sprinkles with archaisms. It is usually characterized with excessive use of antithesis, alliteration and historical allusions, which are not merely ornamental but wholly natural. Moreover, it frequently resorts to the use of adjectives, adverbs and figures of speech. In terms of syntactic and textual organization, it strives for the balance of sentences, of paragraphs and even of the whole text.

6.3 The Laconic Style

Laconic style is a concise and comprehensive style, which rejects redundant words and expressions. Francis Bacon is a master of laconic style. His essays are compact in style, clear in expression and profound in thoughts. The following passage is featured by its incisiveness, terseness and clarity. Bacon makes full use of a meager vocabulary to explicate his theme: the selfish wisdom. The whole text, no more than sixty-three words, is endowed with profound insights and resourceful ideas. The translator chooses some archaic Chinese expressions to make a concise style.

e. g.

Wisdom for a man's self is, in many branches thereof, a depraved thing. It is the wisdom of rats, that will be sure to leave a house, somewhat before it falls. It is the wisdom of the fox, that thrusts out the badger, who digged and made room for him. It is the wisdom of crocodiles that shed tears when they would devour.

(Francis Bacon, *Of Wisdom for a Man's Self*)

为利己而玩弄的诸多聪明,说到底是一种败坏的聪明。它是老鼠的聪明,因大屋将倾,鼠必先逃之;它是狐狸的聪明,因獾掘洞穴,狐占而居之;它是鳄鱼的聪明,因其欲食之,必先哭之。 (曹明伦译)

6.4 The Involved Style

The involved style does not equal with the superfluous style. It manifests itself by detailed and complete writing. Sentences are usually long and complicated. Besides the subject-predicate main clause, more information is provided by the coordination or subordination which is very common in writing of involved style.

6.5 The Ironic Style

Irony is a covert sarcasm which is inherently critical. It ridicules in the guise of compliment or praise. It is the product of a highly conscious mind. Many English writers practice irony in their proses.

6.6 The Humorous Style

It increases the language artistic appeal. It manifests itself by jocular and witty expressions.

【英译汉赏析】

Of Studies

Francis Bacon

Studies serve for delight, for ornament, and for ability. Their chief use for delight, is in privateness and retiring; for ornament, is in discourse; and for ability, is in the judgment and disposition of business. For expert men can execute, and perhaps judge of particulars, one by one; but the general counsels, and the plots and marshalling of affairs, come best, from those that are learned. To spend too much time in studies is sloth; to use them too much for ornament, is affectation; to make judgement wholly by their rules, is the humour of a scholar. They perfect nature, and are perfected by experience: for natural abilities are like natural plants that need pruning by study; and studies themselves do give forth directions too much at large, except they be bounded in by experience. Crafty men contemn studies, simple men admire them, and wise men use them; for they teach not their own use; but that is a wisdom without them, and above them, won by observation. Read not to contradict and confute; nor to believe and take for granted; nor to find talk and discourse; but to weigh and consider. Some books are to be tasted, others to be swallowed, and some few to be chewed and digested; that is, some books are to be read only in parts; others to be read, but not curiously; and some few to be read wholly, and with diligence and attention. Some books also may be read by deputy, and extracts made of them by others; but that would be only in the less important arguments, and the meaner sort of books; else distilled books are, like common distilled waters, flashy things. Reading makes a full man; conference a ready man; and writing an exact man. And therefore, if a man write little, he had need have a great memory; if he confer little, he had need have a present wit; and if he read little, he had need have much cunning, to seem to know that he doth not. Histories make men wise; poets witty; the mathematics subtile; natural philosophy deep; moral grave; logic and rhetoric able to contend. *Abeunt studia in mores*. Nay there is no stand or impediment in the wit, but may be wrought out by fit studies: like as diseases of the body may have appropriate exercises. Bowling is good for the stone and reins; shooting for the lungs and breast; gentle walking for the stomach; riding for the head; and the like. So if a man's wit be wandering, let him study the mathematics; for in demonstrations, if his wit be called away never so little, he must begin again. If his wit be not apt to distinguish or find differences, let him study the schoolmen; for they are cymini sectors. If he be not apt to beat over matters, and to call up one thing to prove and illustrate another, let him study the lawyers' cases. So every defect of the mind may have a special receipt.

【译文】

谈读书

王佐良

读书足以怡情,足以傅彩,足以长才。其怡情也,最见于独处幽居之时;其傅彩也,最见于高谈阔论之中;其长才也,最见于处世判事之际。练达之士虽能分别处理细事或一一判别枝节,然纵观统筹、全局策划,则舍好学深思者莫属。读书费时过多易惰,文采藻饰太盛则矫,全凭条文断事乃学究故态。读书补天然之不足,经验又补读书之不足,盖天生才干犹如自然花草,读书然后知如何修剪移接;而书中所示,如不以经验范之,则又大而无当。

有一技之长者鄙读书,无知者羡读书,唯明智之士用读书,然书并不以用处告人,用书之智不在书中,而在书外,全凭观察得之。读书时不可存心诘难作者,不可尽信书上所言,亦不可只为寻章摘句,而应推敲细思。

书有可浅尝者,有可吞食者,少数则须咀嚼消化。换言之,有只须读其部分者,有只须大体涉猎者,少数则须全读,读时须全神贯注,孜孜不倦。书亦可请人代读,取其所作摘要,但只限题材较次或价值不高者,否则书经提炼犹如水经蒸馏,淡而无味矣。

读书使人充实,讨论使人机智,笔记使人准确。因此不常作笔记者须记忆特强,不常讨论者须天生聪颖,不常读书者须欺世有术,始能无知而显有知。

读史使人明智,读诗使人灵秀,数学使人周密,科学使人深刻,论理学使人庄重,逻辑修辞之学使人善辩:凡有所学,皆成性格。人之才智但有滞碍,无不可读适当之书使之顺畅,一如身体百病,皆可借相宜之运动除之。滚球利睾肾,射箭利胸肺,慢步利肠胃,骑术利头脑,诸如此类。如智力不集中,可令读数学,盖演题须全神贯注,稍有分散即须重演;如不能辨异,可令读经院哲学,盖是辈皆吹毛求疵之人;如不善求同,不善以一物阐证另一物,可令读律师之案卷。如此头脑中凡有缺陷,皆有特药可医。

➢ **Source Text Analysis**

Brief Introduction to *Of Studies*

The source text ***Of Studies*** was written by Francis Bacon, who is a distinguished English lawyer, statesman, essayist, historian, intellectual reformer, philosopher, and champion of modern science and acknowledged by Karl Max as the "genuine founder of British Materialism and entire modern experimental science". ***Of Studies*** first appeared in the first edition of ***The Essays*** in 1597. Early modern English (1500 - 1700), was a transitional stage from Middle English to Modern English.

Of Studies is one of the most influential essays of Bacon's work, which fully shows his writing genius and profound insight into life. Time proves that it is with all enduring charm and is translated into at least eleven versions in Chinese, including Shui Tiantong

(水天同), Liao Yunfan(廖运范), Wang Zuoliang(王佐良), He Xin(何新), Wang Ji (王揖), Yao Zongli(姚宗立), Chen Caiyu(陈才宇), Cao Minglun(曹明伦), Chen Yiping(陈毅平), Gao Jian(高健), and Dong Xu(东旭), among which Wang Zuoliang's translation enjoys an everlasting fame and is the most frequently quoted version. Three renditions by Shui Tiantong, Wang Zuoliang and He Xin are adopted for they are considered correspondingly as the first, the best and the most widely-known.

The Author's Writing Style

As for its style, the language is *concise*, *archaic* and *elegant*, which is realized on the level of words, sentences and rhetorical devices. *Omission* is frequently found. A large proportion of simple sentences is another element that contributes to the brevity of the essay, such as "Studies serve for delight, for ornament and for ability"; "So every defect of the mind may have a special receipt" etc. Archaism is achieved through Latin sentence or phrase, special verb forms for the third singular person and some old words out of use today. On the whole, it has a confident tone; readers are seldom shocked by words like "perhaps", "probably" and "in my opinion" in the article. In terms of structure, the purpose is made clear at the beginning by stating functions of study; in the body, the concentration is on the theme and specified methods are introduced; finally, it presents a conclusive sentence to echo the topic sentence. Consequently, the essay is highly coherent in general.

Rhetorical Devices

Epigram (警句)

Reading makes a full man; conference a ready man; writing an exact man.

Alliteration (头韵)

*S*tudies *s*erve for delight, for ornament , for ability.

For *e*xpert men can *e*xecute, and *p*erhaps judge of *p*articulars, one by one;

If his wit be not apt to *d*istinguish or find *d*ifference, let him *s*tudy the *s*choolman;

Analogy (类比)

Nay, there is no stone or impediment in the wit, but may be wrought out by fit studies; like as diseases of the body may have appropriate exercise.

Personification (拟人)

Some books are to be tasted, others to be swallowed, and some few to be chewed and digested.

Simile (比喻)

They perfect nature, and are perfected by experience: for natural abilities are like natural plants that need pruning by study;

... else distilled books are, like common distilled waters, flashy things.

Antithesis（对偶）

Crafty men contemn studies, simple men admire them, and wise men use them;

Allusion（典故）

Abeunt studia in mores.（Latin）（studies help shape one's character）

➢ General Features of *Of Studies*

a distinct theme: function and method of reading;

idea: full of dialectical luster (without any trace of dogma);

elegance: epigram, analogy, parallelism, contrast and personification;

style: the author has a confident tone, words like perhaps or probably only dot the whole passage;

language: concise, archaic (marshalling, humor, sloth, nay, stand, discourse) and elegant, which is realized on the level of words, sentences and rhetorical devices;

aesthetic beauty: modifier is omitted in the second and third clauses of the second sentence, which makes sentences shorter and clearer. This contributes to the brevity of the essay;

archaism: achieved through Latin sentence or phrase, special verb forms for the third singular person and some old words falling out of use today;

simple sentences: another element that contributes to the brevity of the essay;

coherent in general: purpose is made clear at the beginning by stating the functions of study;

body part: focus on the theme and specified methods introduced;

final: conclusive sentence to echo the topic sentence.

➢ Statistics of the Version of Translation

《论读书》译文数字统计表

	O. Text	王佐良 Version	曹明伦 Version	水天同 Version	何新 Version
Paragraph	1	2	1	3	7
Word	867	612	753	878	780
Sentence	16	17	12	18	36

➢ Appreciation

(1) Studies serve for delight, for ornament, and for ability.

【王佐良译文】读书足以怡情，足以傅彩，足以长才。

【水天同译文】读书为学的用途是娱乐、装饰和增长才识。

(2) Their chief use for delight, is in privateness and retiring; for ornament, is in discourse; and for ability, is in the judgment and disposition of business.

【王佐良译文】其怡情也,最见于独处幽居之时;其傅彩也,最见于高谈阔论之中;其长才也,最见于处世判事之际。

【水天同译文】在娱乐上学问的主要的用处是幽居养静;在装饰上学问的用处是辞令;在长才上学问的用处是对于事务的判断和处理。

(3) For expert men can execute, and perhaps judge of particulars, one by one; but the general counsels, and the plots and marshalling of affairs, come best from those that are learned.

【王佐良译文】练达之士虽能分别处理细事或一一判别枝节,然纵观统筹、全局策划,则舍好学深思者莫属。

【水天同译文】因为富于经验的人善于实行,也许能够对个别的事情一件一件地加以判断;但是最好的有关大体的议论和对事务的计划与布置,乃是从有学问的人来的。

(4) To spend too much time in studies is sloth; to use them too much for ornament, is affectation; to make judgment wholly by their rules, is the humor of a scholar.

【王佐良译文】读书费时过多易惰,文采藻饰太盛则矫,全凭条文断事乃学究故态。

【水天同译文】在学问上费时过多是偷懒;把学问过于用作装饰是虚假;完全依学问上的规则而断事是书生的怪癖。

(5) They perfect nature, and are perfected by experience: for natural abilities are like natural plants, that need pruning by study; and studies themselves do give forth directions too much at large, except they be bounded in by experience.

【王佐良译文】读书补天然之不足,经验又补读书之不足,盖天生才干犹如自然花草,读书然后知如何修剪移接;而书中所示,如不以经验范之,则又大而无当。

【水天同译文】学问锻炼天性,而其本身又受经验的锻炼,盖人的天赋有如野生的花草,他们需要学问的修剪;而学问的本身,若不受经验的限制,则其所指示的未免过于笼统。

(6) Crafty men contempt studies, simple men admire them, and wise men use them; for they teach not their own use; but that is wisdom without them, and above them, won

by observation.

【王佐良译文】有一技之长者鄙读书，无知者羡读书，唯明智之士用读书，然书并不以用处告人，用书之智不在书中，而在书外，全凭观察得之。

【水天同译文】多诈的人渺视学问，愚鲁的人羡慕学问，聪明的人运用学问；因为学问的本身并不教人如何用它们；这种运用之道乃是学问以外，学问以上的一种智能，是由观察体会才能得到的。

(7) Read not to contradict and confute; nor to believe and take for granted; nor to find talk and discourse; but to weigh and consider.

【王佐良译文】读书时不可存心诘难作者，不可尽信书上所言，亦不可只为寻章摘句，而应推敲细思。

【水天同译文】不要为了辩驳而读书，也不要为了信仰与盲从；也不要为了言谈与议论；要以能权衡轻重、审察事理为目的。

(8) Some books are to be tasted, others to be swallowed, and some few to be chewed and digested; that is, some books are to be read only in parts; others to be read, but not curiously; and some few to be read wholly, and with diligence and attention.

【王佐良译文】书有可浅尝者，有可吞食者，少数则须咀嚼消化。换言之，有只须读其部分者，有只须大体涉猎者，少数则须全读，读时须全神贯注，孜孜不倦。

【水天同译文】有些书可供一尝，有些书可以吞下，有不多的几部书则应当咀嚼消化；这就是说，有些书只要读读他们的一部分就够了，有些书可以全读，但是不必过于细心地读；还有不多的几部书则应当全读，勤读，而且用心地读。

(9) Some books also may be read by deputy, and extracts made of them by others; but that would be only in the less important arguments, and the meaner sort of books; else distilled books are, like common distilled waters, flashy things.

【王佐良译文】书亦可请人代读，取其所作摘要，但只限题材较次或价值不高者，否则书经提炼犹如水经蒸馏，淡而无味矣。

【水天同译文】有些书也可以请代表去读，并且由别人替我作出摘要来；但是这种办法只适于次要的议论和次要的书籍；否则录要的书就和蒸馏的水一样，都是无味的东西。

(10) Reading makes a full man; conference a ready man; and writing an exact man.

【王佐良译文】读书使人充实,讨论使人机智,笔记使人准确。

【水天同译文】阅读使人充实,会谈使人敏捷,写作与笔记使人精确。

(11) And therefore, if a man write little, he had need have a great memory; if he confer little, he had need have a present wit; and if he read little, he had need have much cunning, to seem to know that he doth not.

【王佐良译文】因此不常作笔记者须记忆特强,不常讨论者须天生聪颖,不常读书者须欺世有术,始能无知而显有知。

【水天同译文】因此,如果一个人写得很少,那么他就必须有很好的记性;如果他很少与人会谈,那么他就必须有很敏捷的机智;并且假如他读书读得很少的话,那么他就必须要有很大的狡黠之才,才可以强不知以为知。

(12) Histories make men wise; poets witty; the mathematics subtile; natural philosophy deep; moral grave; logic and rhetoric able to contend. *Abeunt studia in mores.*

【王佐良译文】读史使人明智,读诗使人灵秀,数学使人周密,科学使人深刻,伦理学使人庄重,逻辑修辞之学使人善辩:凡有所学,皆成性格。

【水天同译文】史鉴使人明智;诗歌使人巧慧;数学使人精细;博物使人深沉;伦理之学使人庄重;逻辑与修辞使人善辩。“学问变化气质”。

(13) Nay there is no stand or impediment in the wit, but may be wrought out by fit studies: like as diseases of the body may have appropriate exercises.

【王佐良译文】人之才智但有滞碍,无不可读适当之书使之顺畅,一如身体百病,皆可借相宜之运动除之。

【水天同译文】不特如此,精神上的缺陷没有一种是不能由相当的学问来补救的:就如同肉体上各种的病患都有适当的运动来治疗似的。

(14) Bowling is good for the stone and reins; shooting for the lungs and breast; gentle walking for the stomach; riding for the head; and the like.

【王佐良译文】滚球利睾肾,射箭利胸肺,慢步利肠胃,骑术利头脑,诸如此类。

【水天同译文】踢球有益于结石和肾脏;射箭有益于胸肺;缓步有益于胃;骑马有益于头脑;诸如此类。

(15) So if a man's wit be wandering, let him study the mathematics; for in demonstrations, if his wit be called away never so little, he must begin again.

【王佐良译文】如智力不集中,可令读数学,盖演题须全神贯注,稍有分散即须重演。

【水天同译文】同此,如果一个人心志不专,他顶好研究数学;因为在数学的证理之中,如果他的精神稍有不专,他就非从头再做不可。

【汉译英赏析】

落花生

许地山

我们屋后有半亩隙地。母亲说:"让它荒芜着怪可惜,既然你们那么爱吃花生,就辟来做花生园罢。"我们几姊弟和几个小丫头都很喜欢——买种的买种,动土的动土,灌园的灌园;过不了几个月,居然收获了!

妈妈说:"今晚我们可以做一个收获节,也请你们爹爹来尝尝我们的新花生,如何?"我们都答应了。母亲把花生做成好几样的食品,还吩咐这节期要在园里的茅亭举行。

那晚上的天色不大好,可是爹爹也到来,实在很难得!爹爹说:"你们爱吃花生么?"

我们都争着答应:"爱!"

"谁能把花生的好处说出来?"

姊姊说:"花生的气味很美。"

哥哥说:"花生可以制油。"

我说:"无论何等人都可以用贱价买它来吃;都喜欢吃它。这就是它的好处。"

爹爹说:"花生的用处固然很多;但有一样是很可贵的。这小小的豆不像那好看的苹果、桃子、石榴,把它们的果实悬在枝上,鲜红嫩绿的颜色,令人一望而发生羡慕的心。它只把果子埋在地底,等到成熟,才容人把它挖出来。你们偶然看见一棵花生瑟缩地长在地上,不能立刻辨出它有没有果实,非得等到你接触它才能知道。"

我们都说:"是的。"母亲也点点头。爹爹接下去说:"所以你们要像花生,因为它是有用的,不是伟大、好看的东西。"我说:"那么,人要做有用的人,不要做伟大、体面的人了。"爹爹说:"这是我对于你们的希望。"

我们谈到夜阑才散,所有花生食品虽然没有了,然而父亲的话现在还印在我心版上。

【刘世聪译文】

At the back of our house there was half a *mu* of vacant land. "It's a pity to let it go to waste like that," Mother said. "Since you all enjoy eating peanuts, let us open it up and make it a peanut garden." At that my brother, sister and I were all delighted and so were the young housemaids. Some went to buy seeds, some dug the ground and others watered it and, in a couple of months, we had a harvest!

"Let us have a party tonight to celebrate," Mother suggested, "and ask Dad to come for a taste of our fresh peanuts. What do you say?" We all agreed, of course. Mother cooked the peanuts in different styles and told us to go to the thatched pavilion in the garden for the celebration.

The weather was not very good that night but, to our great delight, Dad came all the same. "Do you like peanuts?" Dad asked.

"Yes!" we all answered eagerly.

"But who can tell me what the peanut is good for?"

"It is very delicious to eat," my sister took the lead.

"It is good for making cooking oil," my brother followed.

"It is inexpensive." I said. "Almost everyone can afford it and everyone enjoys eating it. I think this is what it is good for."

"Peanut is good for many things," Dad said, "but there is one thing that is particularly good about it. Unlike apples, peaches or pomegranates that display their fruits up in the air, attracting you with their beautiful colors, peanut buries its fruit in the earth. It does not show itself until you dig it out when it is ripe and, unless you dig it out, you can't tell whether it bears fruit or not just by its frail stems above ground."

"That's true," we all said and Mother nodded her assent. "So you should try to be like the peanut," Dad went on, "because it is useful, though not great or attractive."

"Do you mean," I asked, "we should learn to be useful but not seek to be great or attractive?"

"Yes," Dad said. "This is what I wish you to be."

We stayed up late that night, eating all the peanuts Mother had cooked for us. But Father's words remained vivid in my memory till this day.

【张培基译文】

Behind our house there lay half a *mu* of vacant land. Mother said, "It's a pity to let it lie waste. Since you all like to eat peanuts so much, why not have them planted here?" That exhilarated us children and our servant girls as well, and soon we started buying seeds, ploughing the land and watering the plants. We gathered in a good harvest just after a couple of months!

Mother said, "How about giving a party this evening to celebrate the harvest and invite your Daddy to have a taste of our newly-harvested peanuts?" We all agreed. Mother made quite a few varieties of goodies out of the peanuts, and told us that the party would be held in the thatched pavilion on the peanut plot.

It looked like rain that evening, yet, to our great joy, Father came nevertheless. "Do you like peanuts?" asked Father.

"Yes, we do!" we vied in giving the answer.

"Which of you could name the good things in peanuts?"

"Peanuts tastes good," said my elder sister.

"Peanuts produce edible oil," said my elder brother.

"Peanuts are so cheap," said I, "that anyone can afford to eat them. Peanuts are everyone's favourite. That's why we call peanuts good."

"It's true that peanuts have many uses," said Father, "but they're most beloved in one respect. Unlike nice-looking apples, peaches, and pomegranates, which hang their fruit on branches and win people's admiration with their brilliant colours, tiny little peanuts bury themselves underground and remain earthed until they're ripe. When you come upon a peanut plant lying curled up on the ground, you can never immediately tell whether or not it bears any nuts until you touch them."

"That's true," we said in unison. Mother also nodded. "So you must take after peanuts," Father continued, "because they're useful though not great and nice-looking."

"Then you mean one should be useful rather than great and nice-looking." I said.

"That's what I expect of you." Father concluded.

We kept chatting until the party broke up late at night. Today, though nothing is left of the goodies made of peanuts, Father's words remain engraved in my mind.

【译文比较翻译】

(1)标题:落花生

刘士聪先生译(刘译):The Peanut
张培基先生译(张译):Peanuts

【解析】

The Peanut 更能使人联想到花生的种类(例如:the rich; the poor)。从整体上看,文章主要是赞扬花生这一物种的优良品格,所以 The Peanut 比 Peanuts 要好。

(2)我们屋后有半亩隙地。

刘译:At the back of our house there was half a mu of vacant land.
张译:Behind our house there lay half a mu of vacant land.

【解析】

"屋后"从逻辑上讲应该是房子的"后面",而不是房间的"后部",因此

"behind"更加准确 。译文中"lay"比"was"更具动感。

(3)母亲说:"让它荒芜着怪可惜,既然你们那么爱吃花生,就辟来做花生园罢。"

刘译:"It's a pity to let it go to waste like that," Mother said. "Since you all enjoy eating peanuts, let us open it up and make it a peanut garden."

张译:"It's a pity to let it lie waste. Since you all like to eat peanuts so much, why not have them planted here."

【解析】

刘译中把"Mother said"放在句中作为插入语,使句子的结构更加平衡也更符合英文的行文特点。"爱吃花生"应该表达的是一种习惯,而 like to eat 一般表示心血来潮的想法。因此, enjoy eating 比 like to eat 要好。荒芜着:"go to waste" 是句法性搭配误用,试比较下列句式:

Her hair's going grey. 她的头发变灰白了。

The milk went sour. 牛奶变酸了。

He's gone blind. 他变成了瞎子。

(4)我们几姊弟和几个小丫头都很喜欢——买种的买种,动土的动土,灌园的灌园;过不了几个月,居然收获了!

刘译: At that my brother, sister and I were all delighted and so were the young housemaids. Some went to buy seeds, some dug the ground and others watered it and, in a couple of months, we had a harvest!

张译: That exhilarated us children and our servant girls as well, and soon we started buying seeds, ploughing the land and watering the plants. We gathered in a good harvest just after a couple of months!

【解析】

在翻译"我们几姊弟"时"my brother , sister and I "虽比"us children"略显冗长,但更能对应"买种的买种,动土的动土,灌园的灌园"。接下来在处理中文的此类并列结构时,Verb-ing 形式的使用彰显了孩子们欢快、活泼的劳动场景,"some . . . some . . . and others" 句式较正式,在节奏上略显迟缓。翻译本段最后一句时,"just after" 精练地将"居然收获"的惊喜表达了出来。

(5)妈妈说:"今晚我们可以做一个收获节,也请你们爹爹来尝尝我们的新花生,如何?"我们都答应了。母亲把花生做成好几样食品,还吩咐这节期要在园里的茅亭举行。那晚上的天色不大好,可是爹爹也到来,实在很难得!

刘译:"Let us have a party tonight to celebrate," Mother suggested, "and ask Dad to come for a taste of our fresh peanuts. What do you say?" We all agreed, of course. Mother cooked the peanuts in different styles and told us to go to the thatched pavilion in the garden for the celebration. The weather was not very good that night but, to our great delight, Dad came all the same.

张译:Mother said, "How about giving a party this evening to celebrate the harvest and invite your Daddy to have a taste of our newly-harvested peanuts?" We all agreed. Mother made quite a few varieties of goodies out of the peanuts, and told us that the party would be held in the thatched pavilion on the peanut plot. It looked like rain that evening, yet, to our great joy, Father came nevertheless.

【解析】

"How about"和"invite"显得母亲说话比较温和。"Let us, ask, What do you say",母亲慈爱的意味似乎传递不足。在表示"新"花生时,"fresh"不如张译"newly-harvested"传神。"可是爹爹也到了"中的"也"字的翻译是表达原文意境的关键,"nevertheless"没有"all the same"译得巧妙。后者追求的不只是译语和原语形式的对等,而且是原文语义和意蕴的交融。

另外英语中对父母的称呼也主要有 4 套,father / mother, papa/mama, dad/mum, daddy/mummy. 在同一语篇里,对父母称呼的词语可以交叉但是以对应为基调。

(6)爹爹说:"你们爱吃花生么?"我们都争着答应:"爱!""谁能把花生的好处说出来?"。姊姊说:"花生的气味很美。"哥哥说:"花生可以制油。"

刘译:"Do you like peanuts?" Dad asked. "Yes!" we all answered eagerly. "But who can tell me what the peanut is good for?" "It is very delicious to eat," my sister took the lead. "It is good for making cooking oil," my brother followed.

张译:"Do you like peanuts?" asked Father. "Yes, we do!" We vied in giving the answer. "Which of you could name the good things in peanuts?" "Peanuts taste good," said my elder sister. "Peanuts produce edible oil," said my elder brother.

【解析】

首先,这是一段典型的对话章节,为符合英文的行文习惯,对话部分的灵活对应非常必要,在翻译"姊姊说"、"哥哥说"时刘译按照逻辑对顺序进行了增译 took the lead... followed,这成为译文的一大亮点。"争着答应"用 vied in giving the answer 为一种习语误用,可参考:"vied with each other in giving the answer"或"vied with each other to give the answer"。

(7)我说:"无论何等人都可以用贱价买它来吃;都喜欢吃它。这就是它的好处。"

刘译:"It is inexpensive." I said. "Almost everyone can afford it and everyone enjoys eating it. I think this is what it is good for."

张译:"Peanuts are so cheap," said I, "that anyone can afford to eat them. Peanuts are everyone's favourite. That's why we call peanuts good."

【解析】

贱价,刘译:It is inexpensive 张译:Peanuts are so cheap,用 inexpensive 和 cheap 似乎都没错,可是通过查阅字典我发现 inexpensive:(adj.) low priced; not expensive 主要表示"廉价的,不贵的"。而 Cheap:(adj.) low in price; worth more than the cost offering good value 则有更多意思如"廉价的,实惠的","价钱好的",因此从上下文来看张译的 cheap 更胜一筹。表示花生人人吃得起,刘译 afford it 比张译 afford to eat them 更加简洁。

(8)这小小的豆不像那好看的苹果、桃子、石榴,把它们的果实悬在枝上,鲜红嫩绿的颜色,令人一望而发生羡慕的心。它只把果子埋在地底,等到成熟,才容人把它挖出来。

刘译:Unlike apples, peaches or pomegranates that display their fruits up in the air, attracting you with their beautiful colors, peanut buries its fruit in the earth.

张译:Unlike nice-looking apples, peaches, and pomegranates, which hang their fruit on branches and win people's admiration with their brilliant colours, tiny little peanuts bury themselves underground and remain earthed until they're ripe.

【解析】

鲜红嫩绿这样的颜色词用 beautiful 不够准确、信息量欠缺,缺乏"brilliant"含有的"full of light, having striking color"的含义。最后部分刘译略显不足。

(9)你们偶然看见一棵花生瑟缩地长在地上,不能立刻辨出它有没有果实,非得等到你接触它才能知道。

刘译:It does not show itself until you dig it out when it is ripe and, unless you dig out, you can't tell whether it bears fruit or not just by its frail stems above ground.

张译:When you come upon a peanut plant lying curled up on the ground, you can never immediately tell whether or not it bears any nuts until you touch them.

【解析】

张译文运用条件状语 when,使句子的逻辑比较清晰。curled up 与原文平实的风格相符。

(10)爹爹接下去说:"所以你们要像花生,因为它是有用的,不是伟大、好看的东西。"我说:"那么,人要做有用的人,不要做伟大、体面的人了。" 爹爹说:"这是我对于你们的希望。"

刘译:"So you should try to be like the peanut," Dad went on, "because it is useful, though not great or attractive." "Do you mean," I asked, "we should learn to be useful but not seek to be great or attractive?" "Yes," Dad said. "This is what I wish you to be."

张译:"So you must take after peanuts," Father continued, "because they're useful though not great and nice-looking." "Then you mean one should be useful rather than great and nice-looking," I said. "That's what I expect of you," Father concluded.

【解析】

"像花生"用"take after"更能体现以花生为榜样,体现了学习态度与行动方面的模仿。

原文有 4 个引述句,引述词"说"。汉语传统引述词多为"说"或"道"。可见引述动词在传统汉语中并不发达,英语中的引述动词丰富得多。以 Dickens 的 *A Tale of Two Cities* 为例,30 处引述动词中有 15 个不同表达,said 以 16 次的频率居第一,其次为 replied , cried, restored, called, asked, read aloud, mused, bawled, accost, repeated, inquired, ... 因此语篇角度上英译应适当调整。

(11)我们谈到夜阑才散,所有花生食品虽然没有了,然而父亲的话现在还印在我心版上。

刘译:We stayed up late that night, eating all the peanuts Mother had cooked for us. But Father's words remained vivid in my memory till this day.

张译:We kept chatting until the party broke up late at night. Today, though nothing is left of the goodies made of peanuts, Father's words remain engraved in my mind.

【解析】

短语 in my mind 与 in my memory 的用法上,in my memory 更准确,因为,虽然有 keep / bear in mind 的表达,但 mind 表记忆的时候,搭配为 in mind 或 on one's mind.

第七章综合练习

【英译汉】

以下短文选自英国作家、批评家约翰·罗斯金的散文《爱美之心》。文章语言优美,译文中应当注意各种修辞手段的重现。

The Love of Beauty

John Ruskin

The love of beauty is an essential part of all healthy human nature. It is a moral quality. The absence of it is not an assured ground of condemnation, but the presence of it is an invariable sign of goodness of heart. In proportion to the degree in which it is felt will probably be the degree in which nobleness and beauty of character will be attained.

Natural beauty is an all-pervading presence. The universe is its temple. It unfolds into the numberless flowers of spring. It waves in the branches of trees and the green blades of grass. It haunts the depths of the earth and the sea. It gleams from the hues of the shell and the precious stone. And not only these minute objects but the oceans, the mountains, the clouds, the stars, the rising and the setting sun—all overflow with beauty. This beauty is so precious, and so congenial to our tenderest and noblest feelings, that it is painful to think of the multitude of people living in the midst of it and yet remaining almost blind to it.

【汉译英】

以下短文节选自茅盾先生的散文《白杨礼赞》,作者的文风质朴,翻译时注意风格的转换。

白杨礼赞

(茅盾)

白杨不是平凡的树。它在西北极普遍,不被人重视,就跟北方农民相似;它有极强的生命力,磨折不了,压迫不倒,也跟北方的农民相似。我赞美白杨树,就因为它不但象征了北方的农民,尤其象征了今天我们民族解放斗争中所不可缺的朴质,坚强,以及力求上进的精神。

让那些看不起民众,贱视民众,顽固的倒退的人们去赞美那贵族化的楠木(那也是直干秀颀的),去鄙视这极常见,极易生长的白杨罢,但是我要高声赞美白杨树!

附录1:英译汉作品欣赏

Of Wisdom For a Man's Self

Francis Bacon

AN ANT is a wise creature for itself, but it is a shrewd thing, in an orchard or garden. And certainly, men that are great lovers of themselves waste the public. Divide with reason; between selflove and society; and be so true to thyself, as thou be not false to others; specially to thy king and country. It is a poor centre of a man' s actions, himself. It is right earth. For that only stands fast upon his own centre; whereas all things, that have affinity with the heavens, move upon the centre of another, which they benefit. The referring of all to a man's self, is more tolerable in a sovereign prince; because themselves are not only themselves, but their good and evil is at the peril of the public fortune. But it is a desperate evil, in a servant to a prince, or a citizen in a republic. For whatsoever affairs pass such a man's hands, he crookes them to his own ends; which must needs be often eccentric to the ends of his master, or state. Therefore, let princes, or states, choose such servants, as have not this mark; except they mean their service should be made but the accessory. That which makes the effect more pernicious, is that all proportion is lost. It were disproportion enough, for the servant's good to be preferred before the master's; but yet it is a greater extreme, when a little good of the servant, shall carry things against a great good of the master's. And yet that is the case of bad officers, treasurers, ambassadors, generals, and other false and corrupt servants; which set a bias upon their bowl, of their own petty ends and envies, to the overthrow of their master's great and important affairs. And for the most part, the good such servants receive, is after the model of their own fortune; but the hurt they sell for that good, is after the model of their master's fortune. And certainly it is the nature of extreme self-lovers, as they will set an house on fire, and it were but to roast their eggs; and yet these men many times hold credit with their masters, because their study is but to please them, and profit themselves; and for either respect, they will abandon the good of their affairs.

Wisdom for a man's self is, in many branches thereof, a depraved thing. It is the wisdom of rats, that will be sure to leave a house, somewhat before it falls. It is the wisdom of the fox, that thrusts out the badger, who digged and made room for him. It is the wisdom of crocodiles, that shed tears when they would devour. But that which is specially to be noted is, that those which (as Cicero says of Pompey) are sui amantes, sine rivali, are many times unfortunate. And whereas they have, all their times, sacrificed to themselves, they become in the end, themselves sacrifices to the inconstancy of fortune, whose wings they thought, by their self-wisdom, to have pinioned.

【译文】

谈利己之聪明

（曹明伦译）

若论为己营生，蚂蚁可谓一种聪明的动物，但对果园花圃来说，它却是一种祸害；而毋庸置疑，过分自私的人亦会有害于公众。故人应该理智地再私利与公利之间划出界限,不可利己而有负于他人,尤其不可有负于君王和国家。常人之行为以我为中心实乃不幸,因为那就像地球只绕其轴心而转,而与各重天道有亲和力的所有天体都绕别的中心而运动并有益于它们所围绕的中心。一切以自我为中心,这于帝王君王尚情有可原,因为君王并不仅仅代表其自身,他们的祸福也与公众的安危息息相关;但于普通臣民或公民,一切以自我为中心则是一种大恶,因为凡事经这种人之手,他们都会使其适合自己的目的,而他们的目的往往都与君王和国家的目标背道而驰,由此可见,君王或国家不可选这种人作为臣仆或公仆,除非只让他们做一些无关紧要的琐事。谋私利的更大危害是使纲常失调。置臣利于君利之先已是违常乱纲,而为臣之小利损君之大利则更是大逆不道。然而这正是那些贪官污吏所为,腐败堕落的大臣、司库、使节和将军,无不为其蝇头小利而偏离正道,从而破坏其君王的宏图大业。而总的说来,这些人所获之利通常只与他们的财富相称,可他们为获私利而牺牲的公利则往往与君王的财富成正比。为烤熟自家鸡蛋而不惜烧掉公家房屋,这无疑就是极端利己者的本性;然而这类利己者却往往得到主人的信任,因为他们的心思全在于如何讨好主人,如何替自己捞好处;他们可以为任何一点好处而抛弃主人的利益。

为利己而玩弄的诸多聪明,说到底是一种败坏的聪明。它是老鼠的聪明,因大屋将倾,鼠必先逃之;它是狐狸的聪明,因獾掘洞穴,狐占而居之;它是鳄鱼的聪明,因其欲食之,必先哭之。但值得指出的是,那些除自己之外谁也不爱的人(如西塞罗笔下的庞培),到头来往往都可叹可悲;尽管他们总是为自己而牺牲他人,并自以为已用其聪明缚住了命运的翅翼,但他们终归也会变成无常命运的祭品。

附录2:汉译英作品欣赏

匆匆

(朱自清)

燕子去了,有再来的时候;杨柳枯了,有再青的时候;桃花谢了,有再开的时候。但是,聪明的,你告诉我,我们的日子为什么一去不复返呢?——是有人偷了他们罢:那是谁?又藏在何处呢?是他们自己逃走了罢:现在又到了哪里呢?

我不知道他们给了我多少日子;但我的手确乎是渐渐空虚了。在默默里算着,八千多日子已经从我手中溜去;像针尖上一滴水滴在大海里,我的日子滴在时间的流里,没有声音,也没有影子。我不禁头涔涔而泪潸潸了。

去的尽管去了,来的尽管来着;去来的中间,又怎样地匆匆呢?早上我起来的时候,小屋里射进两三方斜斜的太阳。太阳他有脚啊,轻轻悄悄地挪移了;我也茫茫然跟着旋转。于是——洗手的时候,日子从水盆里过去;吃饭的时候,日子从饭碗里过去;默默时,便从凝然的双眼前过去。我觉察他去的匆匆了,伸出手遮挽时,他又从遮挽着的手边过去,天黑时,我躺在床上,他便伶伶俐俐地从我身上跨过,从我脚边飞去了。等我睁开眼和太阳再见,这算又溜走了一日。我掩着面叹息。但是新来的日子的影儿又开始在叹息里闪过了。

在逃去如飞的日子里，在千门万户的世界里的我能做些什么呢？只有徘徊罢了，只有匆匆罢了；在八千多日的匆匆里，除徘徊外，又剩些什么呢？过去的日子如轻烟，被微风吹散了，如薄雾，被初阳蒸融了；我留着些什么痕迹呢？我何曾留着像游丝样的痕迹呢？我赤裸裸来到这世界，转眼间也将赤裸裸的回去罢？但不能平的，为什么偏要白白走这一遭啊？

你聪明的，告诉我，我们的日子为什么一去不复返呢？

【译文】

Transient Days

(*Zhu Ziqing*)

If swallows go away, they will come back again. If willows wither, they will turn green again. If peach blossoms fade, they will flower again. But, tell me, you the wise, why should our days go by never to return? Perhaps they have been stolen by someone. But who could it be and where could he hide them? Perhaps they have just run away by themselves. But where could they be at the present moment?

I don't know how many days I am entitled to altogether, but my quota of them is undoubtedly wearing away. Counting up silently, I find that more than 8,000 days have already slipped away through my fingers. Like a drop of water falling off a needle point into the ocean, my days are quietly dripping into the stream of time without leaving a trace. At the thought of this, sweat oozes from my forehead and tears trickle down my cheeks.

What is gone is gone, what is to come keeps coming. How swift is the transition in between! When I get up in the morning, the slanting sun casts two or three squarish patches of light into my small room. The sun has feet too, edging away softly and stealthily. And, without knowing it, I am already caught in its revolution. Thus the day flows away through the sink when I wash my hands; vanishes in the rice bowl when I have my meal; passes away quietly before the fixed gaze of my eyes when I am lost in reverie. Aware of its fleeting presence, I reach out for it only to find it brushing past my outstretched hands. In the evening, when I lie on my bed, it nimbly strides over my body and flits past my feet. By the time when I open my eyes to meet the sun again, another day is already gone. I heave a sign, my head buried in my hands. But, in the midst of my sighs, a new day is flashing past.

Living in this world with its fleeting days and teeming millions, what can I do but waver and wander and live a transient life? What have I been doing during the 8,000 fleeting days except wavering and wandering? The bygone days, like wisps of smoke, have been dispersed by gentle winds, and, like thin mists, have been evaporated by the rising sun. What traces have I left behind? No, nothing, not even gossamer-like traces. I have come to this world stark naked, and in the twinkling of an eye, I am to go to back as stark naked as ever. However, I am taking it very much to heart: why should I be made to pass through this world for nothing at all?

O you the wise, would you tell me please: why should our days go by never to return?

Chapter Eight
Translation of Literary Writings—Novel
小说翻译

Translatability vs. Untranslatability（可译性与不可译性）

Translatability and untranslatability refer to the extent to which a translation is close to the original text, rather than the possibility to translate a certain text. Translatability and untranslatability, as the result of the language functions, co-exist in the same text. Any text as a whole is translatable while there are parts untranslatable. Translatability between any two languages serves as the theoretical basis of translation. This, however, does not mean that no differences exist between languages. Untranslatability is a property of a text or of any utterance, in one language, for which no equivalent text or utterance can be found in another language when translated. Quite often, a text or utterance that is considered to be "untranslatable" is actually a lacuna, or lexical gap. That is, there is no one-to-one equivalence between the word, expression or turn of phrase in the source language and another word, expression or turn of phrase in the target language. Besides, untranslatability is also characterized by phonetic untranslatability and cultural untranslatability.

关键词:不可译性;对等文本;语音不可译;文化不可译;语际翻译

About Fiction

Fiction, an artistic genre with a long history, has absorbed the advantages of various types of literature, which is widely applied and appreciated. There are three essentials of fiction: character, plot and setting. The features of fiction are as below: the fabricating quality is the essence of fiction; capturing the sensations and experiences of the life of the character are the artistic contents, and unforgettable typical character. Lu Xun once said that the model of the character doesn't focus on one particular person, and it used to be mouth in Zhejiang, face in Beijing and clothes in Shanxi, it is a part which is pieced together. Finally, the plot of fiction is originated from actual life and is refined from it, but more concentrated and more representative than it. The process, generally, is divided into beginning, development, climax and ending.

1 Categories of Fiction

The picaresque novel (流浪汉小说)

It is built on the tradition of the 16th century Spanish picaresque narrative, which typically portrayed a sharp-witted rogue living off his wits while traveling through a variety of usually low-life settings. It is typically episodic and often lacks a sophisticated plot or psychologically complex characters, for example, Kingsley Amis's *Lucky Jim*(1954).

The epistolary novel (书信体小说)

It is told through letters exchanged between different characters and flourished in particular in the 18th century, for example Emily Bronte's *Wuthering Heights* (1847).

The historical novel (历史小说)

It sets its events and characters in a well-defined historical context, and it may include both fictional and real characters, for example, Sir Walter Scott's novels.

The regional novel (地域小说)

It involves an especial focus of attention onto the life of a particular, well-defined geographical region, usually rural rather than urban, for example, Thomas Hardy's *Wessex* (1906).

The satirical novel (讽刺小说)

It attacks alleged vices and stupidities, either of individuals of whole communities or groups, and its tools are those of ridicule, exaggeration, and contempt, for example, Joseph Heller's *Catch* 22 (1961); Mark Twains's *The Adventures of Huckleberry Finn* (1884).

The educational novel (教育类小说)

It concentrates on one character's development from early youth to some sort of maturity, for example, James Joyce's *Portrait of the Artist as a Young Man* (1916).

The thesis novel (主题性小说)

It has a particular thesis or argument underlying it. It is typically concerned about encouraging social reform, or the correction of a particular abuse or wrong, for example, Harrit Beecher Stowe's *Uncle Tom's Cabin* (1852).

The gothic novel (哥特式小说)

It introduces stock characters, situations and settings that will survive in the modern horror film: gloomy medieval settings, ancient castles with secret rooms and passages ruled over by a sinister nobleman tortured by a guilty secret, and a strongly supernatural element, for example, Jane Austen's *Northanger Abby* (1816).

The roman-fleuve（系列长篇小说）

It denotes a series or sequence of novels which deal with recurring characters and common events and which can be read and appreciated individually, for example, Anthony Powell's *A Dance to the Music of Time*（1975）.

The science fiction（科幻小说）

It is characterized by settings involving interplanetary travel, advanced technology, and is typically set in the future, for example, Herbert George Wells' *The Time Machine*（1895）, *The Invisible Man*（1897）.

The new novel（新潮流小说）

It is a comparatively new development stemming from France in which the accepted conventions of fictional composition are deliberately distorted or flouted in order to disorient the reader and to achieve a different sort of effect. For example, John Barth's *Lost in the Funhouse*（1968）.

Metafiction（元小说）

It is a fiction about fiction—normally denoting the sort of novel or short story which deliberately breaks fiction illusions and comments directly upon its own fictive nature or process of composition, for example, John Fowels' *The French Lieutenant's Woman*（1969）.

The faction（纪实小说）

It brings actual historical events to life for the reader. It is a work that is on the borderline between fact and fiction, concerning primarily with a real event or persons, but using imagined detail to increase readability, for example, Truman Capote's *In Cold Blood*（1966）.

The sentimental novel（言情小说）

It was popular in the 18th century England. It concentrated on the distresses of the virtuous and attempted to show that a sense of humor and moral behavior were justly rewarded. It also tried to show that the effusive emotion was evidence of kindness and goodness. For example, Goldsmith's *The Vicar of Wakefield*（1766）.

Novel of the soil（现实题材小说）

It is work of fiction whose main theme is the struggle of human beings against the natural forces of the earth, for example, John Steinbeck's *Grapes of Wrath*（1936）.

2. Elements of Novel

2.1 Characterization

The creation of characters includes the creation of the protagonist (the main character or the hero), and the antagonist (the enemy, the character that opposes the protagonist). The most important methods of characterization are by description or reports, by action, through a character's thought or conversation, and by using symbols or images to reveal and develop a character.

2.2 Plot

Plot is a literary term defined as the events that make up a story, particularly as they relate to one another in a pattern, in a sequence, through cause and effect, or by coincidence. One is generally interested in how well this pattern of events accomplishes some artistic or emotional effect. An intricate and complicated plot is called an imbroglio, but even the simplest statements of plot may include multiple inferences, as in traditional ballads. To create good plots, the writer must have three qualities: curiosity, intelligence and a good memory.

2.3 Structure

Structure and plot are closely related to each other. It involves plot, theme, and form, the overall patterning of the novel, the chapters and sections, the way in which its component parts fit together to produce a totality.

2.4 Setting

The ***where*** and ***when*** of a story. The setting is the background in terms of time and place. For example, a novel could be set in modern Chicago, in New York City in the 1950s, in Spain in the 1820s or in an imaginary future society.

Setting does not just mean the geographical setting; social and historical factors are also important. Sometimes, a suitable choice is important, which can be an essential factor in the creation of mood or moral environment.

2.5 Theme

The theme of a novel is its main idea, which may be stated directly or indirectly. For instance, a main theme of the novel *The Adventures of Huckleberry Finn* by Mark Twain is whether racism is correct or not.

2.6 Symbol and Symbolism

A symbol is characterized by a translucence of the special in the individual. Scales for example symbolize justice; the orb and scepter, monarchy and rule; a dove, peace; a goat, lust; the lion, strength and courage; the bulldog, tenacity; the rose, beauty; the lily, purity; the Stars and Stripes, America and its states; the Cross, Christianity... Actions and gestures are also symbolic. The clenched fist symbolizes aggression. Beating of the breast signifies remorse. Arms raised denote surrender. A literary symbol combines an image with a concept.

e.g.

In Nathaniel Hawthorne's masterpiece *The Scarlet Letter*, the letter "A" begins as a symbol of sin. It then becomes a symbol of alone and alienation, and finally it becomes a symbol of able, angel and admirable. The change is significant. The scarlet letter is meant to be a symbol of shame, but instead it becomes a powerful symbol of identity and shows growth in characters.

颜色词的象征意义与翻译

RED：红色

The president was treated to the red carpet in Rome. 总统在罗马受到了隆重的接待。

It was a red-letter day in the history of Chinese. 这是中国历史上值得纪念的日子。

WHITE：白色

They treated us white. 他们公正地对待我们。

My children have bled me white. 我的一切都为孩子花光了。

BLACK：黑色

The black dog is over him. 他意气消沉。

Tom is the black sheep of his family. 汤姆是个败家子。

YELLOW：黄色

He is too yellow to stand up and fight. 他太胆怯，不敢奋起战斗。

I dislike Tom for he is a yellow dog. 我讨厌汤姆，他是个卑鄙小人。

GREEN：绿色

He is still green to his job. 他对其工作尚无经验。

Do you see any green in my eye? 你认为我幼稚可欺吗？

BLUE：蓝色

He is proud of his blue blood. 他因出身名门贵族而骄傲。

True blue will never stain. 真金不怕火炼。

2.7 Tone

The reflection of a writer's attitude, a tone of a literary work may be one of the following: friendly; detache; humorous; solemn; ironic; sarcastic...

2.8 Writing style

Writer's style includes these elements: tone, sentence structure and length; literary devices, such as figurative language, symbol, dialogue and imagery.

3. On Fiction Translation

The genre of fiction translation in literary translation stands out with its own characteristics. The preservation of rhythmic, phonological properties is much less essential to the fiction genre. The translation is inclined to establish equivalence at the level of material content. For instance, in translating Jane Austen's work, if one fails to capture the effect of her voice as conveyed by her subtle linguistic choices, the loss of a substantial part of her artistry may occur.

3.1 On Word Translation

3.1.1 Dialectal Words Translation

Dialect is a particular kind of culture-loaded word, which expresses the regional variety and suggests the place where the story occurs and a person's position. In literary works, applying some dialects properly often can create some atmosphere and increase the cordial feeling, and engender a kind of unexpected result.

天明未久,华大妈已在右边的一座新坟前面，排出四碟菜，一碗饭，哭了一场。化过纸，呆呆的坐在地上。(《呐喊 · 药》)

杨宪益译：Shortly after daybreak, Old Chuan's wife brought four dishes and a bowl of rice to set before a new grave in the right section, and wailed before it. When she had burned paper money she sat on the ground in a stupor as if waiting for something. (*Medicine*)

"化纸"在绍兴方言中指烧纸钱祭祀死者、亡灵，译为"paper money"表明译者对词汇的文化内涵有一定了解,但英语中"paper money"的意思为"money in the form of small sheets of paper"(*Longman Dictionary of Contemporary English*)，所以可以考虑译为"spirit money"。

高克毅在翻译 ***The Great Gatsby*** 时文中多次运用吴语。

The very phrases were worn so threadbare that they evoked no image except that of a turbaned "character" leaking sawdust at every pore as he pursued a tiger through the Bois de Boulogne. (*The Great Gatsby*)

高克毅译：他这样信口开河，没有一句令人可信的话，我听了脑中没有别的构想，似乎只见到一个裹了头巾的印度"阿三"，像塞满木屑的傀儡玩具一样，在巴黎郊外布龙林园里东奔西跑、追打着老虎。

"印度'阿三'"是旧上海老居民在上海公共租界时期对印度巡捕的俗称，一般含贬义，属于江浙方言吴语的范畴。翻译时原文意象没有再现，译者通过运用旧中国老上海含轻蔑意味的方言替代之，不仅传达了原文的讽刺口吻，而且给译文读者以浓重的旧日情怀，倍感亲切熟悉。

3.1.2 On Translation of Culture-Loaded Words 文化内涵词汇翻译

Every language has the so-called culture-bound terms, which are closely related to the culture background of those speaking that language, and which represent the concepts of those things produced from that peculiar culture. There are no equivalent words and expressions since such things do not exist in another culture.

In the Chinese novel ***Weicheng*** (***Fortress Besieged***), a lot of cultural-loaded expressions can be found. In Jeane Kelly & Nathan K. Mao's translation version, a lot of annotations were used to reinforce the cultural information. Here are some examples.

e.g.

这是七月下旬，合中国旧历的三伏，一年最热的时候。

It was toward the end of July, equivalent to the "san-fu" period of the lunar calendar—the hottest days of the year.

这真是"有缘千里来相会"了。

It's certainly a case of "fate bringing people together from a thousand li away."

Annotation: Li is a measure of length reckoned at 360 paces or about 1,890 feet in English measure.

鸿渐给酒摆布得失掉自制力道："反正你会摆空城计。"

Under the influence of alcohol, Hung-chien had lost his self-control, as he blurted out, "Anyway, you could always pull the 'empty-town bluff'."

Annotation: A reference to a story in the *Romance of the Three Kingdoms* in which Zhuge Liang, left to defend a town with no soldiers, feigned nonchalance by playing music in the tower on the town walls to give the enemy commander the impression that the town was confident and would prepare for an attack.

3.2 Representation of Portrait Depiction

Portrait description in literary works occupies an extremely important position. The author often uses all sorts of rhetorical tactics to impress us. Portrait depiction is an essential element in character depiction. Successful portrait depiction gives reader a direct impression. A good translator can make the translation more adequate and the content more understandable with appropriate words and implements. A good portrait of the character can be very impressive and lay a good foundation for the development of the character. The following example will show the way of portrait depiction and version of translation.

《傲慢与偏见》

Mr. Darcy soon drew the attention of the room by his fine, tall person, handsome features, noble men; and the report which was in general circulation within five minutes after his entrance, of his having ten thousand pounds a year. . . He was looked at with great admiration for about half the evening, till his manners gave a disgust which turned the tide of his popularity; for he was discovered to be proud, to be above his company, and above being pleased; and not all his large estate in Derbyshire could then save him from having a most forbidding, disagreeable countenance, and being unworthy to be compared with his friend.

达西却立即引起了全场的注意,因为他身材魁梧,眉清目秀,举止高贵,于是他进场不到五分钟,大家都纷纷传说他每年有一万镑收入……人们差不多有半个晚上都带着爱慕的目光看着他,最后人们才发现他为人骄傲,看不起人,巴结不上他,因此对他起了厌恶的感觉,他那众望所归的极盛一时的场面才黯然失色。他既然摆起那么一副惹人厌的面貌,那么,不管他在德比郡有多大的财产,也挽救不了他,况且和他的朋友比起来,他更没有什么大不了。

Here Jane Austen, in a satirical tone, tells of how the neighborhood swiftly change from admiration to disgust towards this wealthy but proud hero of the novel.

在《傲慢与偏见》(***Pride and Prejudice***)中,主人公达西的出现引发了人们的注意,译文用了三个四字短语描述了他的个人魅力"身材魁梧,眉清目秀,举止高贵",但是因为他"为人骄傲,看不起人,巴结不上他"而情况急转直下。寥寥数语为人物性格发展作了铺垫。从"爱慕"到"惹人厌",这样的人物形象极富喜剧张力,译文中将此种转变忠实地传递出来,完成了对人物的刻画。

《爱玛》

Emma Woodhouse, handsome, clever and rich, with a comfortable home and happy disposition seemed to unite some of the best blessings of existence; and had lived nearly twenty-one years in the world with very little to distress or vex her.

爱玛·伍德豪斯简直是一个得天独厚的人,又美丽,又聪明,又有钱,不但在家里生活舒适,而且性格开朗。她快满二十一岁了,一直过着无忧无虑的生活。

张经浩先生翻译的《爱玛》使一个"handsome, clever , rich"的少女形象跃然纸上。Although the original sentence of English is a long one, by carefully choosing words and skillfully arranging the structure, the Chinese version reproduced the style and meaning of the original.

《飘》

下面是《飘》的作者对女主角美丽容貌的经典描写,显然傅东华先生的译本更胜一筹。其译文优美流畅,惟妙惟肖地刻画出了郝思嘉的美貌。第一句将"face"、"chin" 和"jaw" 都译成了儿化词语"脸蛋儿"、"下巴颏儿"、"牙床骨儿",这些儿化音很带有女孩子的娇态。而"pointed of chin, square of jaw"译为"下巴颏儿尖尖的,牙床骨儿方方的",不但做到了和原文一样的对仗工整,而且还因为儿化词与叠音词"尖尖"、"方方" 的结合使用,使译文另外透出一种精致的韵味美。第二句通过几个"一味、一丝儿、一圈儿",使译文读起来特别生动,并且琅琅上口。而三个动词词组"竖着、斜竖着、划出" 用得生动贴切,把原文 "star, slant, cut" 的形象传神准确地移植了过来,让一个有着绿色眼睛和姣好容貌的女子跃然纸上。

e. g.

But it was an arresting face, pointed of chin, square of jaw. Her eyes were pale green without a touch of hazel, starred with bristly black lashes and slightly tilted at the ends. Above them, her thick black brows slanted upward, cutting a startling oblique line in her magnolia-white skin.

【傅东华译】

她那一张脸蛋儿却实在迷人得很,下巴颏儿尖尖的,牙床骨儿方方的。她的眼珠儿是一味的淡绿色,不杂一丝儿茶褐,周围竖着一圈儿粗黑的睫毛,眼角微微有点翘,上面斜竖着两撇墨黑的蛾眉,在她那木兰花一般白的皮肤上,划出两条异常惹眼的斜线。

【戴侃等译】

不过这张脸,连同那尖尖的下巴和四四方方的牙床骨,是很引人注意的。她那双淡绿色的眼睛纯净得不带一丝褐色,配上刚硬乌黑的睫毛和稍稍翘起的眼角,显得别具风韵。

3.3 Translation of Writing Style of the Author

Hemingway

Hemingway's writing style owes much to his career as a journalist. His use of language is different from others. Short words, straightforward sentence structures, vivid descriptions and factual details are combined to create an almost transparent medium for his engaging and realistic stories, which is showed in his representative work of ***The Old Man and the Sea.***

The boy went out. They had eaten with no light on the table and the old man took off his trousers and went to bed in the dark. He rolled his trousers up to make a pillow, putting the newspaper inside them. He rolled himself in the blanket and slept on the other old newspapers that covered the springs of the bed.

He was asleep in a short time and he dreamed of Africa when he was a boy and the long golden beaches and the white beaches, so white they hurt your eyes, and the high capes and the great brown mountains. He lived along that coast now every night and in his dreams he heard the surf roar and saw the native boats come riding through it. He smelled the tar and oakum of the deck as he slept and he smelled the smell of Africa that the land breeze brought at morning.

【译文】

孩子去了。他俩吃饭的时候,桌上连个灯都没有点,孩子走开以后,老头儿脱掉裤子,人摸黑上了床。他把裤子卷成枕头,把那些报纸塞在里面,然后用军毯裹住身子,睡在破床弹簧垫上面的一些旧报纸上。

他不一会就睡去,梦见了孩提时见到的非洲,迤长的金色海滩和白色刺眼的海滩,高耸的海岬和褐色的大山。现在,他每晚住在那海边。在梦中听到海潮的怒号,看见本地的小船从海潮中穿梭来去。睡着的时候,他闻到甲板上柏油和填絮的味道,闻到了地面上的风在早晨送来的非洲气息。

海观的译文充分体现了作者的文风,译文多用短句,简洁明快,遣词造句朴实无华。

Mark Twain

Mark Twain's use of sarcasm is his central characteristic; another literary trick of Twain's is his use of slang and regional dialect rather than the use of flowery language: Twain often wrote the way that people spoke. He lived in a repressive Christian culture with Puritan roots; therefore, it is easy to see how Twain's no-holds-barred style of writing could offend people. What the greatest work can do is to influence people and help create social change.

下文选自马克吐·温的《百万英镑》,译文采用口语化的语言,轻松诙谐幽默。

"Let me just stand here a little and look my fill. Dear me! It's a palace—it's just a palace! And in it everything a body could desire, including cozy coal fire and supper standing ready. Henry, it doesn't merely make me realize how rich you are; it makes me realize, to the bone, to the marrow, how poor I am—how poor I am, and how miserable, how defeated, routed, annihilated!"

让我在这儿站一会吧,我要看个够,好家伙!简直是个皇宫——地道的皇宫!这里面一个人所能希望得到的,真是应有尽有,包括惬意的炉火,还有现成的晚饭。亨利,这不仅叫我明白你有多么阔气;还叫我深入骨髓地看到我自己穷到了什么地步——我多么穷,多么倒霉,多么泄气,多么走投无路,真是一败涂地!

钱钟书

《围城》(***Fortress Besieged***) is a representative of the scholar's novel, which is filled with humor, satire and metaphors. It is noticed that the unique elements in this book are especially metaphors. According to some scholars, there are nearly seven hundred metaphors in the whole book. Ch'ien Chung-shu regards metaphor as "main feature of literary language", and he is skillful at linking two seemingly non-related things together to achieve wonderful unexpected effect. Besides, satire is widely used in this book. A lot of ironic descriptions towards social phenomenon and the fickleness of the world can be found. The metaphors, vivid and fancy, give a lot of discussion on translation work. For example:

鸿渐恼道:"说得好漂亮!为什么当初我告诉了你韩学愈薪水比你高一级,你要气得掼纱帽不干呢?"

"Oh, doesn't that just sound beautiful?" said Hungchien crossly, "When I first told you Han Hsueh-yus' salary was a grade higher than yours, why did you get so mad that you wanted to throw away your cone-shaped hat?"

Jane Austen

Pride and Prejudice is one of the greatest and most brilliant English novels in the 18th century. It portrays a vivid picture of middle class in regency England under the author's sharp perception of its snobberies and absurdities. The technique Austen often used to make humorous effect is the employment of irony and satire, which is often used to highlight the faults and ridiculous features of the characters. To help the target readers perceive the humor of the author and get the similar amusement, translators should have their own strategies.

Playfulness and epigrammatism hit off the character of the narrative style of ***Pride and Prejudice***, which give birth to ironies. Moreover, the structure and style of Jane Austen's writing are neat and ordered with an inherent feeling for rhythm and balance. One can experience the rhythm underneath the surface of language, such as the dialogue between Mr. Bennet and his wife, with the clarity of a musical chord contrasting with the muddle of their conversation. It is vital for the translator to reproduce this stylistic feature in her work.

4. Change of Translation Strategies

Language change, including change of sound, vocabulary and grammar, produces all kinds of language varieties, which includes diachronic variety and synchronic variety. The use of domestication and foreignization has been a disputed problem in translation researches. At the very beginning of Chinese translation history, the techniques of domestication were the main stream in translation activities. With the change of time, foreignization, represented by Lu Xun, took the lead in translation activities in China. Literature translation in this period paid more attention to the fluency and smoothness of target texts than the transformation of the forms of original texts.

4.1 On Name and Place Translation

The choice of domestication and foreignization is showed on name translation of different versions of ***Gone with the Wind***. 傅东华 nearly domesticated all the names of person and places appearing in the novel so as to ease the reading. In addition, Fu also borrowed certain suffix words denoting the places in Chinese.

On Name Translation (傅东华, 戴侃)

Original Text	傅东华	戴侃
Scarllet O' Hara	郝思嘉	思嘉·奥哈拉
Rhett Butler	白瑞德	瑞德·巴特勒
Ashley Wilkes	卫希礼	艾希里·威尔克斯
Malenia Hamilton	韩媚兰	媚兰·汉密尔顿
Dicey	蝶姐	艾尔西
Port	阿宝	吉姆斯
Georgia	肇佳州	佐治亚
Altanta	饿狼陀	亚特兰大
Virginia	佛金泥	佛吉尼亚
Charleston	曹氏屯	查尔斯顿

4.2 On Sentence Level—Historical Consciousness

e.g.

His sisters were very anxious for his having an estate of his own; but though he was now established only as a tenant, Miss Bingley was by no means unwilling to preside at his table; nor was Mrs. Hurst, who had married a man of more fashion than fortune, less disposed to consider his house as her home when it suited her.

——*Pride and Prejudice*

【王科一译】他的姐妹们倒反而替他着急,希望他早些购置产业;不过,尽管他现在仅仅是以一个租户的身份在这儿住下来,彬格莱小姐还是非常愿意替他掌管家务,再说那位嫁了个穷措大的赫斯脱太太，每逢上弟弟这儿来作客，依旧像是到了自己家里一样。

【孙致礼译】他的两个姐妹都热切希望他能有一份自己的房地产。不过，尽管他现在仅仅是以房客的身份在这里住了下来，但宾利小姐还很愿意替他掌管家务，而那位赫斯特夫人嫁了个家财不足、派头有余的绅士。因而一旦得便，也很情愿把弟弟的家当作自己的家。

Here, Sun's translation "家财不足、派头有余" is symmetrical, and preserved the flavor of the original. Wang translated it into"穷措大", which is a typical Chinese word to describe the poor scholars. And for the word "estate", Wang and Sun's translations are"产业"and"房地产" respectively. In the 1950s, many Chinese knew little or nothing about western culture; and among the readers, there was resistance against the western culture for a time. Hence, many translators adopted domestication to meet readers' demands.

However, in the 1990s, after China's reform and opening-up, Chinese readers began to understand and accept the new things in foreign literature. "房地产"was a so popular word that nearly everyone knew it. Both"穷措大"and"房地产" are the representative words of the times. Just as what we talked about in Chapter Two, the act of understanding is historical, hence the interpreter must understand and interpret the text with historical consciousness.

e. g.

Scarlett O'Hara was not beautiful, but men seldom realized it when caught by her charm as the Tarleton twins were. ——*Gone with the Wind*

傅东华译：那郝思嘉小姐长得并不美，可是极富于魅力，男人见了她，往往要着迷，就像汤家那一对双胞胎兄弟似的。

陈良廷译：斯嘉丽·奥哈拉长得并不美，但是男人一旦像塔尔顿家孪生兄弟那样给她的魅力迷住就不大会理会这点。

就具体的译法而言，傅东华的译文中大量的归化手法使译文的可读性大大增加。

You are well enough, I see. Then, tell me this. Was I the only iron you had in the fire? His eyes were keen and alert watching every change in her face.

——*Gone with the Wind*

傅东华译我看是可以的了。那么，请你告诉我一句话，你所要钓的鱼儿是不是只有我一条？他一面问，一面尖着眼睛，注意观察着她脸上的变化。

戴侃译：我看你是完全好了。那么，请你告诉我，我是你火中惟一的一块铁吗？他的眼光犀利而警觉，审视着她脸上的每一丝变化。

傅东华把 iron you had in the fire（火中的一块铁）译成要钓的鱼儿，很形象很幽默。以归化为主的口语化翻译是傅译显著的特征，同时贯穿整个译本的幽默化语言又是傅译本的另一大特色。而戴侃照搬原文译为"火中惟一的一块铁"。

第八章综合练习

1）

我可能是天津人

（侯宝林）

还是从火车上说起吧！大约在我四岁多的时候，我坐过火车。当时带我坐车的人，是我的舅舅，叫张全斌。我记得那时我的打扮挺滑稽的，穿着蓝布大褂、小坎肩，戴瓜皮小帽。那时候，小孩子打扮成那个样子，够不错了。在我的童年中，也就只有过这么一次。在火车上，因为小，没坐过火车，也很少见过家里以外的人，觉得挺新鲜。也许人在幼年时代终归想要些温暖吧！那时舅舅抱着我，哄着我，我觉得很温暖。一路上吃了半斤炒栗子，睡了一会儿觉，就到了北京。

根据这个情况，现在估计起来，我可能是从天津来的。我现在对我原来的父母还有个模糊不清的印象，父亲、母亲的形象还能回忆起一点儿，但很模糊。究竟家里姓什么？哪里人？不知道。我只知道自己的生日和乳名。生日是自己长大以后听家里大人说的，是农历十月十五酉时生人。所以我的乳名叫“酉”，北京人爱用儿化韵，前面加个小，后面加“儿”，就叫“小酉儿”。关于我个人的历史情况，我就知道这一些，再多一点都记不起来了。

2）I love my love with an E, because she's enticing; I hate her with an E, because she's engaged; I took her to the sign of the exquisite, and treated her with an elopement; her name's Emily, and she lives in the east. ——*David Copperfield*

3）She was quite a child—perhaps seven or eight years old—slightly built, with a pale, small-pictured face, and a redundancy of hair falling in curls to her waist. (*Wuthering Heights*)

4）以后飞机接连光顾，大有绝世佳人一顾倾城、再顾倾国的风度。（《围城》）

5）吃的是西菜。“海军大将”信基督教，坐下以前，还向天花板眨白眼，感谢上帝赏饭。（《围城》）

6）Miss Ophelia, as you now behold her, stands before you, in a very shining brown linen travelling-dress, tall, square-formed, and angular. Her face was thin, and rather sharp in its outlines; the lips compressed, like those of a person who is in the habit of making up her mind definitely on all subjects; while the keen, dark eyes had a particularly searching, advised movement, and travelled over everything, as if they were looking for something to take care of. (*Uncle Tom's Cabin*)

7）咱俩的事，一条绳子拴着两只蚂蚱——谁也跑不了！（《骆驼祥子》）

8）阿 Q 又很自尊，所有未庄的居民，全不在他眼睛里。（《阿 Q 正传》）

9）It is a truth universally acknowledged that a single man in possession of a good fortune must be in want of a wife. (*Pride and Prejudice*)

10) "An unhappy alternative is before you, Elizabeth. From this day you must be a stranger to one of your parents. Your mother will never see you again if you do not marry Mr. Collins, and I will never see you again if you do." (*Pride and Prejudice*)

Chapter Nine
Translation of Literary writing—Poetry
诗歌翻译

Lawence Venuti（韦努蒂）

Lawence Venuti（1953—），an Italian-American translation theorist，has published several important books，among which *The Translator's Invisibility*：*A History of Translators* has established his position as an influential translation theorist. He constructively put forward the resistant foreignizing translation strategy，aiming to "force the translators and their readers to reflect on the ethnocentric violence of translation and hence to write and read translated texts in ways that seek to recognize the linguistic and cultural difference of foreign texts". Different from the traditional criterion，which regards "fluent" as the most important feature of a good translation，Venuti switches attention to reserving differences so as to preserve the exotic feature.

关键词：韦努蒂；阻抗式翻译；异化；民族中心

Prose is words in the best order；
Poetry is the best words in the best order.

——Coleridge

散文是井然有序的文字，
诗是井然有序的绝妙好词。

——柯尔律治

1. Introduction to Poetry Translation

诗是一种最集中地反映社会生活的文学样式，它饱含着丰富的想象和感情，常常以直接抒情的方式来表现，而且在精炼与和谐的程度上，特别是在节奏的鲜明上，它的语言有别于散文的语言。

——何其芳

诗歌的特点

第一，高度集中、概括地反映生活（a full reflection of life）。

第二，抒情言志，饱含丰富的思想感情（outflow of strong emotion）。

第三,丰富的想象、联想和幻想（imagination and fancy）。

第四,语言具有音乐美（musical beauty）。

As one of the literary forms, poetry is regarded as the crystallization of artistic expressions. Its translation has been a topic of common concern in the field of translation studies. The translatability of poems has also been a controversial issue. Some think that poems are translatable while others do not. Among those who advocate the translatability of poems, there are still disputes about which is the better way, to render them in the form of free verse or to put them in that of classical poetic composition.

2. *Linguistic Features of English Poetry*

Unlike Chinese poetry, English poetry differs to a great degree from Chinese one, not only in language features, but also in form, style and image, especially in grammatical rules.

The first aspect of poetry is sound pattern. This includes rhyme, alliteration, assonance, reverse rhyme and consonant patterning. These are features of language which poets employ to create effects such as beauty or emphasis in their writing.

The second aspect of poetry we will consider is the stress patterns of spoken English. These are used in poetry to create rhythmical effects, and some of the conventional arrangements of rhythm (also called meter) and rhyme will be illustrated.

The language of poetry is musical. The musical poetic language lies in that it has not only strong rhythm but also melodious and graceful rhyme, which makes it distinctive from prose.

2.1 The Rhyme

Rhyme is the repetition of the same or similar sounds often occurring at set intervals. There are generally two kinds of rhymes: internal rhyme and end rhyme.

押韵是诗体与其他文体的最大区别之一。押韵是语流中相同音素的重复和组合所造成的共鸣和呼应。英诗常用的韵有:头韵(alliteration);谐元音/腹韵(assonance),即词中重读元音的重复;尾韵(rhyme),即词尾相同音素的重复。诗歌除了音韵美外,其有规律的轻重抑扬变化连同韵式的变化,一同构成了诗的节奏美。

英语格律诗分为诗节(stanza),诗节又分为诗行,每一诗行又分为几个音步(foot)。音步是由一个重读音节和一个或数个非重读音节有规律地排列构成,常见的有抑扬格五音步,扬抑格四音步,抑扬格七音步以及扬抑抑格两音步、抑抑扬格三音步等。无韵诗(blank verse)虽然不讲究押韵,但传统的无韵诗仍十分讲究节奏,一般是以抑扬格五音步为一行,如莎士比亚的诗剧。至于当代诗人写的一些无韵自由诗(free verse)则完全不受韵式和音步的限制,完全听凭思想的自然流露和语言自然节奏的流动。

2.1.1 Internal Rhyme

Internal rhyme is the repetition of the same or similar sounds occurring within a line. It takes the following forms.

Alliteration: the repetition of an initial sound of two or more words within a line

e.g.

fire-folk, and bloody blameful blade

Assonance: the repetition of same or similar vowels within a line

e.g.

Though wise men at their end know dark is right

Consonance: the repetition of the same ending consonants of two or more words within a line

e.g.

At once a voice arose among (the bleak twigs overhead)

Reverse Rhyme: the repetition of the initial arises containing the same consonants and vowels of two or more words within a line

e.g.

A boy's will is the wind's will

Para Rhyme: the repetition of the initial and ending consonants of two or more words within a line

e.g.

Your looks were like the raven

2.1.2 End Rhyme

End rhyme refers to the repetition of the same or similar sounds of the ending words of lines occurring between or among lines. End rhyme can be classified into perfect rhyme and imperfect rhyme (or half rhyme).

Perfect rhyme occurs when the initial consonants change, but succeeding vowels and consonants remain the same. Such rhyming tends to produce a pronounced or emphatic effect, as in Byron's *Don Juan*:

The Senior Don Alfonso stood confused;
Antonia bustled round the ransacked room,
And turning up her nose, with looks abused
Her master, and his myrmidons, of whom
Not one, except the attorney, was amused

Half rhyme or imperfect rhyme occurs when there are changes within the vowel sounds of words which mean to rhyme. It occurs when the two or more rhymed words have the same stressed vowels but different consonants coming before and after the vowels, such as *fern-bird*, *faze-late*, *and like-right*.

2.1.3 Rhyming Scheme

There are three sorts of rhyme schemes in general: running rhyme, alternating rhyme and enclosing rhyme.

Running rhyme means that the neighboring two lines of a stanza or a poem are rhymed. The scheme is as bb cc. For instance:

Tiger! Tiger! burning bright (*a*)
In the forests of the night, (*a*)
What immortal hand or eye (*b*)
Could frame thy fearful symmetry? (*b*)
In what distant deeps or skies (*c*)
Burnt the fire of throe eyes? (*c*)
On what wings dare he aspire? (*d*)
What the hand dare seize the fire? (*d*)

Alternating rhyme scheme, the interlacing rhyme, refers to a rhyme going every other line, which can be ordered as ab ab.

In a four-line stanza, the first line rhymes with the fourth line; the second with the third line, which is called enclosing rhyme scheme. The scheme is ab ba.

2.2 Meter

When we speak of the rhythm of a poem, we mean the recurrence of stresses and pauses in it, or the pattern of stressed and unstressed syllables. It is possible to be aware of rhythms in poems read silently, too. The rhythm of English poetry comes from its meter and foot; and foot is the basic unit of meter.

A poem often consists of certain lines and each line is composed of several feet. Foot is a regular arrangement of certain arsis and theses. The way feet are arranged forms the meter of English poetry. According to the different ways arsis and theses are arranged in each foot, there are four kinds of meter (foot patterns).

2.2.1 Iambus: the Iambic Foot

Iambus refers to the combination of a thesis and an arsis in one foot.

She walks/in beau/ty, like/the night
Of cloud/less climes/and star/ry skies;

2.2.2 Trochee: the Trochaic Foot

Trochee refers to the combination of an arsis and a thesis in one foot.

Men of/England,/Wherefore/plough
For the/Lords who/lay yel/low?

2.2.3 Dactyl: the Dactylic Foot

Dactyl contains an arsis and two theses in one foot.

Cannon to/right of them,
Cannon to/ left of them.
Cannon in/front of them
Volley'd and/thunder'd

2.2.4 Anapest: the Anapestic Foot

Anapest consists of two theses and one arsis in one foot.

For the moon/never beams/without bringing me dreams

According to the numbers of metrical foot or scansion, there are eight meters:

1) monometer(one foot a line)
2) dimeter (two feet a line)
3) trimeter(three feet a line)
4) tetrameter (four feet a line)
5) pentameter (five feet a line)
6) hexameter(six feet a line)
7) heptameter(seven feet a line)
8) octometer(eight feet a line)

3. *Translation of Poetry*

Poems call for beauty in form, sound and meaning. A translator of them should not be satisfied with the mere conveying of artistic conception and style in the original, but must strive for the reproduction of the original beauty. To achieve this, he ought to, first of all, retain the original meaning and artistic conception and secondly, do his best to make his translation bear a certain due form, rhythm, and rhyme when necessary. Owing to the differences in the characteristics of various languages, it is both impossible and unnecessary for the translator to render the original poems word for word. The translator is allowed to make up the loss in the meaning of some foregoing or following words somewhere within the whole poem.

3.1 On Translatability and Untranslatability of Poetry

Chinese is tonal language, while English is syllabic language. Classical Chinese poems have fixed pattern of prosody, which makes them beautiful in sound just like music, while it is also difficult in translating. The variation of the four tones (level, rising, entering and falling) constitutes the modulation in pitch which plays a very important role in Chinese versification. By contrast, the musicality of English poetry is based upon a fixed arrangement of stressed and unstressed syllables.

Liu Zhongde, among many other scholars, believes that it is possible, though quite difficult, to translate poems satisfactorily and successfully. He gives two reasons for his argument. First of all, there exist many things in common among men. For instance, they all have the thinking powers to reason logically and the feelings to express joy or sorrow, love or hatred, and possess the same nature, world and universe no matter what races they may be. In other words, all human beings are endowed by nature with the same mind which has the same function so that they can commune with one another. As a consequence, poetry, a product of the mind, is understandable, enjoyable and translatable. And secondly, the fact that large quantities of poems have been translated between many language pairs also proves the translatability of poems.

The translation work of Xu Yuanchong is a good representation of the standard of "three beauty", which is really a demonstration of translatability.

春晓

(孟浩然)

春眠不觉晓,处处闻啼鸟。
夜来风雨声,花落知多少。

A Spring Morning

This morn of spring in bed I'm lying,
Not wake up till I hear birds crying.
After one night of wind and showers,
How many are the fallen flowers!

(许渊冲译)

Beauty in Sense: Xu's version is basic in consistence with the original meaning in general, especially the last sentence "How many are the fallen flowers!", which not only shows the poet's regretful and sorrowful feeling, but also shows the hazy beauty in sense of the original poem.

Beauty in Form : metrical verse (格律诗) replaces the original five-character quatrains(五言绝句), and the stich (诗行) is characterized by the same length, antithesis neat, rhyming couplets, forming a shape of rectangle.

Beauty in Sound: in Xu's translation, the beauty in sound is well dealt with. The rhyme is also well kept. The end rhyme of his translation is AABB, "lying" and "crying", "shower" and "flower", almost in accordance with the original end rhyme, "晓", "鸟", "少". Thus Xu Yuanchong's version remains close to the original beautiful sound.

3.2 Reproduction of Original Sound in Poems

3.2.1 Rhythm and End Rhyme

It is said that sound is the heartbeat of the poem. Poetry is music in words and music in sound. Sound beauty can be viewed from rhythm, rhyme and other metrical devices. Reading a good poem is like enjoying a sweet melody with the echo and rhyme, the ups and downs of the rhythm lingering forever. Because the rhyme scheme of Chinese poetry is very similar to that of English poetry in principle, Xu Yuanchong follows the common practice to substitute "feet" for "顿" and uses heroic couplets and Alexandrines to replace the five character and seven-character lines. In the following example, Xu successfully represents the beauty in rhythm and end rhyme by applying corresponding metrical patterns in the English poetry. Look at the following example, the original is a seven-syllabic quatrain. It is found that Xu's version is a highly regular iambic hexameter. The six feet replace the original four pauses in each line and the iambic pattern reflects the alternation of level and deflected tones. The original simple rhyme scheme is turned into *aabb* rhyme scheme. Different in sound values and forms, the English version is faithfully in musicality.

庐山仙人洞(七绝)

(毛泽东)

暮色苍茫看劲松,
乱云飞渡仍从容。
天生一个仙人洞,
无限风光在险峰。

The Immortal's Cave

A sturdy pine, as viewed in twilight dim and low,
Remains at ease while riotous clouds come and go.
The Fairy Cave's a wonder wrought by Nature's hand,

The view from perilous peak is sublime and grand.

（许渊冲译）

Switch of Rhyme（换韵脚）

Love

She wept with pity and delight,
She blush'd with love and virgin shame;
And, like the murmur of a dream,
I heard her breathe my name.

爱

情窦初开羞答答，怜爱欣喜落泪花；
犹如梦呓低声语，红云满面呼唤他。

原诗2、4行押韵，shame和dream押尾韵和辅音韵/m/，给人以节奏感；译诗1、2、4行押/a/韵，同样读来朗朗上口，节奏鲜明。韵脚换了，方式不同，却异曲同工。

Reorder the Verse（调换语序）

Dull is My Verse

Dull is my verse: not ever thou
Who movest many cares away
From this lone breast and weary brow,
Canst make, as once, its fountain lay;
No, nor those gentle words that now
Support my heart to hear thee say:
"The bird upon its lonely bough
Sings sweetest at the close of day."

我的诗句变得无聊

我的诗句变得无聊，
我的文辞多么单调；
你曾一次次慰藉我胸中的孤独，
你曾一回回抚平我额头的烦恼；
可你无法让我才思的清泉重新喷涌，
可你不能使我灵感的火花再次闪耀；
不，尽管你用温柔的话语把我激励，
我的信心已经瓦解冰消：
"枝头的小鸟虽然孤独，
黄昏的歌唱最为美妙。"

原文为英国诗人瓦尔特·萨维奇·兰德(Walter Savage Landor 1775—1864)的诗文,字字哀叹,句句自怜。可以看出译文的句式有一定的变化规律。特别是原诗的7、8两行,属于典型的欧式句型;而译作中对应的9、10行是典型的汉语句式,而且译诗韵脚也有转化。

Rearrange the Lines (诗行调整)

Parting at Morning

Round the cape of a sudden came the sea,
And the sun look'd over the mountain's rim:
And straight was a path of gold for him,
And the need of a world of men for me.

晨别

送君过岬角,浪海扑面涌;
太阳偷眼看,山顶红彤彤。
君有阳光道,笔直一线通;
我有小天地,心系情爱中。

译文把原诗的四句译为八句,而译文采用偶句押韵,读来朗朗上口,富有很强的节奏感。

3.2.2 Translation of Reduplicated Words in Classical Chinese Poetry

Reduplicated words are a figure of speech. It is an active rhetorical device, according to Cheng Wangdao, the father of modern Chinese rhetorician. By using this figure of speech properly, literature works may seem more impressive and rhythmic. Reduplicated words have more force of expression than plain words and could strongly emphasize the subject of literature. Their description of objects is more artistic and visual. Dong Jitang from Taiwan also thinks high of reduplicated words. He once remarks in his *Rhetoric Analysis and Discussion* that reduplicated words can greatly increase the vigor of an article when used in narration. A feeling of continuity is given when reduplicated words are used to express emotion. Look at the following example:

青青河畔草,	Green, green riverside grass she sees,
郁郁园中柳。	Lush, lush the garden's willow trees.
盈盈楼上女,	Fair, fair, she waits in painted bower,
皎皎当窗牖。	Bright, bright like a window-framed flower.

娥娥红粉妆， In rosy, rosy dress she stands,
纤纤出素手。 She puts forth slender, slender hands.

（汪溶培译）

In the original poem, the six pairs of reduplicated words have made the whole poem full of musicality and harmony. At the same time, the simple and short reduplicated words act as the pen to draw a lifelike picture of beautiful scenery and the charming young lady; "Qingqing" depicts the green grass; "yuyu" paints the thick willows in the garden; "yingying", "ee" and "qianqian" portray a beautiful and slender young lady; "jiaojiao" describes the clear and bright moon light across the window. It is surely that the reduplicated words make the whole poem achieve the three beauties: beauty in sound, beauty in form and beauty in sense. In order to keep the style of the original, Professor Wang Rongpei adopts the iteration for the reduplicated words.

3.2.3 Translation of Onomatopoeia

English onomatopoeia or imitative words are created by imitating sounds of humans, animals, natural phenomena and other things. As a very useful figure of speech, it cannot only imitate or echo the natural sounds, but also can portray people and depict scenery, stir imagination and arouse interest of the reader.

Elegy Written in a Country Church-Yard

Thomas Gray

The breezy call of incense-breathing morn,
The swallow twittering from the straw-built shed,
The cock's shrill clarion, or the echoing horn,
No more shall rouse them from their lowly bed.

墓园挽歌

（托马斯·格雷）

香气四溢的晨风轻松的呼召，
燕子从茅草棚子里吐出的呢喃，
公鸡的尖喇叭，使山鸣谷应的猎号，
再不能唤醒他们在地下的长眠。

（卞之琳）

In this translation, "twittering" is converted from a verb into a noun, because "no more" in the last sentence means no more "call, twittering, clarion and horn". In order to be accordant with other words, the translator puts all of them into nouns, together with "twittering".

3.3　Translation of Poetic Image

Image is the soul of poetry. Poets use images to make their meaning strong and vocative, but the image transmission is the greatest barrier to the translation of poems.

An image could be a verbal picture of a concrete object, a behavior and idea, or a specific sensation. "Image" (象) is the load of "meaning" (意), therefore, "reflecting through image" and "expressing through image" are affirmation and belief of Chinese classic language philosophy, especially poetics. English, however, has an evident character of "expressing through language", so there must be problems with image transference.

Images, in accordance with the five senses of man, could be classified into several groups as visual images, auditory images, tactile images and gustatory images. Usually one image could stimulate several different sensory perceptions of the reader at the same time. For instance, flowers touch reader's smelling and visual nerves. Birds arouse man's auditory and tactile sensibilities.

Ezra Pound (1885—1972), the famous American poets, poem critic and vanguard of imagism, said that "'an image' is that which presents an intellectual and emotional complex in an instant of time." Pound and other imagists laid down three imagist poetic principles: to treat things directly whether subjective or objective; to use absolutely no word that does not contribute to the presentation; to compose in sequence of musical phrase, not in sequence of a metronome as regarding rhythm.

In *Tune of Tian Jing Sha: Autumn Thoughts* twelve images can be classified into groups in accordance with word-formation: all these images are pure and real objects in nature.

天净沙·秋思

（马致远）

枯藤老树昏鸦，
小桥流水人家，
古道西风瘦马，
夕阳西下，
断肠人在天涯。

Word-formation	Images in the poem
Modifier + noun	（枯）藤；（老）树；（昏）鸦， （小）桥；（流）水；（人）家， （古）道；（西）风；（瘦）马， （断肠）人
noun	人家;夕阳;天涯

元朝马致远的《天净沙·秋思》精妙绝伦地描绘出了秋郊黄昏之景以羁旅之愁，是负有盛名的情景交融的佳作：一幅苍茫肃杀的深秋夕照图，作者使用了一组有形的、可感的、灰色基调的意象群，用纯白描手法勾勒出一幅生动的生活图景，意境优美，各意象之间的方位和逻辑关系在原诗中没有明示。

Version 1

Tune: Sunny Sand
Autumn Thoughts
Over old trees wreathed with rotten vines fly crows;
Under a small bridge beside a cot a stream flows;
On ancient road in western breeze a lean horse goes,
Westwards declines the setting sun.
Far, far from home is the heart-broken one.

（许渊冲译）

Version 2

Autumn Thoughts
To the Tune of Tianjingsha
Withered wines, old trees, crows at dusk,
a small bridge over the flowing water, a few houses,
an ancient path, the west wind,
a lean horse, and sun setting...
A heart-broken traveler at the end of the world.

（裘小龙译）

Version 3

Autumn

Crows hovering over rugged trees wreathed with rotten vine—the day is about done. Younger is a tiny bridge over a sparkling stream, and on the fair bank, a pretty little village. But the traveler has to go on down this ancient road, the west wind moaning, his bony horse groaning, trudging towards the sinking sun, farther and farther away from home.

(翁显良译)

In the first version, the translator creates prepositional and verbal words to connect the images, such as "over, with, under, besides, on, in" and verbs like "wreath, fly, flow, go", in which the original poem are drowned in a bunch of connective words. The following versions adopt a similar way in image transference. They directly translate images with the fewest rhetoric words; meanwhile, nouns stand separately and naturally in connecting themselves. It seems that translators try to maintain the concise imagery of the source text and conform to the principle of "directness" of Imagism.

Image Substitution

Sometimes the translator has to find another image which conveys a similar meaning and produces a similar effect on the target reader as the original image does in the source language. The following example is quoted from *Ancient Wind* by Li Bai (李白《古风》):

七十紫鸳鸯,双双戏庭幽。

Seventy purple ducks and drakes,
Pair by pair, play in the dark of the court.

(叶维廉译)

鸳鸯 (an Asian duck, or mandarin duck) is the kind of bird symbolizing merry couples in Chinese, but it is unavailable to find an exact equivalent in English. To retain the graphic vividness of the original image, the translator flexibly exploits "ducks and drakes" to go with its counterparts, namely the merry-making couple of mandarin ducks. Though the mood of original text is not fully reproduced, the compensation is made for the meaning which may otherwise be lost due to the zero equivalent of the image.

Loss of Image

Sometimes the translator sacrifices images to sound, in other words, the representation of rhyme and rhythm is at the expense of images. For example, "江山如此多娇,引无数英雄竞折腰" is put into "our land has such a charming show, that countless heroes love it so". The rhyme is achieved by "show" and "so" but the image "折腰" is sacrificed.

何满子

（张祜）

故国三千里，
深宫二十年，
一声何满子，
双泪落君前。
Home-sick a thousand miles away,
Shut in the palace twenty years.
Singing the dying swan's sweet lay,
Oh! How can she hold back her tears.

（许渊冲）

该译文基本表达了原诗的含义，但是，"何满子"是中国唐代的歌曲，而"天鹅的绝唱"却是西方文化中的典故，以"天鹅的绝唱"译"何满子"，虽然容易被英语语言使用者所理解，却使原诗作品中包含的生活画面失去了历史和民族色彩。

3.5 Translation on Numbers of Hyperbole

飞流直下三千尺，疑是银河落九天。
Its torrent dashes down three thousand feet from high,
As if the Silver River fell from the blue sky.
千山鸟飞绝，万径人踪灭。
A hundred mountains and no birds,
A thousand paths without a footprint.
布被秋宵梦觉，眼前万里江山。
I woke up in thin quilt on autumn night,
The boundless land I dreamed of still remains in sight.

4. Case Study

The following English versions of the Tang four-lined poems will be discussed to verify the difficulty of translating poems.

赠别

（杜牧）

多情却似总无情，
唯觉尊前笑不成。
蜡烛有心还惜别，
替人垂泪到天明。

Parting

How can a deep love seem a deep love,
How can it smile, at a farewell feast?
Even the candle, feeling our sadness,
Weeps, as we do, all night long.

(Bynner)

In the original, it is the candle that weeps for the heroine, but in the English version the expression "as we do" means that the candle weeps just as the parting couple. Thus what is expressed in the translation is not so delicate as in the Chinese. The translator may think since the couple can't smile at the farewell feast, naturally they have no choice but to shed tears. What does their tear-shedding signify? No doubt, it is a sign of the outburst of deep love. This constitutes a contradiction in the context of the translation. In fact, the girl parting is neither in a position to put on a smile on her face, nor does she know how to express her deep love in a smile. She is merely able to look dejected in absolute silence.

在追求形似上,我们认为,王佐良先生提倡的以诗译诗是完全正确的,诗歌毕竟不是散文。因此,原诗如果有韵,那么译诗也应尽量沿用;原诗如果无韵,译诗也应无韵,即使用韵,也不能太过整齐,只应在个别诗句中用韵。原诗的节奏应尽量用汉语的自然起落体现,但不可偏执,非要找到所谓"顿"与"音步"的等量齐观不可。形似应尽量在用韵与否以及诗行长短上予以体现,这样既保存了原诗的形,又再现了原诗的音美。比如我们虽不赞成将英语格律诗全都译为中国五言或七言诗,但以这种形式译出的某些诗如能做到传神,却也不失为好的译作。诗歌形式中确有一些不可译因素,但诗的意义、意境、神韵却大都可以被意会、被言传,尽管难以全部传达。因此译者应在词语的锤炼上下苦功夫,写诗者常常是"语不惊人誓不休",试比较下面一个英语诗节的汉译。

The curfew tolls the knell of parting day,
The lowing herd wind slowly o'er the lea,
The plowman homeward plods his weary way,
And leaves the world to darkness and to me.

Version 1

暮钟鸣,昼已暝,
牛羊相呼,迂回草径,
农人荷锄归,蹒跚而行,
把全盘世界剩给我与黄昏。

(郭沫若译)

Version 2

晚钟响起来一阵阵给白昼报丧,

牛群在草原上迂回,吼声起落。
耕地人累了,回家走脚步踉跄,
把整个世界给了黄昏与我。

（卞之琳译）

Version 3

晚钟殷殷响,夕阳已西沉,
群牛呼叫归,迂回走草径,
农人荷锄犁,倦倦回家门,
惟我立旷野,独自对黄昏。

（丰华瞻译）

第九章综合练习

1）**春晓**（孟浩然）

春眠不觉晓,
处处闻啼鸟。
夜来风雨声,
花落知多少。

2）**枫桥夜泊**（张继）

月落乌啼霜满天,
江枫渔火对愁眠。
姑苏城外寒山寺,
夜半钟声到客船。

3）**再别康桥**（徐志摩）

轻轻的我走了,
正如我轻轻的来;
我轻轻的招手,
作别西天的云彩。

那河畔的金柳,
是夕阳中的新娘,
波光里的艳影,
在我的心头荡漾。

软泥上的青荇,
油油的在水底招摇;
在康河的柔波里,
我甘心做一条水草!

那榆荫下的一潭，
不是清泉，是天上虹
揉碎在浮藻间，
沉淀着彩虹似的梦。

寻梦？撑一支长篙，
向青草更青处漫溯，
满载一船星辉，
在星辉斑斓里放歌。

但我不能放歌，
悄悄是别离的笙箫；
夏虫也为我沉默，
沉默是今晚的康桥！

悄悄的我走了，
正如我悄悄的来；
我挥一挥衣袖，
不带走一片云彩。

4) **Ode to the West Wind**

by Percy B. Shelley

O wild West Wind, thou breath of Autumn's being,
Thou, from whose unseen presence the leaves dead
Are driven, like ghosts from an enchanter fleeing,
Yellow, and black, and pale, and hectic red,
Pestilence-stricken multitudes: O thou,
Who chariotest to their dark wintry bed
The winged seeds, where they lie cold and low,
Each like a corpse within its grave, until
Thine azure sister of the Spring shall blow
Her clarion o'er the dreaming earth, and fill
(Driving sweet buds like flocks to feed in air)
With living hues and odors plain and hill:
Wild Spirit, which art moving everywhere;
Destroyer and preserver; hear, oh, hear!

5) **The Lost Love**

By William Wordsworth

She dwelt among the untrodden ways
Beside the springs of Dove;
A maid whom there were none to praise,
And very few to love:
A violet by a mossy stone
Half hidden from the eye!
—Fair as a star, when only one
Is shining in the sky.
She lived unknown, and few could know
When Lucy ceased to be;
But she is in her grave, and oh,
The difference to me!

翻译练习参考答案

Chapter One

1.

1）要了解一个人,通常除了可以通过他所交往的朋友之外,也可以通过他所阅读的书籍来认识他。因为一个人除了与朋友之间有友情之外,与书也有交情。一个人应该经常生活在最佳友伴之中,不管其是书籍,抑或是人。

2）一本好书往往是一个人生命精华的缩影,因为人最主要的就是他的精神世界。因此,好书就是美好言辞和高尚思想的宝库,这些珍藏在心中的话语和思想会随时随地地陪伴并安慰我们。Philip Sidney 爵士曾说过:“有着高尚理想的人从不感到孤独。”

3）青春并非人生的一段时间,而是一种心态。它不仅仅表现于满面红光,嘴唇红润,腿脚灵便,更意味着坚强的意志,卓越的想象力和充沛的情感。青春是生命之源泉,它清澈常新。

4）这是最美好的时期,这是最坏的时期;这是智慧的年代,这是愚蠢的年代;这是充满信仰的时代,这是顾虑重重的时代;这是光明的季节,这是黑暗的季节;这是富有希望的春天,这是充满绝望的冬天;我们拥有一切,我们一无所有;我们正笔直地走上天堂,我们正笔直地走下地狱。

5）Translation means the conversion of an expression from one language into another. To say it plainly, translation is an art to reproduce the exact idea of the author by means of a language different from the original. From the above definition of translation we know that the original thought of the expression must be kept as far as possible. Nothing should be added or taken away from the original work. The duty of the translator is simply to change the vocabulary, not the thought. In translation therefore, there are two essential elements: accuracy and expressiveness. Accuracy is the first indispensable quality of translation. The translator must cautiously stick to the author's idea. Words selected and sentences constructed must be such as to convey the exact thought. Expressiveness is to make the translation readily understood. In other words, the translator must express his author's idea as clearly and as forcibly as he can by the medium he employs. Accuracy is to make the thought definite and exact; while expressiveness is to make the translation vivid and attractive.

6.3

1）润滑油的浓度必须适当，太稀起不到应有的润滑效果，太稠则流不到需要润滑的所有零件。

2）早知今日，何必当初。

3）他老是见异思迁。

4）他离乡背井十载，从未回去过。

5）话不投机半句多。

6）江山易改，本性难移。

7）前途是光明的，道路是曲折的。

8）We will not attack unless we are attacked.

9）Crows hovering over rugged old trees wretched with, rotten vine—the day is about done. Yonder is a tiny bridge over a sparkling stream. And on the far bank, a pretty little village, but the traveler has to go on down this ancient road, the west wind moaning, his bony horse groaning, trudging forwards the sinking sun, farther and farther away from home.

10）You have little cause to make excessive demands from others and make yourself disappointed.

6.4

1）人造材料通称为合成材料。许多人造材料正在代替某些天然材料，这或者是由于天然物产的数量不能满足日日增长的需要，或者是由于人们选择了合成材料的一些物理性质并加以突出而造成的，因此，合成材料在其应用领域将有极大的用途。

2）科学家的思维活动和普通人的思维活动之间存在着差别，这种差别就像一个面包师或者卖肉者和一个化学家在操作方法上的差别一样。前者用普通的秤称东西，而后者则用天平和精密砝码进行艰难复杂的分析。其差别不过如此。

3）Sometimes it is interpersonal skills rather than professional skills that really count in your career. Interpersonal skills are nothing but the ability to be a good listener, to be sensitive toward other's needs, to take criticism well. People with skill in social relations admit their mistakes, and take their share of blame, which is a mature and responsible way to handle an error.

4）The successful launching of China's first experimental communication satellite, which was propelled by a three-stage rocket and has been in operation ever since, indicates that our nation has entered into a new stage in the development of carrier rockets and electronics.

6.5

1）我突然想到一个主意。

2）他们欣喜若狂。

3）一踏上中华人民共和国的国土,我们就随时随地地受到关怀与照顾。

4）我走在厚厚的地毯上,一点脚步声也没有。

5）Three main categories of foods have been recognized as essential for the life process. The first is carbohydrates which are widely distributed throughout the plant and animal worlds, including such substances as sugar, starch, and cellulose molecules, which can help to supply energy for the body.

6.6

1）I was astounded that he was going to give me a job.

2）I'm sorry to say that the visit to the museum has to be put off till tomorrow because of the heavy rain.

3）All teachers and students of the department are requested to meet in the conference room at 2:00 p. m. on Wednesday for a speech.

4）One country, two systems has been adopted to suit China's conditions and is not an expedient measure.

5）The child was seriously wounded and was treated by the hospital immediately.

6）Whenever work is being done, energy is being converted from one form into another.

7）Kissinger was alarmed by China's first atomic blast in October, 1964.

8）Air resistance must be given careful consideration when the aircraft is to be manufactured.

6.7

1）好书就是美好言辞和高尚思想的宝库,这些珍藏在心中的话语和思想会随时随地陪伴并安慰我们。

2）他能吃能睡。

3）看着我们的喷气式飞机,听着隆隆的机器轰鸣声,我感到心驰神往。

4）电视通过无线电波传输和接收活动物体的影像。

5）发言人一个接一个地表示要打倒帝国主义,消灭人剥削人的制度,解放世界上被压迫的人民。

6）Families upstairs have to carry pails to the taps downstairs for water.

7）He usually rides subways to and from work.

8）The adoption of this new device will greatly cut down the percentage of defective product.

9) Lin Zexu believed that a successful ban of the trade in opium must be preceded by the destruction of the drug itself.

10) China's entry into the WTO will instill new vitality into the economic growth of China, Asia and other countries and regions of the world.

6.9

1) 我觉得身体好极了。

2) 我太赞成你的看法了。

3) 他很想尽快和你见面。

4) 这本书我实在看不懂。

5) 人人都有不挨饿的权利。

6) 如果你有小汽车,就不用去坐火车或挤公共汽车了。

6.10

1) We answer that the Long March is the first of its kind in the annals of history, that it is a manifesto, a propaganda force, a seeding-machine.

2) A proton has a positive charge and an electron a negative charge, but a neutron has neither.

3) 他讨厌失败,他一生中曾战胜失败,超越失败,并且藐视别人的失败。

Chapter Two

3.2.2

1) 字母 I 代表电流的安培数,E 代表电动势的伏特数,R 代表电阻的欧姆数。

2) 佣金多少取决于订货数量。

3) 气温随着温度的升高而提高。

4) 水的压力随着深度的加深而加大。

5) 该报告总结了在热塑料和热固性塑料等两方面取得的成就。

3.3.2

1) 受热固体冷却过程中的收缩作用被利用在铆接上。

2) 如果氢和氧这两种气体的混合物被加热,就会出现氢原子失去电子的现象。

3) 必须找到新的能源,但这需要时间。

4) 全世界都将通信卫星用于国际间的实况转播。

5) 许多规范容器的制造,部分是在工厂,部分是在现场进行的,锅炉尤其如此。

6) 信息接收人可以迟些时候取出这些语音信息。

7) 已经注意到采取防腐新措施。

8）运用计算机算法进行比较和核实身份。

9）迅速冷凝是靠冷凝器来完成的。

10）钚是用来引爆核弹的。

3.3.3

1）

T. 并非供给热机的所有热量都被转变为有用的功。

F. 所有供给热机的热量都没有被转变为有用的功。

2）

T. 并非人人都能做这些试验。

F. 每个人都不能做这些试验。

3）

T. 两台仪器并不都是精密的。

F. 两台仪器都不是精密的。

4）

T. 这个工厂并不总是制造这样的机床。

F. 这个工厂总是不制造这样的机床。

5）引擎并不是因为燃料耗尽而停止运转。

6）发光的不一定都是金子。

3.4.1

1）

T1：只要有足够的电差位，所有的物体都允许一些电流通过。

T2：只要有足够的电差位，电流便可以通过任何物体。

2）

T1：通过在炉壁周围使用耐火砖，热损失可以被大大降低。

T2：炉壁采用耐火砖可以大大降低热耗。

3）

T1：电视是通过无线电波的活动物体的图像的传播和接收。

T2：电视通过无线电波传输和接收各种活动物体的图像。

4）最近十年来，由于不断积累新的资料数据，从而完善了以前的一些观点和概念。

5）如果太阳收缩到这种状态，就会把海洋变成冰，把大气变为液化气。

第二章综合练习

1）这就是说，传统的程序设计之所以可被称为单线索，是因为程序员在小心地设计一个接一个的指令时，只负责管理一个单线索。

2）如果一个窗口在你的屏幕上冻结了，要按 Ctrl + Alt + Del 键（同时按这三个键）。

3）最新的发现给双方提供了更多的证据，从而使有关这些作物安全环境的争论变得更加激烈。

4）我们正生活在一场意识的变革之中。在过去的数十年里，遗传学家、神经学家、心理学家、社会学家、经济学家等研究人员，在人类心理领域的深入探索已经取得长足的进步。他们的研究工作远远不是枯燥无味的唯物主义，而是照亮了暗藏在水下的丰富世界，那正是我们性格形成和才智滋长的地方。他们让我们更好地理解情感、直觉、偏见、渴望、倾向、性格特征和社会联系，这些东西恰恰是我们的文化所极少谈及的。

5）但是实际上，某些变化已经悄悄进入高级语言中，使得没有一种高级语言对带有该语言编译程序的所有计算机系统是可以完全移植的。

6）对用户来说，可重复利用性也可能是一种好坏难说的事情，因为程序员必须能够找到他所需要的对象。

7）简短的浏览使你初涉门径，等你熟悉了 Windows 95 以后，你就为每天的工作做好了准备。

8）事实上，网络可以结束"地理专制"。

9）今天我们可以说，美国是靠汽车轮子运转的，四个橡胶轮子推动着美国人的工作和娱乐。

10）这种遥测系统源源不断地送回地面大量最新的计算机数据，每秒达 1 000 次。

【汉译英】

1）

译文 1：The box for the tools, which is made of steel, is kept in the room for stores. In addition to the standard tools, it should contain a ruler for measuring up to 12 inches, some wires made of copper, some 10 centimeters long nails, a number of plugs with two pins, some wires for fuses and a can containing oil. If any tools are missing, the manager of the workshop should be told.

译文 2：The *steel tool box* is kept in the *storeroom*. In addition to the standard tools, it should contain a 12-*inch ruler*, some *copper wires*, some 10-*centimeter nails*, and a number of 2-*pin plugs*, some *fuse wires* and an *oil can*. If any tools are missing, the *workshop manager* should be told.

2）We can see color only because object reflects light. Something red reflects mostly red light, while a green object reflects mostly green light. White objects reflect all colors of light, but black objects do not reflect any light at all.

3) The value of industrial diamonds lies in their hardness, not in their beauty, and in the thousands of jobs they do.

4) Science deals with things in a practical way. Science means honest, solid knowledge, allowing not an iota of falsehood, and it involves Herculean efforts and grueling toil, but on the other hand, science also calls for creativeness and imagination; only with imagination is it possible to break away from the confines of conventionalities and to make headway in science.

5) What is one avenue to increase productivity in your organization while saving time and money? Videoconferencing is now a practical alternative for almost any organization. State-of-the-art advances in performance, economical pricing, local area networks, and the benefits of digital telephone networks have enabled the research, development and acquisition community to discover the competitive advantages and power of videoconferencing.

Passage One

英国:入厕无隐秘

英国工业与设计的又一个第一:带屏幕的便池。这种设施被评为“视屏便池”,其特征是在眼睛的水平位置安装一个小电视屏幕,显示广告内容。人们希望这种装置不会太分散入厕人的注意力。这种新设施已经安置在大约100家夜总会和酒吧间,其生产制造者是一家叫做“数码视图”的公司,他们希望看到这类产品在世界各地得到应用。

“视屏便池”只不过是最新的(也是最特殊的)一个例子说明电影正在怎样取代传统的广告宣传。现今在超市、街角商店、服务站前院等地随处都可以见到屏幕。这些屏幕或者能够为店主带来收益,或者能够促销店内特定商品。

液晶显示技术是促成这一新产品问世的部分原因。液晶显示屏的价格已经下降,而好处却举不胜举。液晶屏幕不像阴极射线监视器,液晶屏幕很薄,因此可以牢固地装嵌在挤满物件的狭小空间中和墙壁上。它也不费电,并且便于保护,不容易受破坏。

此外,“视频便池”的屏幕现在可以直接与国际互联网络连接,这样一来就可以接收来自世界各地的商业广告节目,而这些广告节目靠适用最新的视频压缩技术来传送。因此“视屏便池”便处于现代技术的前沿。

“数码视图”已经把广告屏推广到了商店、公共汽车和火车上,以及一些非比寻常的地方。目前,一些夜总会安装了“数码视图”生产的带有嵌入式电视的售烟机,以炫耀现场的各个不同侧面。公司同样也打算在出租车和现金出纳机上安装屏幕，甚至为一些小玩意儿，如在啤酒唧筒上安装屏幕以促销各类饮料。

“视频便池”能流行于世吗？广告商可以密切注视每个广告究竟看了多少次。而另一方面，设施过于先进的洗手间有遭电脑黑客破坏的风险，因此没有必要考虑修建。所以，尽管“数码视图”公司也将厕所视屏高雅地安装在便池旁，但是却没有为女性也安装“视屏便池”的打算。谢天谢地。

Passage Two

首席干细胞专家造假获罪

据12月29日韩国首尔国立大学发布的一份报告，曾在该校任职的黄禹锡已于6天前正式提出辞职。此前他故意捏造科研数据，和24位同事一道将一篇关于人类胚胎干细胞的论文发表在2005年5月的《科学》杂志上。

具体地说，黄博士曾声称他已培育出11组人类胚胎干细胞的克隆体，其遗传基因与某些特定的病人相匹配。他承认其中9个有假，但他说这是偶然的失误所致，其他两个还是真的。然而一个由首尔大学指派的负责调查这一事件的专家组却不同意他的说法。他们发现，论文记载的用于干细胞的DNA指纹图形曾被篡改，使得看起来所有的11个干细胞都和特定的病人相匹配。而事实上，这些干细胞中没有任何一个与脊柱受伤和糖尿病患者志愿提供的做研究用的皮肤细胞相匹配。为了达到预期的“成果”，黄博士从每个捐赠者身上要了两组DNA样本做测试，而不是一组捐赠者的样本，一组被认为是接受DNA移植手术者的干细胞样本。

专家小组还发现了论文中的另一处造假。该论文声称，只有185个卵子被用于培养11个干细胞系。而调查者们认为，尽管无法确定一个精确的数字，但实际所用到的卵子数量远大于此数，大概有数千个。

这次双重造假事件给人们以很大的打击，其原因是人类对胚胎干细胞寄予厚望。干细胞还没有进入特化程序，因此原则上可以发育成任何组织或器官，可以用来治疗包括糖尿病和帕金森综合征在内的各种疾病。他们甚至可以用来治愈脊椎伤，而且从患者身上克隆的干细胞不会被当成异体组织受到免疫系统排斥。

当然，黄博士现在已名声扫地。首尔国立大学现在正在调查他以前所声称的两项开创性的实验——世界上第一个克隆人类胚胎及提取的干细胞，以及世界上第一只克隆狗。他也因违背伦理道德、使用该小组成员捐献的卵子而处境不妙。

Chapter Three

3.6

1)

T. 失去体重,省下英镑。

E. The parallel structure and adjectives used in the advert remind us of some idioms about penny and pound, such as "penny wise, pound foolish"; "save pennies, lose pounds". 此句表明该食品不会发胖,还能帮人减肥。

2)

T. 吸烟还是不吸烟,这是个问题。

E. 这则广告仿拟了人们耳熟能详的 Shakespeare's famous line "to be or not to be, that is a question".(生存还是毁灭,这是个问题)。

3)

T. 质量铸就成功。

E. 仿拟了"Familiarity breeds contempt."(各自识老底,互相瞧不起)。

4)

T. 车到山前必有路,有路必有丰田车。

E. 此广告仿英谚"Where there is a will, there is a way"。为复述或再现此广告创意,可仿"船到桥头自然直,车到山前必有路"来表达。

5)

T. Apple thinks different.

E. 原文仿拟了成语"不同凡响"。其含意十分明确:苹果电脑,品质卓绝,与众不同。这种好奇心正是该广告所追求的目标之一。译文似乎和原文不谋而合,它套用了英语谚语"Great minds think alike."。隐含了慧眼识英雄的寓意,可谓一箭双雕。

6)

T. He who lasts last laughs best.

E. 此广告仿照谚语"谁笑在最后,谁笑得最好"而成,并且采用拟人化的修辞法突出了轮胎的坚固耐久的特性。译文套用"He who laughs last laughs best"的句式,将第一个 laughs 改为 lasts,不仅有效地传达了这则广告的本意,而且保留了与原谚语相同的头韵和谐音,可谓是妙趣天成。

7)

T. East, west, Hangtian is the best. / All roads run Hangtian.

E. 原文仿拟了古汉语诗词的风格。五字连用,对仗工整,节奏明快。译文仿照谚语"East or west, home is best."和"All road leads to Rome.",采用了套译的方法将

“非航天莫属”的寓意展示了出来。

8）

T. 一天一块 Mars 巧克力，保您工作休息娱乐随心意。

E. 该广告融合了两则英语谚语：“An apple a day keeps the doctor away.”和“All work and no play makes Jack a dull boy.”仿佛每天吃一块巧克力就能使人身体健康，心情愉悦。另外，原文中的 day 和 play 押韵。

9）

T. Billi sliming cream—using is believing.

10）

T. 百事可乐口味好，十二盎司真不少，花五便士喝个够，百事可乐真享受。

E. 这是一则仿篇广告，仿拟英国一首民间曲调编写的百事可乐小韵文，英语叫 Pepsi-Cola Jingle，行文抑扬顿挫。押韵严谨，和谐匀称，格调优美，容易记忆，被视为一则十分成功的广告。仿照前人著名诗歌、曲调等，并作一定改动，创造出新的意境。

11）

T. 一个人的灾难就是另一个人的福气！大甩卖正在进行中。

这一广告是仿拟了英语的谚语“One man's meat is another man's poison.”而来的。告诉人们商店大甩卖对店主而言是“灾”，而对顾客来讲却是“福”，幽默而俏皮。

12）

T. Give the plum to all, and to all a good time.

E. An imitation of the well-known advert for the “Timex watch”. Give the Timex to all and to all a good time. The repetition of “to all” implies the popularity of the product. A good time is a perfect reproducing of 准时乐道.

3.8

1）

T. 我们这里有充足的阳光，清新的空气，对您的儿子和财产的继承人大有裨益。

E. 某海滨浴场的宣传广告；其中 sun—son，air—heir 两对谐音词的妙用，使广告和谐悦耳，具有感召力。

2）

T. 相信我们吧。历经 5 000 多只耳朵的检验，有着 5 000 多年的经验。

E. The literal meaning is that the product has experienced a lot of tests, while ears and years are a pair of homonymy, which implies that the product has a long history and has a high quality. 从字面看，它说明了该产品已经接受了众多消费者的考验，但字里行间巧妙地嵌入一对谐音字 ears—years，充分暗示了该产品悠久的历史，久经考验的

上乘质量。

3）

T1. 树上是长不出钱来的，但它会在我们的树枝上开花结果。

T2. 你的钱会不断增值。就像枝头上的蓓蕾一样年年不断地绽放、开花、结出累累硕果，永不枯竭。

E. 这则广告里的 branch 这个词有两层含义，The word "branch"：1. refers to the stem or limb of a tree 2. the division of bank 第一层含义是字面意思，即树枝；而更深一层含义是指该银行的各个支行。

4）

T. 尽情大吃，不增体重。

E. 这是 Weight-Watcher 冰淇淋的广告标题，这种冰淇淋是专为节食者生产的。双关不仅存在于商品商标名称中，标题中的 spoil 也是双关所在。spoil oneself 意为"尽兴"；而 spoil one's figure 则意为"破坏了体形"。这则广告通过一语双关，使减肥者在轻松幽默的语气中很自然地接受该广告，并能使其产生购买欲望。

5）

T. 哪种大罐啤酒可称得上是地道的德国货？这一罐。

E. 这是一则 Lager 牌淡啤酒的广告。句中的 can 既可作情态动词，又可作名词（饮料罐）。由于 can 一语双关，加上 Lager 的品牌名称双关，使广告产生了一定的幽默效果，给读者以深刻的印象。

6）

T. 纳克斯坚果让你爱不释口。

E. 从广告的字面意义看，to go nuts 是"去买坚果"，但它同时还是一句成语，意为"疯狂、发疯"。双关语的运用表明了纳克斯牌坚果对人们的吸引力是无以抗拒的。*Go nuts* means *go to buy nuts*, at the same time it is also an idiom of being crazy. This pun indicates that people can not resist the temptation of this kind of nuts.

7）

T. 尝尝我们的甜玉米，包你乐得合不拢嘴。

E. ear 具有"穗"和"耳朵"双层含义。成语 from ear to ear 一语双关，既表示了因满意而乐得合不拢嘴，又表示因喜欢而吃了一穗又一穗。广告词中的双关语构思巧妙，新颖别致，令人难忘，收到了极好的宣传效果。

8）

T. 一天一块玛斯巧克力，让您工作像工作，娱乐像娱乐。

E. 这则广告让人们联想起两条非常熟悉的成语："An apple a day keeps the doctors away"和"All work and no play makes Jack a dull boy."。该广告不仅在语言形

式上借用了成语的模式,同时还引用了两条成语的内容,让人们从久已熟知的成语中得出一个新的判断:玛斯牌巧克力不仅能使人们健康,而且让人们工作时精力充沛,休息时放松自如。

第三章综合练习

1)

T. Located in Shanhaiguan, a picturesque summer resort, and the famous historic town, where the east end of the Great Wall called "head of dragon" extending to the sea, Shanhaiguan Brewery was set in 1982 and has been technically transformed twice and expanded to the present scale with an annual capacity of 80,000 tons of beer and 9,000 tons of malt. The brewery has become one of the key enterprises producing beer in China.

2)

T. 柔情四季,萨拉那,呵护您/ 我们的秀发,爱护您/我们的健康,天然配方,令秀发光泽柔顺,情有独钟,萨拉那。生物降解,不伤水土,爱护自然,数它第一。萨拉那。

3)

T. PRINCE OF PEACE DELUXE PACK is a combination of specially chosen products which are picked with the high class consumer in mind.

E. 原文中的"是礼品市场之需求"是汉语广告的套话,旨在诉诸顾客的从众心理(group-oriented),这里就没有必要翻译出来,所以省略不译。"是对各界人士一份诚意的贡献"也是汉语的表达习惯,强调了卖方,也容易使译文消费者产生心理反感。

4)

T. Bits of all types manufactured in the factory conform to the API standards. With novel design and fine workmanship, they are made of quality steel in advanced technology. All the products have passed strict quality test and reached in all aspects the advanced level of the domestically made bits of the kind.

5)

T. The refrigerators of 112 and 145 liters manufactured by our plant are noted for their graceful style, reliable quality, low noise and low power-consumption. It can be operated conveniently.

6)

T1. We have been in the silk garment trade for 35 years. The products find a ready market in 50 countries and regions. They are made of high quality pure silk, soft and smooth, an easy fit in the latest style. Fast to washing and sunlight, the silk garment is a must for ladies of good taste. Contact us for more information.

T2. Our factory has been producing silk clothing for 35 years and its products have been sold in 50 countries and areas all around the world. The clothes are of genuine silk, top quality, fine making and novel style. They are smooth and soft, and endurable in washing and drying without fading their colors. Comfortable and elegant, they are a must for ladies. Contact us for more information.

7)

Version 1. Tianjin Arts & Crafts Import & Export Company was established in July 1965 and is one of the leading specialized exporters in North China. Along the seashore with the convenient traffic and the prosperous commerce in the city, we exert ourselves to do business with countries and regions all over the world on the basis of equality and mutual benefits. We make friends in wide range and offer them excellent service, thus we have won great reputation.

Version 2. Established in July 1965, Tianjin Arts & Crafts Import & Export Company was and is one of the leading specialized exporters in North China. With the convenient traffic along the seashore and the prosperous commerce in the city, we spare no pains to do business with countries and regions all over the world on the basis of equality and mutual benefits.

8)

T. All shoppers must present this coupon to receive discount 30% off toward the purchase of fifty bottles of Mineral Water. With this coupon, limit one per family.

E. 七折是汉语的习惯表达，按照中国文化，它可被译为“ a 70% charge”，但是西方消费者会被这种中国式的英语搞糊涂。按照西方文化，“七折”应从视角相反的角度译为 a 30% discount 或 discount 30% off 。

9)

T. Founded in May 1945, with a history over 40 years, FARENCOL has established business relations all over the world. FARENCOL is a comprehensive transportation business specializing in shipping.

E. 这则用汉英双语制作的企业广告，译文语言朴实简洁，表达自然，令人信服。通过汉英对比还会发现，对于汉语原文中那些华丽辞藻，译者并未把这些四字词组完整地传译到译语中。译者有意对汉语习以为常的华丽辞藻弃之不译，其目的不过是使译文更好地适应英语文风和文化习惯。

10)

T. Beginning in 1992, with its quality exhibition, facilities and excellent services,

Intex Shanghai has been host to a variety of well organized international exhibitions.

该广告语介绍展览中心的成功史，若按等量原则译出全句，要译出：international standard, large—scale, winning favorable comments from the organizing institutions, exhibitors and audience of various countries 等词。但把原语中信息全盘传译到目的语中，将加大接收者的信息负担，使客户不易抓住主要信息，也就达不到做广告宣传的目的。所以，对文本中不同地位的信息，译者必须做出适当的选择。

11）

<table>
<tr>
<td>
Lose 5 kg in 10 days!
This is not magic
It's Dr. Guo's Healthy-slim Extract
YES, it's only NATURAL
Dr. Guo's Healthy-slim Extract is not a medicine, but a completely natural food. It is rich in various nutrients that are especially important to dieters, including proteins, vitamins, amino acids and trace elements. Take it as dietary supplement to your dieting program—It's natural and safe.
YES, it's indeed EFFECTIVE
Dr. Guo's Healthy-slim Extract helps you start and maintain a successful weight loss program. It burns out fat, keeps you energized, and you don't have to suffer at all. Wouldn't it be great if you can keep fit and keep slim at the same time? Actually, you can! Because you have Dr. Guo's! Thousands of women have been benefited from it, and it has been selected as the authorized weight-control food of the Women's Gymnastic Team of China. So, why should you wait for miracles to happen?
Just let Dr. Guo's work out the magic on you!!
</td>
<td>
胆固醇的天然克星
在与胆固醇的抗争中，人类似乎有个天然的盟友。
深海冷水鱼类体内含有一种成为“欧米加－3”的特别油脂。新近科学研究表明，这种油脂有助于抑制胆固醇。
司桂波公司现奉献给您含有“欧米加－3”的营养补充食品，隆重推出“降胆固醇鱼油”。
这种油脂仅取于含有丰富“欧米加－3”的深海冷水鱼类，浓缩后置于便于吞服的密封胶内，故无鱼腥味。
当然，服用“降胆固醇鱼油”只是抑制胆固醇整个方案的一部分，还需经常锻炼，食用低脂肪食品和定期到医院检查。
劝君采取行动，早日降低胆固醇。
胆固醇是您必须每日与之斗争的顽敌。
美国新泽西州普林斯顿市
Squibb & Sons 公司
</td>
</tr>
</table>

Chapter Four

3.1.1

1）UN = United Nations

伊拉克大选在即 联合国官员加紧讨论

2）PC = personal computer

个人电脑和传真机销量看涨

3）MPs = members of parliament

民众游行呼吁增加黑人议员

4）NPC = National People's Congress

人大草拟新法，遏制腐败

5）WB = World Bank

世银：中国脱贫成绩显著

3.1.2

1）八国峰会志在抗击贫困

2）普京因恐怖事件受媒体严厉批评

3）奥运盛妆开幕 泳将喜夺首金

4）英国第一寿星谢世 享天年百岁又十五

3.1.3

1）勇气不分男女

2）繁华好景不再，萧条接踵而来（保持原修辞格）

3）足球开踢拳打脚踢（保持原修辞格）

4）自由是发明之母（保持原修辞格）

5）中东：恐怖主义的摇篮（保持原修辞格）

6）只要意志坚，不怕征途远

7）储蓄劳务，未雨绸缪（四字短语）

8）载人难，难于上青天

9）德国整装待发，球迷心花怒放

10）老人与经济

11）投资还是不投资

12）工党失宠了吗？

13）房产投资五步法

14）无暇读书，忙于上网

15）克氏就职典礼 花费空前巨大

16）布什着手为社保方案寻求民主党支持

17）布莱尔前助手：安南曾被英间谍监视

18）油价年末将达每桶 100 美元，并将继续上涨

19）Yuan Rate against Dollar：Hit New High

20）Chong Qing Nail House Challenges Property Injustices

21）Looking Back to Look Ahead

22）Other People's Advice Is of Help

23）Changsha experiencing exceptional autumn drought

24）Beijing population exceeds 17.4 million

3.2.2

1）经过包括美国最高法院在内的五周的法庭讨论，美国选举团星期一投票选举共和党获选人德克萨斯州州长乔治·布什为美国第43届总统。

2）世界卫生组织总干事哈夫登·马勒尔先生昨天预言，今后四五年内全世界可能将有一亿人感染艾滋病；随着时间的推移，艾滋病病毒可能会发生变异，因而更加难以控制。到那时，每年可能至少需要花费15亿美元来对付艾滋病。

3）A Chinese sturgeon was found dead Saturday afternoon in the Yangtze River of Taichang, a small city in east China's Jiangsu province.

4）A photo exhibition on the life of Zhou Enlai and his wife Deng Yingchao kicked off Friday in Nanjing Meicun Memorial. Zhou became China's premier in 1949 and held the post until his death in 1976.

5）【路透社北京8月19日电】此间新闻界认为，总统此次来访为两国关系揭开了新的一页。

6）【新华社转路透社伦敦10月20日电】此间人士称，伦敦股市开市时股市上扬，交易相当活跃。由于一些持股者获利抛股，由此收盘时有涨有跌。

7）A program to ease city traffic got under way in Beijing this afternoon. This program, run by China's Public Security Ministry, will involve thirty-six cities across the country.

8）Passengers can take 24 round-trip charter flights across the Taiwan Straits during the Mid-Autumn Festival, a traditional Chinese feast, said the Civil Aviation Administration of China(CAAC) here Friday.

9）这些疫苗的疗效问题成为印度消除小儿麻痹症运动的最大障碍。

10）正在上海访问的耐克公司首席执行官如是说："中国的市场无限巨大"。

11）电子邮件是一条通向来自几乎所有行业的千千万万个专家的纽带，它可以使你与志趣相投或问题相同的人们交往。

12）Rescuers have found another corpse in Sunjiawan coal mine in Fuxin City, northeast China's Liaoning Province, where a gas explosion occurred on Monday, bringing the death toll to 211.

13）美国前第一夫人、现任参议员希拉里·克林顿 在纽约州西部城市布法罗出席公开活动时突然晕倒。

14）【路透社伦敦10月16日电】来自警方的消息称，速度高达每小时170公里的狂风于今天横扫了此间的大街小巷和房屋建筑。在这场有史以来最严重的风暴中，至少已有13人死亡。英国南部地区已处于瘫痪状态。

第四章综合练习

【英译汉】

美国与中国的贸易逆差突破千亿大关

美国与中国的贸易逆差已超过了 1 000 亿美元水平。

美国商务部昨天公布的数字显示,去年美国与中国的贸易逆差为 1 030 亿美元。这几乎相当于美国当年 4 350 亿美元总贸易逆差的 1/4。这一总贸易逆差是历史上最大的贸易失衡,超过了 2000 年创下的 3 790 亿美元的纪录。

如按月计算,去年 12 月美国与中国的贸易逆差达到了 95 亿美元,比 2001 年 12 月大幅增长了 73%。商务部没有提供这一强劲同比增长的原因。

中国是 3 年前超过日本成为美国与之有最大贸易逆差的国家的,这种情况一直保持到现在。

今年 1 月份,中国与其全球贸易伙伴的总贸易逆差达到了 12.5 亿美元。这是过去 5 年来中国第一次出现月度贸易逆差。中国把这种情况归之于石油进口的增加。

【汉译英】

1)

Moyan Winning the 2012 Nobel Price

The 2012 Nobel Prize in Literature was awarded to Mo Yan "who with hallucinatory realism merges folk tales, history and the contemporary". Through a mixture of fantasy and reality, historical and social perspectives, Mo Yan has created a world reminiscent in its complexity of those in the writings of William Faulkner and Gabriel Garcia Marquez, at the same time finding a departure point in old Chinese literature and in oral tradition.

2)

Mo Yan, a wildly prolific and internationally renowned Chinese author, was awarded on Thursday the 2012 Nobel Prize in Literature. In his novels and short stories, Mr. Mo paints sprawling, intricate portraits of Chinese rural life, often using flights of fancy—animal narrators, the underworld, elements of fairy tales—that evoke the techniques of South American magical realists.

Michel Hockx, professor of Chinese at the School of Oriental and African Studies at the University of London, said that Mr. Mo was part of a generation of post-Cultural Revolution writers who began looking at Chinese society, particularly in the countryside, through new eyes . "But instead of writing about socialist superheroes," Mr. Hockx continued, while at the same time portraying rural China as a "magical place where wonderful things happened, things that seemed to come out of mythology and fairy tales."

3）

Beijing Downpours Kills 37

The 20-hour storm that hit Beijing on Saturday claimed the lives of 37 people—25 of the deaths were caused by drowning, six were killed in house collapses, the Beijing municipal government said Sunday night.

4）

Black Tea Could Help Prevent Cancer

Drinking tea has a number of health benefits. Now, add one more to the list—a cup of the beverage a day can help slash the risk of developing cancer by shrinking tumors, say researchers.

5）

Mass Transit Encourages Exercise and Weight Loss

City planners and citizens alike frequently push for better public transportation. They argue that it can lessen traffic and reduce emissions from cars. Now there's a new reason to be gung-ho about public transit-it helps make people skinner. That's according to a study published in the August issue of the American Journal of Preventive Medicine.

Chapter Five

第五章综合练习

1）

T1. If you can reduce your price of urea to 1,200 dollars per ton, we may be able to place an order of 150—180 tons.

T2. If you can reduce your price of urea to US $1200 per metric ton, we may be able to place an order of 150—180 metric tons.

E. In American System, there are long ton and short ton. 1 short ton is equivalent to 0.9072 metric ton, while 1 long ton equals to 1.016 metric ton. 1 metric ton is equivalent to 100 kilograms, so "吨" should be translated into metric ton. Secondly, dollar is also used in other countries, such as in Canada, Australia, Singapore and New Zealand. In order to avoid confusion, the translator should translate "美元" into US $, whereas "dollar" is used in other contries as:

Canadian Dollar Can $ 加拿大元
Australian Dollar A $ 澳大利亚元
Singapore Dollar S $ 新加坡元

2）

T. 至于直接出口业务和间接出口业务，哪一种方式最好取决于许多因素，比如公司的大小，出口数量的多少，公司业务所牵涉国家的多少，出口所需投资的多少，所赚利润的多少，存在风险的大小，以及海外买主的要求等等。

E. For the sake of natural and clear expressions, certain part of speech can be added such as verb, noun, adverb, adjective and measure word. In this example,“公司业务” is added to make it more clear and logical.

3）

T. 所有与合同有关或在合同履行中发生的争执，均应通过友好协商方式解决。如果得不到解决，应将争执提交仲裁。

E：The adverbial clause introduced by “where” is usually translated into condition clause with“如果、若”。

4）

T. 卖方应在收到船舶公司出具有关单据之日起，20 天内向买方支付款项。

E. Adverbial clause introduced by“after” is usually translated into“……之日起”。

5）

T. 我们对该货物投保全险。

E. In business and in letters of insurance , ***cover*** has the meaning of “to protect by insurance”, whose literal Chinese equivalent is “入保险加以保护”. To make it more idiomatically , we can put it into“对……投保”。

6）

T. 劳务工程常常以交钥匙工程的方式进行，即以合同形式规定承建商在承建生产设备投入运行时移交给业主。

7）

T. 跨国银行提供的服务包括开立信用证、买卖外汇、开证行承兑、接受欧洲货币储存、提供欧洲货币以及发行推销欧洲货币债券。

E. “issuing bank's acceptances ”should be put into “开证行承兑”, instead of “开立银行承兑”。“assisting in the marketing of Eurobonds” should be put into“发行推销……” instead of “发行……”, for apart from issuing Eurobonds, multinational banks market bonds as well.

8）

T1. 现有各种不同重量、尺寸、颜色和形状的大理石供君选择。价格绝对公道，按需报价。

T2. 我方有各种不同重量、不同体积、颜色丰富、形状各异的大理石，数量甚巨，价格合理，受函报价。

E. To ensure that the translated text performs the same function as the source text, the second version is clearer in meaning and much more stylistically equivalent to the original. A number of four-character words are used, which make the sentence smooth, balanced and formal.

9)

T1. 我方报价已考虑到大批量订货的因素。相信贵公司了解我们在一个竞争十分激烈的市场上经营销售业务,因而已不得不把利润减到最低限度。

T2. 我们的价格已经是大量批发的价格。另外,你也知道,我们所处的行业竞争十分激烈,因而已不得不把价格压至最低。

E. The Original business letter is made informal by such colloquial words as : 我们的价格,批发价格,你也知道 and 将价格压至最低。The courtesy existing between the addresser and addressee is not conveyed. As a result, the tenor and the mode of discourse are neglected.

10)

T. 除非合同中已指明承包商代表的姓名,承包商应在开工日期前,将其拟任命为承包商代表的人员姓名及详细资料提交雇主,以取得同意。

E. Prior to the Commencement Date 不包括开工日期这一天,也就是说如果承包商在开工日期那一天提交资料,则视为违约。

11)

T. "竣工时间"系指投标书附录中写明的,自开工日期算起至工程或某分项工程(视情况而定)根据第 8.2 款[竣工时间]规定的要求竣工的全部时间。

E. "自"(from)开工日期始,意思是不包括开工日期当天,而是从该日期后的一天起算;结束是在最后一天的午夜。

12)

T . 承包商检查、照管、监护和控制的义务,不应解除雇主对目视检查时难发现的任何短少、缺陷或缺项所负的责任。

E. shortage, defect 和 default 都有缺陷的意思, shortage 强调数量上的短少, defect 强调质量上的缺陷, default 强调整体上的缺项。只有准确地译出三者的区别,才能明确地阐述出雇主的责任。不管是数量上的短少,质量上的缺陷,或者整体上的缺项,雇主都负有责任。

13)

T. 本公约中的任何规定,都不禁止承运人或托运人就承运人或船舶对海运货物在装船前或卸货后的保管、照料和搬运或与之相关的义务,以及货物的丢失或损害的责任,订立任何协议、规定、条件、保留或免责条款。

14)

T. 当事人或当事人的任何代理人不得就案件与任何首席仲裁员候选人进行单方联系。

15)

T. 本协议由中国进出口公司(以下简称甲方)与美国斯密斯威尔斯公司(以下简称乙方)拟定并订立。据此甲方同意委托乙方在指定的地区内按如下条例任甲方为下述商品的独家经销商。

Chapter Six

第六章综合练习

1) In heaven (there) is the paradise, and on earth (there) are Suzhou and Hangzhou.

As there is the paradise in heaven, so there are Suzhou and Hangzhou on earth.

2) Like a bright pearl set on the Taihu and situated in the center of the beautiful and fertile Changjiang Delta in southern Jiangsu Province, Wuxi is one of China's major tourist cities, with its pleasant climate, rich natural resources and picturesque scenery. Cutting through the city is the Beijing-hangzhou Grand Canal, an ancient project equal in fame to the Great Wall.

3) Laoshan Scenic Area is thickly covered with trees of many species, which add credit for its scenery. Among them over 300 ale considered rare and precious, half of which ale plants under top-level protection. The most famous species include gingko and cypress.

4) Valuable articles and cash should be handed to General Service Desk for safekeeping.

5) Situated on the Huangpu River and at the point of Lujiazui in Pudong, the Oriental Pearl Radio and Television Tower is surrounded by waters on three sides and faces a row of buildings of variegated international architectural styles in the Bund across the river. This 468-meter-tall tower ranks first in Asia and third in the world in height.

6) Our tourists are kindly expected to notice the rules and regulations. Your corporation will be highly appreciated in making our services effective.

7) HIGHLIGHTS OF CHINA TOUR

SPECIAL FEATURES OF 10 DAYS TOUR PACKAGE

★A WALK ON THE GREAT WALL

★ENJOY THE FAMOUS "ROAST DUCK"

★SEE TERRA-COTTA FIGURES

★ENJOY THE MAGNIFICENT ACROBATIC SHOW

ITINERARY AS FOLLOWS:

DAY 1.: ARR BEIJING, INTERNATIONAL HTL. (DOWNTOWN)

DAY 2.: FORBIDDEN CITY, TEMPLE OF HEAVEN, BEIJING OPERA

DAY 3.:GREAT WALL, MING TOMBS, TEA HOUSE

DAY 4.:SUMMER PALACE, ZOO, ROAST DUCK

...

DAY 10:EXIT

TOTAL PRICE FOR OVER 10 PAX GROUP:

PER PAX 690 US $

798 CA $

8）前往“锦绣中华”观光，交通极为方便，从落马洲口岸乘车仅10多分钟便可到达。香港中国旅行社的直通旅游巴士，深圳市每日川流不息的中巴、小巴，经深南公路、广深公路和北环快速公路均可抵达。

欢迎您到“锦绣中华”来。

9）尊敬的旅客：

本店不受理信用卡，住店客人可以用现金、旅行支票或者私人支票结账。为了您的方便，本店备有银行取款单。

客房服务费或小费之类的新近费用可能尚未移到账台，在结账时，请您提醒出纳员，以免在您离店之后再开账收款。

副董事长兼总经理

罗伯特·巴特菲尔德

10）夏威夷

对于大部分人来说，那些星星点点的关于夏威夷的印象，足以让我们沉浸于她的魅力中。金色的海滩金色的人们。阳光、沙子、大海、浪花……在蓝天和棕榈树之间，我们流连忘返。夏威夷岛是世界上最美丽的地方之一。这里天气晴朗，气温整年在华氏60—90度之间变化。夏天稍暖，冬天稍凉，但对于某些人来说每天都是晒太阳的好日子。在这人间天堂没有陌生人。也许夏威夷人与生俱来的热情才是这里真正的魅力所在。我们称之为爱的精神。它是世界上最文明的地方之一，世界各地的文化都可以在这熔炉中找到共同点，生根发芽。

Chapter Seven

3.2

1）The Americans have sprinkled some relief flour in Peiping, Tientsin and Shanghai to see who will stoop to pick it up. Like Chiang TaiKung fishing, they have cast the line for the fish who want to be caught. But he who swallows food handed out in contempt will get a bellyache.（王佐良译）

E. 虽然在译文读者文化中有“playing willingly in someone's hands”但没有“姜太公钓鱼，愿者上钩”这一具有中国文化特色的文化意象，采用直译翻译策略可以传达出作者的信息意图，这个译文能够使作者的意图与译文读者的审美期盼相吻合。

2) The old saying, "Three cobblers with their wits combined would equal Zhuge Liang, the master mind," simply means the masses have great creative powers.（王佐良译）

E. 在英语中可找到两个英语谚语："Two heads are better than one; Collective wisdom is greater than a single wit"。但为防止两个文化意象"臭皮匠"和"诸葛亮"丢失,在原文明示的基础上，王佐良采用了直接翻译增加隐含意义"with their wits combined; the master mind"的翻译策略，使整个译文释义性相似于作者的信息意图和交际意图。

3) They were sure Ah Q had met his Waterloo.（梁社乾译）

E. "met his Waterloo"是"拿破仑在滑铁卢战役中（1815年6月18日）遭到了决定性失败"，其文化隐含的意思是"损失惨重的失败"。译者在英语读者的认知语境中寻找关联。

4) 男人送花，送情书，送时运给她。可她梦幻无边。这一百五十块钱！这一百五十块钱！真像藏着神灯的山洞为阿拉丁打开了门。

E. 间接翻译方法增加了"真像藏着神灯的山洞为阿拉丁打开了门"，补偿了仅靠直译作者的信息意图可能会产生的文化亏损。

第七章综合练习

【英译汉】

爱美之心是健全人性的必然组成部分。它是一种精神品质。不爱美不一定不好,但爱美则是心地善良的恒久标志。爱美的程度可能与性格高贵美好的程度成正比。

自然之美无处不在。宇宙是其殿堂,美在春天无数花蕊中绽放,美在树枝绿草间摇曳,美在陆地和海洋的深处萦绕,美在贝壳和宝石的光芒中闪烁。除了这些微小的事物,海洋、高山、云层、群星、朝阳和落日,都充满了美。这种美是如此珍贵,与我们内心最温柔、最高贵的情感又如此契合,因此一想到大多数人身在其中,却又几乎视若无睹,就令人倍感痛心。

【汉译英】

Tribute to the White Poplar

Mao Dun

White poplars are no ordinary trees. But these common trees in Northwest China are as much ignored as our peasants in the North. However, like our peasants in the North, they are bursting with vitality and capable of surviving any hardship or oppression. I pay tribute to them because they symbolize our peasants in the North and, in particular, the spirit of honesty, tenacity and forging ahead—a spirit central to our struggle for national liberation.

The reactionary diehards, who despise and snub the common people, can do whatever they like to eulogize the elite nanmu (which is also tall, straight and good-looking) and look down upon the common, fast-growing white poplar. I, for my part, will be loud in my praise of the latter!

Chapter Eight

第八章综合练习

1)

I Might Have Come from Tianjin

Hou Baolin

(Translated by Liu Shicong)

Let me begin with my trip on the train. When I was about four years old I had traveled by train. The man I traveled with was my uncle Zhang Quanbin. I still remembered how funny I looked the way I was dressed—in a blue cloth gown with a short sleeveless jacket over it and a skullcap on the head. In those days it was good enough for small kids to be dressed like that. However, it was my only experience to boast about in my childhood. As I had never traveled by train or met anyone outside my family before, I felt everything on the train was new to me. Probably in childhood, one always needs some comfort. Sitting in my uncle's lap, being humored all the way, I was very happy. We ate half a *jin* of roast chestnuts, had a nap and soon arrived in Beijing.

With the hints mentioned above I assume I might have come from Tianjin. Even today I can recollect what my own parents looked like but, of course, my impression is blurry. As for what my family name was and where my parents came from, I really don't know. I only remember my birthday and my infant name. I was told about my birthday by my foster-parents when I grew up. I was born in the "you" period (between 5 - 7 p. m.), 15th of the 10th lunar month. So I was named You. Prefixed with xiao-young, and suffixed with a diminutive er—an intimate way of addressing young and small things by Beijingers, my name, therefore, became Xiao You'r. This is all I know about my childhood and beyond that I do not remember much else.

2)译文:我爱我的心上人,因为她是那样地叫人入迷;我恨我的心上人,因为她已订婚将作他人妻;我的心上人花容月貌无可比拟,我劝她离家出走跟我在一起;她的名字叫爱米莉,她的家就在东城里,我爱我的心上人呀,一切都因为这个E!(陆乃圣译)

E. 在上面的原文中,从句的最后一个单词都是以E开头,富于节奏感,并朗朗上口。在译文中,译者在每个从句中都以汉语拼音的yi音结束,如迷,妻,拟,起,莉,里。因此原文的语言特色被较完好地保留了下来。

3）她完全是个小孩，七八岁光景，身材纤细，脸色苍白，五官小巧，过长的头发卷垂到腰际。（祝庆英译）

4）Later, the planes kept coming in much the same manner as the peerless beauty whose "one glance could conquer city and whose second glance could vanquish an empire."

5）They had Western food. "Admiral Nelson", who was a Christian, rolled his eyes up toward the ceiling and thanked God for bestowing the food before he sat down.

6）你眼前的奥菲利亚小姐，身穿一套崭新的黄色亚麻布旅行服，身材高挑，瘦削的体态方方正正，清瘦的脸上眉目分明。她双唇紧闭，显得果断而有主见。她那双锐利的黑眼睛转动起来明察秋毫，凡事都要探究个明白，总像在寻找什么需要照顾的东西。

7）We're like two grasshoppers tied to one cord, neither can get away!

8）Ah Q, again, had a high opinion of himself. He looked down on all the inhabitants of Weizhuang.

9）

孙致礼译：有钱的单身汉总要娶位太太，这是一条举世公认的真理。

王科一译：凡是有钱的单身汉，必定需要娶位太太，这已是举世公认的真理。

E. At first sight, the reader would expect something solemn, something important to occur in the end of the sentence. Nothing magnificent occurs, but a very common phenomenon—a rich man wants a wife. The use of the periodic sentence and the anticlimax at the end of the sentence achieves the effect of irony and humor.

10）

王科一译："摆在你面前的是个很不幸的难题，你得自己去抉择，伊丽莎白。从今天起，你不和你父亲成为陌路人，就要和母亲成为陌路人。要是你不嫁给柯林斯先生，你的妈就不要再见到你，要是你嫁给他，我就不要再见你了。"

孙致礼译："伊丽莎白，你面临着一个不幸的抉择。从今天起，你要和你父母中的一个成为陌路人。你要是不嫁给柯林斯先生，你的母亲就永远不再见你了；你若嫁给柯林斯先生，我就永远不再见你了。"

E. 上述两种翻译都译出了班纳特先生话语的意思，但我们仍然可以发现当中存在假象等值。王把"From this day you must be a stranger to one of your parents"翻译成"你不是和你父亲成为陌路人，就要和母亲成为陌路人"，表面上看来意思和孙的版本一样。但再仔细地想一想，以因长期受到妻子粗俗地压制而沉默寡言的班纳特先生不太可能会那样说话。他说话经常带点讽刺意味，但不会太明显。从这一点看来，孙的翻译很好地把班纳特先生说话的风格翻译出来了。

Chapter Nine

第九章综合练习

1) **Version** 1

Spring Mornings（徐忠杰）

One slumbers late in the morning in spring,
Everywhere, one hears birds warble or sing.
As the night advances, rain spatters; winds moan,
How many flowers have dropped? Can that be known?

Version 2

The Spring Dawn(吴钧陶)

Slumbering, I know not the singing dawn is peeping,
But everywhere the spring birds are cheeping.
Last night I heared the rain dripping and wind weeping,
How many petals are now on the ground sleeping?

2) **A Night-Mooring Near Maple Bridge**

Moon going down, Crow cawing, frost filling all over the sky,
Maple-trees near the river and torch in the fisher opposite the sleeping anxiety.
From the temple on Cold Mountain out of Suzhou,
The midnight ding touches my boat.

3) **Goodbye Again, Cambridge!**

I leave softly, gently,
Exactly as I came.
I wave to the western sky,
Telling it goodbye softly, gently.
The golden willow at the river edge
Is the setting sun's bride.
Her quivering reflection
Stays fixed in my mind.
Green grass on the bank
Dances on a watery floor
In bright reflection.
I wish myself a bit of waterweed
Vibrating to the ripple.
Of the River Cam.
That creek in the shade of the great elms
Is not a creek but a shattered rainbow,

Printed on the water
And inlaid with duckweed,
It is my lost dream.
　　Hunting a dream?
Wielding a long punting pole
I get my boat into green water,
Into still greener grass.
In a flood of starlight
On a river of silver and diamond
I sing to my heart's content.
But now, no, I cannot sing
With farewell in my heart.
Farewells must be quiet, mute,
Even the summer insects are silent,
Knowing I am leaving.
The Cambridge night is soundless.
I leave quietly
As I came quietly.
I am leaving
Without taking so much
As a piece of cloud.
But with a quick jerk of my sleave
I wave goodbye.

4）西风颂　（王佐良）

呵,狂野的西风,你把秋气猛吹,
不露脸便将落叶 扫而空,
犹如法师赶走了群鬼,
赶走那黄绿红黑紫的一群,
那些染上了瘟疫的魔怪——
呵,你让种子长翅腾空,
又落在冰冷的土壤里深埋,
象尸体躺在坟墓,但一朝
你那青色的东风妹妹回来,
为沉睡的大地吹响银号,
驱使羊群般的蓓蕾把大气猛喝,
就吹出遍野嫩色,处处香飘。

狂野的精灵！你吹遍了大地山河，
破坏者，保护者，听吧——听我的歌！

5）失去的爱（郭沫若）

她居住在白鸽泉水的旁边，
无人来往的路径通往四面；
一位姑娘不曾受人称赞，
也不曾受过别人的爱怜。
苔藓石旁的一株紫罗兰，
半藏着没有被人看见！
美丽得如同天上的星点，
一颗唯一的星清辉闪闪。
她生无人知，死也无人唁，
不知她何时去了人间；
但她安睡在墓中，哦可怜，
对于我呵是个地异天变！

参考文献

[1] AUSTEN J. Pride and prejudice[M]. Hertfordshire: Wordsworth Editions Limited, 1993.

[2] CATFORD J C. A lingustic theory of translation[M]. Oxford: Oxford University Press, 1965.

[3] KRAMSCH C. Language and culture [M]. Shanghai: Shanghai Foreign Language Education Press, 2000.

[4] CONNOR U. Contrastive rhetoric[M]. New York: Cambridge University Press, 1996.

[5] HALLIDAY M A K. Linguistic function and literary style [M]. London: Edward Arnold Cpublishert) Ltd., 1971.

[6] HAWTHORN J. Studying the novel[M]. London: Edward Arnold (Publishers) Ltd., 1986.

[7] LAKOFF G, JOHNSON M. Metaphors we live by. [M] Chicago and London: University of Chicago Press, 1980.

[8] LEECH G N, SHORT M H. Style in fiction: an linguistic introduction to English fiction prose [M]. Beijing: Foreign Language Teaching & Research Press, 2001.

[9] MICHEL M. Gone with the wind[M]. New York: Simon & Schuster Inc, 2008.

[10] NEWMARK P A. Textbook of translation[M]. New York: Prentice Hall International Ltd., 1988.

[11] NIDA E, TABER C. The theory and practice of translation[M]. Shanghai: Shanghai Foreign Language Education Press, 2004.

[12] NIDA E A. Language and culture: contexts in translating[M]. Shanghai: Shanghai Foreign Language Education Press, 2001.

[13] NORD C. Translation as a purposeful activities: functional approaches explained [M]. Shanghai: Shanghai Foreign Language Education Press, 2001.

[14] NEWMARK P. A Textbook of translation [M]. Shanghai: Shanghai Foreign Language Education Press, 2001.

[15] NEWMARK P. Approaches to translation [M]. Shanghai: Shanghai Foreign Language Education Press, 2001.

[16] NEWMARK P. More approaches on translation [M]. Bristol: Multilingual Matters Ltd., 1998.

[17] REISS K. Text type, translation types and translation assessment [A]//CHESTERMAN A. Readings in translation theory. Helsinki: Finnlectura, 1987.

[18] VERSCHUEREN J. Understanding pragmatics[M]. London: Edward Arnold (Publishers) Ltd., 1999.

[19] 陈宏薇,李亚丹.新编汉英翻译教程[M].上海:上海外语教育出版社 2007.

[20] 陈新.文体翻译教程[M].北京:北京大学出版社,1999.

[21] 蔡基刚.英汉写作对比研究[M].上海:复旦大学出版社,2001.

[22] 冯庆华.文体翻译论[M].上海:上海外语教育出版社,2002.

[23] 冯庆华.实用翻译教程[M].上海:上海外语教育出版社,2002.
[24] 郭著章,李庆生.英汉互译实用教程[M].武汉:武汉大学出版社,1998.
[25] 华先发.新实用英译汉教程[M].武汉:湖北教育出版社,2000.
[26] 刘宓庆.翻译美学理论[M].北京:外语教学与研究出版社,2011.
[27] 刘宓庆.英汉对比与翻译[M].南昌:江西教育出版社,1992.
[28] 刘宓庆.文体与翻译[M].北京:中国对外翻译出版公司, 1998.
[29] 刘宓庆.翻译美学导论[M].北京:中国对外翻译出版公司,2005.
[30] 刘士聪.英汉·汉英美文翻译与鉴赏[M].上海:译林出版社,2010.
[31] 连淑能.英汉对比研究[M].北京:高等教育出版社,1993.
[32] 玛格丽特·米歇尔.飘[M].傅东华,译.杭州: 浙江文艺出版社, 1985.
[33] 邵志洪.汉英对比翻译导论[M]. 上海:华东理工大学出版社,2005.
[34] 孙致礼.新编英汉翻译教程[M].上海:上海外语教育出版社,2003.
[35] 王宏印.英汉翻译综合教程[M].西安:陕西师范大学出版社,2002.
[36] 王佐良.王佐良文集[M].北京:外语教学与研究出版社,1997.
[37] 王佐良,丁往道.英语文体学引论[M].北京:外语教学与研究出版社,1987.
[38] 许建平.英汉互译实践与技巧[M].北京:清华大学出版社,2000.
[39] 许启华,王乃文.实用英译汉教程[M].上海:上海外语教育出版社,1989.
[40] 杨莉藜.英汉互译教程[M].开封:河南大学出版社,1993.
[41] 喻云根,吕瑞昌,张复星.汉英翻译教程[M].西安:陕西人民出版社,1983.
[42] 张培基.中国现代散文选[M]. 上海:上海外语教育出版社,2007.
[43] 周志培,邵志洪.英汉对比与翻译中的转换[M].上海:华东理工大学出版社,2003.